Constructions and the Analytic Field

Constructions and the Analytic Field questions the relationship between psychoanalysis, history and literature. Does the analyst help the analysand construct a narrative, or is their task more of a historical reconstruction?

In seeking to answer this question, Domenico Chianese examines Freud's writing, beginning with 'Constructions in Analysis' and ending in 'Moses and Monotheism', as well as the impressions of analytic method reflected in contemporary writers such as Thomas Mann, and historical writings from both sides of the Atlantic. Drawing on vivid and persuasive clinical examples, he argues that psychoanalysis creates a 'scenic space' between analysand and analyst, a theatrical space wherein the cast of the patient's interior world enters and exits the scene.

Drawing on the rich Italian psychoanalytic tradition, this original approach to the analytic field will be of interest to psychoanalysts, historians and literary experts.

Domenico Chianese is a psychiatrist and training analyst of the Italian Psychoanalytic Society, of which he is former president. He has published two books, and lives and works in Rome.

THE NEW LIBRARY OF PSYCHOANALYSIS
General Editor Dana Birksted-Breen

The New Library of Psychoanalysis was launched in 1987 in association with the Institute of Psychoanalysis, London. It took over from the International Psychoanalytical Library which published many of the early translations of the works of Freud and the writings of most of the leading British and Continental psychoanalysts.

The purpose of the New Library of Psychoanalysis is to facilitate a greater and more widespread appreciation of psychoanalysis and to provide a forum for increasing mutual understanding between psychoanalysts and those working in other disciplines such as the social sciences, medicine, philosophy, history, linguistics, literature and the arts. It aims to represent different trends both in British psychoanalysis and in psychoanalysis generally. The New Library of Psychoanalysis is well placed to make available to the English-speaking world psychoanalytic writings from other European countries and to increase the interchange of ideas between British and American psychoanalysts.

The Institute, together with the British Psychoanalytical Society, runs a low-fee psychoanalytic clinic, organises lectures and scientific events concerned with psychoanalysis and publishes the *International Journal of Psychoanalysis*. It also runs the only UK training course in psychoanalysis which leads to membership of the International Psychoanalytical Association – the body which preserves internationally agreed standards of training, of professional entry, and of professional ethics and practice for psychoanalysis as initiated and developed by Sigmund Freud. Distinguished members of the Institute have included Michael Balint, Wilfred Bion, Ronald Fairbairn, Anna Freud, Ernest Jones, Melanie Klein, John Rickman and Donald Winnicott.

ALSO IN THIS SERIES

Impasse and Interpretation Herbert Rosenfeld
Psychoanalysis and Discourse Patrick Mahony
The Suppressed Madness of Sane Men Marion Milner
The Riddle of Freud Estelle Roith
Thinking, Feeling, and Being Ignacio Matte-Blanco
The Theatre of the Dream Salomon Resnik
Melanie Klein Today: Volume 1, Mainly Theory Edited by Elizabeth Bott Spillius
Melanie Klein Today: Volume 2, Mainly Practice Edited by Elizabeth Bott Spillius
Psychic Equilibrium and Psychic Change: Selected Papers of Betty Joseph Edited by Michael Feldman and Elizabeth Bott Spillius
About Children and Children-No-Longer: Collected Papers 1942–80 Paula Heimann. Edited by Margret Tonnesmann
The Freud–Klein Controversies 1941–45 Edited by Pearl King and Riccardo Steiner
Dream, Phantasy and Art Hanna Segal
Psychic Experience and Problems of Technique Harold Stewart
Clinical Lectures on Klein and Bion Edited by Robin Anderson
From Fetus to Child Alessandra Piontelli
A Psychoanalytic Theory of Infantile Experience: Conceptual and Clinical Reflections E. Gaddini. Edited by Adam Limentani
The Dream Discourse Today Edited and introduced by Sara Flanders
The Gender Conundrum: Contemporary Psychoanalytic Perspectives on Femininity and Masculinity Edited and introduced by Dana Breen
Psychic Retreats John Steiner
The Taming of Solitude: Separation Anxiety in Psychoanalysis Jean-Michel Quinodoz
Unconscious Logic: An Introduction to Matte-Blanco's Bi-logic and Its Uses Eric Rayner
Understanding Mental Objects Meir Perlow
Life, Sex and Death: Selected Writings of William Gillespie Edited and introduced by Michael Sinason
What Do Psychoanalysts Want? The Problem of Aims in Psychoanalytic Therapy Joseph Sandler and Anna Ursula Dreher
Michael Balint: Object Relations, Pure and Applied Harold Stewart
Hope: A Shield in the Economy of Borderline States Anna Potamianou

Psychoanalysis, Literature and War: Papers 1972–1995 Hanna Segal
Emotional Vertigo: Between Anxiety and Pleasure Danielle Quinodoz
Early Freud and Late Freud Ilse Grubrich-Simitis
A History of Child Psychoanalysis Claudine and Pierre Geissmann
Belief and Imagination: Explorations in Psychoanalysis Ronald Britton
A Mind of One's Own: A Kleinian View of Self and Object Robert A. Caper
Psychoanalytic Understanding of Violence and Suicide Edited by Rosine Jozef Perelberg
On Bearing Unbearable States of Mind Ruth Riesenberg-Malcolm
Psychoanalysis on the Move: The Work of Joseph Sandler Edited by Peter Fonagy, Arnold M. Cooper and Robert S. Wallerstein
The Dead Mother: The Work of André Green Edited by Gregorio Kohon
The Fabric of Affect in the Psychoanalytic Discourse André Green
The Bi-Personal Field: Experiences of Child Analysis Antonino Ferro
The Dove that Returns, the Dove that Vanishes: Paradox and Creativity in Psychoanalysis Michael Parsons
Ordinary People and Extra-Ordinary Protections: A Post-Kleinian Approach to the Treatment of Primitive Mental States Judith Mitrani
The Violence of Interpretation: From Pictogram to Statement Piera Aulagnier
The Importance of Fathers: A Psychoanalytic Re-Evaluation Judith Trowell and Alicia Etchegoyen
Dreams That Turn Over a Page: Paradoxical Dreams in Psychoanalysis Jean-Michel Quinodoz
The Couch and the Silver Screen: Psychoanalytic Reflections on European Cinema Edited and introduced by Andrea Sabbadini
In Pursuit of Psychic Change: The Betty Joseph Workshop Edited by Edith Hargreaves and Arturo Varchevker
The Quiet Revolution in American Psychoanalysis: Selected Papers of Arnold M. Cooper Arnold M. Cooper. Edited and introduced by Elizabeth L. Auchincloss
Seeds of Illness, Seeds of Recovery: The Genesis of Suffering and the Role of Psychoanalysis Antonino Ferro
The Work of Psychic Figurability: Mental States Without Representation César Botella and Sára Botella
Key Ideas for a Contemporary Psychoanalysis: Misrecognition and Recognition of the Unconscious André Green
The Telescoping of Generations: Listening to the Narcissistic Links Between Generations Haydée Faimberg

Glacial Times: A Journey Through the World of Madness Salomon Resnik
This Art of Psychoanalysis: Dreaming Undreamt Dreams and Interrupted Cries Thomas H. Ogden
Psychoanalysis as Therapy and Storytelling Antonino Ferro
Psychoanalysis and Religion in the 21st Century: Competitors or Collaborators? Edited by David M. Black
Recovery of the Lost Good Object Eric Brenman
The Many Voices of Psychoanalysis Roger Kennedy
Feeling the Words: Neuropsychoanalytic Understanding of Memory and the Unconscious Mauro Mancia
Projected Shadows: Psychoanalytic Reflections on the Representation of Loss in European Cinema Edited by Andrea Sabbadini
Encounters with Melanie Klein: Selected Papers of Elizabeth Spillius Elizabeth Spillius edited by Priscilla Roth and Richard Rusbridger
Yesterday, Today and Tomorrow Hanna Segal
Constructions and the Analytic Field: History, Scenes and Destiny Domenico Chianese

TITLES IN THE NEW LIBRARY OF PSYCHOANALYSIS TEACHING SERIES

Reading Freud: A Chronological Exploration of Freud's Writings Jean-Michel Quinodoz

THE NEW LIBRARY OF PSYCHOANALYSIS

General Editor: Dana Birksted-Breen

Constructions and the Analytic Field

History, Scenes and Destiny

Domenico Chianese

Routledge
Taylor & Francis Group
LONDON AND NEW YORK

First published 2007
by Routledge
27 Church Road, Hove, East Sussex BN3 2FA

Simultaneously published in the USA and Canada
by Routledge
270 Madison Avenue, New York, NY 10016

Routledge is an imprint of the Taylor & Francis Group, an Informa business

Typeset in Bembo by RefineCatch Limited, Bungay, Suffolk
Printed and bound in Great Britain by TJ International Ltd, Padstow, Cornwall
Paperback cover design by Sandra Heath
Translated by Ian Harvey

This publication has been produced with paper manufactured to strict environmental standards and with pulp derived from sustainable forests.

British Library Cataloguing in Publication Data
A catalogue record for this book is available from the British Library

Library of Congress Cataloging-in-Publication Data
Chianese, Domenico.
[Costruzioni e campo analitico. English]
Constructions and the analytic field : history, scenes and destiny / Domenico Chianese,
p. cm. – (The new library of psychoanalysis)
Includes bibliographical references and index.
ISBN-13: 978-0-415-38404-9 (hardback)
ISBN-10: 0-415-38404-4 (hardback)
ISBN-13: 978-0-415-38405-6 (pbk.)
ISBN-10: 0-415-38405-2 (pbk.)
1. Psychoanalysis. 2. Psychoanalysis and literature. I. Title.
BF175.C525 2007
150.19′5—dc22

2006037981

ISBN 978-0-415-38404-9 (hbk)
ISBN 978-0-415-38405-6 (pbk)

Contents

Acknowledgements

I should like to thank Ian Harvey for his work in translating this book from the Italian. Ian Harvey is based in Genoa and is the translator of a number of books from both German and Italian, including *Guilt: Revenge, Remorse and Responsibility after Freud* by Roberto Speziale-Bagliacca (1994, London: Brunner-Routledge).

Foreword

'The individual', wrote Freud, 'does actually carry on a twofold existence: one to serve his own purposes and the other as a link in a chain, which he serves against his will, or at least involuntarily' (Freud 1914c: 78).

'At the end of his analysis,' writes the author of this book (subtitled, recall, *History, Scenes and Destiny*), 'a patient dreamt of an old convent which had previously stood in an isolated position outside the city but which had gradually, with the passing of time, been absorbed into it. There were no monks and it had been completely restructured. The restructuring work had in part respected the old buildings and made them suitable for new functions. The place had become a cultural centre, a place of intense human exchange. At the centre, an effigy of a 'Madonna with child of the fourteenth century' had been preserved over the gate. The place had lost the gloomy, holy atmosphere it once had, the product of its isolation and abandonment' (p. 58). Associations of analyst and patient follow along with the analyst's understanding.

As the reader of the clinical story I have excerpted from his work will find, Domenico Chianese is a gifted and experienced practising psychoanalyst. He works in Rome, is extensively involved with painters, writers and philosophers and lives in a modernised apartment with features and foundations made up from the architectural styles of the last 2000 years. No doubt this happenstance leaves him particularly well placed to appreciate and illuminate Freud's work and to have developed the profound clinical understanding of what a psychoanalyst can do to construct what has happened to his patients and (as in the case of the dreamer just quoted) use it to free them from its involuntary determination of their destiny.

Today, psychoanalysis (as with the various psychotherapies based on it) is an assemblage of theories and practices all loosely based on Freud's works. Differences are great – sometimes superficially but also, I think, at depth – to the extent that one friend of mine once commented that his analyst provided fewer interpretations in the course of his whole analysis than another friend of mine had just described providing to his patient in one session. Even allowing for hyperbole, this comment reflects a major difference in the style and conception of the analytic process and, implicitly, in the analysts' theories of transformation, the states of mind analyst and patient must experience, the definition and location of transference, the meaning of the term unconscious, and so on.

Chianese's writing (which has been well translated from Italian into English by Ian Harvey for this volume in the New Library) is both rigorous and evocative, creating for the reader a rich fabric of images, ideas and thoughts. Its fascination for me comes from the way the author welds his clinical thinking together with his extensive knowledge of Italian psychoanalysis, Freud's writing and philosophy and a series of dialogic exegeses with historiographers, philosophers and epistemologists to take us on a compelling journey in which he uses his own dialogic writing style both to argue and to evoke meaning. As one reviewer put it, the author's many quotations, 'constitute a kind of cultural plankton of the utmost diversity on which he feeds as he trawls through it' (Bolognini 2002: 520). They range, for example, from the pre-Socratics to Schafer, from Laplanche to Calvino, from Green to Hoffmann, from Piera Aulagnier to Hempel, and from Tobie Nathan to Wittgenstein – Italian, French, German, British, American, South American. The freedom with which Chianese chooses his dialogists is matched by the rigour of his in-depth theoretical and epistemological studies and comparisons. He leads the reader beyond reductionist positions (such as that psychoanalysis is only remembering, only joint construction, only empathy and the like) to an eventual conception of the rich treasure house of the complex analytic space, in which the potential creativity of the couple and the 'archaeological' aspect alternate and sometimes merge unpredictably.

The starting point is two late Freud works – *Moses and Monotheism* (1939a) and *Constructions in Analysis* (1937b). These are works in which Freud develops thoughts both about the nature of historical evidence and the ways historical experience is inscribed and 'visible' in the living, explicitly and implicitly developing his specific contribution to temporality. The radical and original nature of these works and particularly of the Freudian view of the meaning and experience of time are discussed in the context of a rigorous and scholarly survey of philosophical and historiographical contributions before leading eventually to a consideration of what in Chianese's view is specific about a psychoanalytic session: the regular meeting of patient and analyst in the analyst's consulting room within the framework of the Freudian conception. Freud wrote:

> The work of analysis consists of two quite different portions, that it is carried on in two separate localities, that it involves two people, to each of whom a distinct task is assigned . . . We all know that the person who is being analysed has to be induced to remember something that has been experienced by him and repressed; and the dynamic determinants of this process are so interesting that the other portion of the work, the task performed by the analyst, has been pushed into the background. The analyst has neither experienced nor repressed any of the material under consideration; his task cannot be to remember anything. What then is his task? His task is to make out what has been forgotten from the traces which it has left behind or, more correctly, to construct it. The time and manner in which he conveys his constructions to the person who is being analysed, as well as the explanations with which he accompanies them, constitute the link between the two portions of the work of analysis, between his own part and that of the patient . . . His work of construction, or, if it is preferred, of reconstruction, resembles to a great extent an archaeologist's excavation of some dwelling-place that has been destroyed and buried or of some ancient edifice. The two processes are in fact identical, except that the analyst works under better conditions and has more material at his command to assist him, since what he is dealing with is not something destroyed but something that is still alive.
>
> (Freud 1937b: 258–259)

In his second attempt to consider the question as to whether Moses was an Egyptian, Freud wrote:

> I have tried to strengthen by a new argument the suggestion that the man Moses, the liberator and law-giver of the Jewish people, was not a Jew, but an Egyptian. That his name derived from the Egyptian vocabulary had long been observed, though not duly appreciated. I added to this consideration

> the further one that the interpretation of the exposure myth attaching to Moses necessitated the conclusion that he was an Egyptian whom a people needed to make into a Jew. At the end of my essay I said that important and far-reaching conclusions could be drawn from the suggestion that Moses was an Egyptian; but I was not prepared to uphold them publicly, since they were based only on psychological probabilities and lacked objective proof. The more significant the possibilities thus discerned the more cautious is one about exposing them to the critical attack of the outside world without any secure foundation – like an iron monument with feet of clay. No probability, however seductive, can protect us from error; even if all parts of a problem seem to fit together like the pieces of a jigsaw puzzle, one has to remember that the probable need not necessarily be the truth and the truth not always probable. And, lastly, it is not attractive to be classed with the scholastics and talmudists who are satisfied to exercise their ingenuity – unconcerned how far removed their conclusions may be from the truth.
>
> (Freud 1939b: 1)

Is psychoanalysis real or just 'made up'? What must the *Moses* story reveal (if understood as a construction) or cover up (if understood as a legend), asks Chianese? Freud kept at his preoccupation and did not write about Moses lightly or without a great deal of self-reflection. Why did he compose it and the *Constructions* paper at this stage in his career?

As well as tracing the development of these ideas from the inception of Freud's work, Chianese's argument on these points is subtle and delicate. What he 'constructs' about Freud's exploration of the *Moses* story is the structure of the way he sets out and explores his thesis; using three mutually referring poles of reference: his efforts at historical reconstruction, his efforts at self-analysis and his efforts at developing a theory to resolve the question of the primacy of imagination or memory in the mind – just as he had done when approaching two earlier defining moments in his work – his discovery/invention of the significance of Oedipus in 1897, based on his own dreams, and his construction of the Wolf Man's Grusha episode in 1914, where he established the concept of *Nachträglichkeit* and positioned it and primal phantasies at the centre of analytic practice. Psychoanalysis, Chianese suggests, 'grows out of and through the "failure" of history and its limitations . . . the repressed becomes historical truth through the work of analysis' (p.15) and a process of resignification takes place in phantasies: they contain 'things heard by children at an early age and only understood later'.[1] Chianese notes how in each case Freud hesitated and delayed publication but how each case, and the personal struggle tied up in apprehending it, illustrates the functioning of what he thinks is fundamental about the psychoanalytic apparatus – formed by three referential poles, as just mentioned, which in the clinical situation become the analyst, the patient and the theory. 'One might be tempted,' says Chianese, as indeed Freud often was, 'to privilege one of these points of reference, making the other two part of the one we choose: self-analysis and the history of the patient translated into the referential language of theory; or theory and history understood through self-analytic referentiality. Any attempt in one of these directions cancels out the virtual space which is created between the poles and which we can call the analytic field' (p. 119).

It is the analytic field as a virtual space and its special peculiarly fertile characteristics that Chianese (following and clarifying an important Italian tradition in this area[2]) goes on to elucidate and exemplify clinically in the last third of the book. In doing so he makes profound points about what is (and is not) important about approaching and understanding his countertransference that allows an analyst to function, linking this to self-analysis. Quoting John Klauber (1976: 283) he writes: 'The analyst also needs the patient in order to crystallize and communicate his own thoughts . . . It is also in his relationship with his patients that the analyst refreshes his own analysis' (p. 120).

As Chianese writes: 'Placing theory as the third "subject" in the analytic field may arouse some puzzlement in analysts who consider theory as a defence . . . But theory does not come along in the end and arrive from outside: it is the origin of the process and internal to it.' It is to the great credit of the New Library of Psychoanalysis that this fascinating argument is now available in English. Its style is refreshing and its argument and mode of argument rigorous but unlike English writing. It is a rich feast of evocation. Moreover, for the Anglo-Saxon psychoanalyst and psychotherapist – particularly at this time when relational and here and now perspectives are so pervasive – the proposition, that the theory of psychoanalysis (Freudian metapsychology) must be lived into the clinical situation in order to create a real psychoanalytic engagement with the patient, is perhaps the most timely, interesting and provocative point: one which it can be nothing but invigorating to engage with.

David Tuckett

1

Turning over a new leaf

> Man tries to form for himself a clear, simplified image of the world in the way best suited to him. . . . This is what the painter, the speculative philosopher and the natural scientist all do, each in his own way. He locates the centre of gravity of his emotional life inside this image and its formation in order to attain the peace and serenity he cannot find within the narrow confines of his ever-changing personal experience.
>
> (Albert Einstein)

> The more time passes, the more I come to think that although we honestly believe that the various questions we focus on at various points along our theoretical path depend on the importance of a certain clinical phenomenon or a new interpretation, the fact is that all we are doing is examining, under different guises, what I would call the fundamental questions that are peculiar to each analyst. Perhaps these designate the point both of resistance and fascination that marks his relationship with analytic theory.
>
> (Piera Aulagnier)

I have been interested in Freud's *Constructions in Analysis* (1937b) ever since I first became an analyst. It is one of those 'fundamental questions' that Aulagnier talks about and likewise it occupies that 'centre of gravity of emotional life' to which Einstein refers.

I have decided to bring together in one book the results of my research and reflections on this subject over the years not merely so as to talk about my own questions – it is in any case difficult to have more than a very vague notion of the genesis of our ideas and of the traces that lie scattered along the path we have taken.

The sole reason that justifies publication lies in my deep conviction that these 'personal' questions are intertwined and articulated with some fundamental questions that had their origin in Freud and which are still today part of the psychoanalytic debate.

History, narrative, external reality, memory, the position and role of the analyst are inseparable. They are interconnected elements which form the meshes of a web. Each analyst weaves his own web during the course of his experience, but it is inconceivable that some web or other should be missing entirely from an analyst's thinking. The web I have created does not claim to be the only one, nor certainly the best. There is, however, one thing I am certain about: if these links were to be lost or if only one took over absolutely, this would produce real oppositions (one example would be the opposition between history and narration) whose prime effect would be to tear through the fabric of theory and analytical practice.

My research has been an attempt at an historical-critical study of the Freudian oeuvre, constantly enriched and supported by what I have learned from analytic practice. The pattern that emerges has been woven out of 'new objects' and 'new meanings' (for example, *virtual space*, chiasmus).

This book is itself a construction: it is a collage of unpublished chapters and reworkings of previous articles, which have been put together irrespective, however, of the chronological order of their publication. After all, writing does not proceed in a linear fashion (nor, for that matter, does analysis). There are openings, insights, returns, stylistic deformities. Psychoanalytical works – sometimes even by the same author, as Pontalis suggests (1977) – are written in different styles: they can be theoretical, poetic, abstract, allusive, novelistic.

The chapters on the analytical field – as anticipated by the title – come after those on the constructions. This order in some way reflects a kind of logical – though not chronological – derivation: the analytical field is defined and delineated at and by the edges of historical reconstruction in psychoanalysis. The order does not, however, correspond to my own path: my interest in the analytical field developed side by side with my interest in constructions. There is more than one chiasmus between the two levels.

Although the concept of 'field' applied to the analytical situation has been a clear hallmark of Italian psychoanalysis over the last 15 years, its use has never been unambiguous. There are still divergent points of view and clashes between different research traditions. Despite an abundance of clinical descriptions and theoretical hypotheses, no sufficiently stable conceptual model has been reached that is both shared and useful. What we really need is a more in-depth discussion in a spirit of what Freud called 'intellectual communism' where no one scrutinises too carefully what has been given and what has been received (letter to Jung, 7 April 1907). The latter part of this book attempts to set this dialogue in motion. I hope that what I try to see through the eyes of the future does not ultimately turn out to be a utopian landscape.

Writing a book is like turning over a new leaf. A path is seen as completed; the questions that remain open cannot be answered by continuing along routes already taken; other paths are glimpsed, other landscapes whose contours one hopes will come into focus once the page has been turned for good.

Construction, or, if it is preferred, reconstruction

> Frightened by the immense complication of events, our investigations take the side of one correlation as against another and set up contradictions which do not exist but have arisen owing to a rupture of more comprehensive relations.
>
> (Freud 1939a: 107–108)

> If we have the courage to proceed in the same way, we shall be setting foot on a path which will lead us first to something unexpected and incomprehensible, but which will perhaps, by a devious route, bring us to a goal.
>
> (Freud 1913a: 293–294)

Interrupted itineraries

'Silence and long periods of time are worth more than constructions and memory: this could be the moral of the analytical stories that are being written today.' This is how Aulagnier expressed her misgivings in 1970 at the first signs of a 'revolution' in psychoanalytic technique. This was just the start. It is not easy to summarise what happened subsequently: the expansion of the concept of countertransference, the emphasis on the here and now, the reference to ever more archaic experiences which in the therapeutic process have necessarily had to rely increasingly on theoretical frameworks since they can find no confirmation in the patient's memory. Finally, in more recent times, 'analyst–patient interaction' appears to have become the definition of therapy par excellence. These are all undeniable advances and expansions which rest on a basic question that has become ineluctable. There is more than a simple gap between the strand of psychoanalysis that continues to refer to repression, *rememoration* and construction and the other strand where these elements fade ever more into the background until they finally disappear; the difference is one of style and theory. This second model does not correspond to anything based on Freud's work, and this difference represents one of the problems present-day psychoanalysts have to address. What is at stake is not only the practice but also the ethics of psychoanalysis, by which I mean the 'project which inspires the work of the analyst' (Aulagnier 1970). In the Freudian model ethics were based on and in concord with method: this is what led to a psychoanalytic ethic. What has become of this project today?

'Constructing a well-formed, more coherent story', 'analyst and patient together construct many possible stories, many tales' – these are expressions of a contemporary psychoanalysis which can easily lead to infinite hermeneutics and narratological drift and whose project (assuming there is only one) is difficult to fully understand.

Prompted by what are in many ways radical doubts, I have decided to go back over the path starting from the beginning. This is not meant to be yet another return – we are aware that each return implies distance – but rather a way of reconstructing the links, of forging anew forgotten paths, reflecting on what have in the course of time become oppositions.

Reconstructing a path is thus an act of beginning again – although, at the moment one sets foot on the path, there is no guarantee of a result, irrespective of whether the story is repeated or a new one is set in motion. *Constructions in Analysis* lends itself particularly well to this work of return and opening. We shall start from there – from this boundary work. It brings together strands which run through Freud's work. It is the starting point of itineraries, later interrupted by his death, which can give us glimpses of a new and different analytical purpose.

We shall start by briefly illustrating the structure of Freud's 1937 work and then work backwards, picking up the various threads and reconstructing the interrupted itineraries. At various points as we go along, in the light of analysts' present experience, we shall make necessary critical shifts away from Freud's position. As we follow this trajectory we shall outline our theses and try to respond to the doubts that propel us along our path. Needless to say, however, the replies will be found on the path itself, in the act of becoming that defines all research.

Constructions in Analysis

Some 50 years before the controversy aroused by Grunbaum, Freud found himself, when writing *Constructions in Analysis* (1937b), faced with the problem of verifiability which had presented itself at the very beginning of his enterprise and which, after Freud, went on to involve both psychoanalysts and epistemologists, detractors and defenders of psychoanalysis. At the time a 'well-known man of science' had expressed a 'derogatory and unjust' opinion about psychoanalysis, saying that the psychoanalyst provided the patient with interpretations and treated him according to the 'famous principle of heads I win, tails you lose' (Freud 1937b: 257).

Freud took up the challenge and started his defence in the first part of *Constructions in Analysis* by illustrating in detail the way in which analysts 'are accustomed to arrive at an assessment of the 'Yes' or 'No' of [. . .] patients during analytic treatment'. Analytic work 'involves two people, to each of whom a distinct task is assigned': the patient must 'be induced to remember something that has been experienced by him and repressed', the analyst must 'make out what has been forgotten from the traces which it has left behind or, more correctly, to construct it'. The aim is to obtain 'a picture of the patient's forgotten years that shall be alike trustworthy and in all essential respects complete'. The analyst's work is one of '*construction, or, if it is preferred, of reconstruction*' (pp. 257–259, emphasis added). It is worth looking more closely at this expression (which we have used as the title of this section). It is ambiguous but in our opinion precisely for this reason highly creative. Freud suggests that there is an equivalence between the two terms, that they are interchangeable and it is almost as if he is leaving the choice between them up to the reader. We are convinced, however, that Freud was amply aware of what was in many respects a substantial difference, one which stood at the centre of the methodological problem that had come to the fore during the troubled writing of *Moses and Monotheism* (1939a). The debate between narrative construction and historical reconstruction was one which occupied Freud from the very beginning of his career and in the last period of his life led him to new and unexpected conclusions; it is also a debate which continues to rage (one thinks of Spence 1982).

The quotation we have just commented on introduces the celebrated archaeological metaphor which is developed over two detailed sections and which we shall not quote or comment on here because it will be the object of more in-depth discussion elsewhere in this book.

The first section of *Constructions in Analysis* – in a pattern to be found in the other two sections as well – ends with a break, a drastic variation, the prelude to the different level of discourse on which he then develops the subsequent section. The comparison with archaeology had led Freud to say that it 'depends only upon analytic technique whether we shall succeed in bringing what is concealed completely to light'. It is a question, that is, of skill and experience. But just a few lines later comes the unexpected conclusion: while for 'the archaeologist *reconstruction* is the aim and end of his endeavours', in analysis 'the *construction* is only a preliminary labour' (p. 260, emphasis added). It is to be noted that he uses the terms construction and reconstruction differently, the former referring to the work of the analyst and the latter to that of the archaeologist – reflecting a difference present in his mind. An archaeologist would, however, have strong objections to Freud's thesis because he too would see the interpretive-constructive work as an important part of his endeavour. The text changes tack at this point: a dialogic dimension is opened up in the initial debate between true and false. Here we have a substantial change, one which can be applied by extension to psychoanalysis as a whole; and *Constructions in Analysis* represents its opening moment.

In the second section, Freud tries to identify coherent and credible guarantees; probably he is afraid that working with constructions will lead to errors. His long line of reasoning emphasises the importance of the indirect form of confirmation coming from the patient: the influx of further material, faulty actions, repetitions, transference, but also the 'unmistakable aggravation of his symptoms' (p. 265) and opposition to the analyst's help – in short, negative therapeutic reactions. The decidedly assertive and vigorous tone of the beginning of the section (let us not forget that he is defending himself against a 'derogatory and unjust' accusation) gives way to a more moderate and prudent register towards the end: 'We do not pretend that an individual construction is anything more than a conjecture which awaits examination, confirmation or rejection. We claim no authority for it' (p. 265).

In the prelude to the third, and crucial, section, we find 'remarks which open up a wider perspective'. Not always does the road which starts from construction lead to the memory of the analysand; instead we sometimes get an 'assured conviction' of the truth of the construction. This conviction, Freud continues, 'achieves the same therapeutic result as a recaptured memory'. He adds: 'The problem of what the circumstances are in which this occurs and of how it is possible that what appears to be an incomplete substitute should nevertheless produce a complete result – all of this is matter for a later enquiry' (p. 266). Here opens the (previously announced) broad perspective and Freud returns to the psychoanalytically longstanding *topos* of hallucinations and delusions. He talks about *überdeutlich* ('ultra-clear'), visually vivid memories of places, objects, furniture that can emerge in response to the constructions, in the place of the repressed: a compromise between 'the "upward drive" of the repressed' and 'resistance'.

At this point Freud makes his first generalisation: 'Perhaps it may be a general characteristic of hallucinations to which sufficient attention has not hitherto been paid that in them something that has been experienced in infancy and then forgotten returns – something that the child has seen or heard at a time when he could hardly speak' (p. 267). He then moves on to delusions, which, together with distortions and the wrong positions of what is remembered, convey a 'fragment of historical truth'. At first Freud treads carefully – 'I am aware,' he says, 'that it is of small service to handle so important a subject in the cursory fashion that I have here employed' – but then gives a real acceleration to the text, saying that he has been unable to 'resist the seduction' of the analogy between the constructions of the analyst and the delusional constructions of the psychotic – both are attempts 'at explanation and cure'. The difference between the analyst and the psychotic lies in the fact that the latter can do no more than 'replace the fragment of reality that is being disavowed in the present by another fragment that had already been disavowed in the remote past'. This is how he introduces the hypothesis of double *Verleugnung* (disavowal) in the genesis of the psychosis – a hypothesis which has yet to be sufficiently examined. He finally goes on to say: 'The delusion owes its convincing power to the element of historical truth which it inserts in the place of the rejected reality' (p. 268). The conclusion of *Constructions in Analysis* is paradoxical and ironical. Freud had started out by defending himself against an unjust opinion and after trying to defend the validity of constructions he had entrusted their outcome to analytic dialogue, finally reaching an embarrassing analogy that might confirm his adversary's accusation against the arbitrariness of the analyst's construction.

The article finishes with another generalisation: Freud comes back to the historical and religious themes which, as we shall see, were the focus of his speculation, and maintains that the delusions of mankind (he is thinking of religions) 'contradict reality' and 'owe their power to the element of *historical truth* which they have brought up from the repression of the forgotten and primeval past' (Freud 1938d: 387).

The short, long-forgotten article by Freud we have summarised here was later reappraised not only by psychoanalysts but also by philosophers (Rella 1977), historians (Bori 1979) and literary figures (Lavagetto 1985). The early difficulties can perhaps be attributed to the fact that constructions, interwoven as they are with reason, might have appeared incompatible with the supposed spontaneity of the analytic act. Moreover, a certain amount of unease will have been due to the clear position Freud takes on the reality of infantile traumas at the end of the article. This is one of the most tormented aspects of Freud's theory – and one we shall be looking at again in the following chapters. Reality – and the tyranny of reality – will come back in late Freud to interrogate, or perhaps it would be better to say, attack the symbolic order, to point out the limits and the power of language.

The paper portrays the Freudian trajectory in various ways. It starts from the perspective of *Rechtfertigung*, justification, and goes on to the intermediary phase of *Mitteilung*, communication, thus opening up analysis to dialogue. Freud is clear about what kind of dialogue he means: a dialogue between two people – the analyst and the patient – 'to each of whom a distinct task is assigned' (p. 258). In an excellent article Humphrey Morris (1993) makes a suggestion we can usefully follow up. He considers this as a dialogue between two aspects of Freud himself: the part that 'reflects and is reflected, the subjective and the objective, the theorised and the theoriser'. Looked at in this way, the entire text becomes a kind of meditation. Freud was over 80 when he wrote *Constructions in Analysis* (published immediately after *Analysis Terminable and Interminable*, 1937a) and was revising his life's work, re-examining it and opening himself up to doubts and new hypotheses. Like Descartes (again, this is Morris's supposition), Freud based his reflections on doubts and his first question was: how can we know whether an interpretation is correct? He then created difficulties for construction by suggesting that it does not always lead the patient to remember. Then, having called into question the bases of his knowledge, he turned, like Descartes, towards dreams, hallucinations and delusions. 'What we are in search of is a picture of the patient's forgotten years that shall be alike, trustworthy and, in all essential respects, complete' (p. 258). This is what Freud says about the analyst's aim. It implies a stable relationship between construction, language and image. But soon Freud was faced with a lack of traces, images and *rememoration* (something confirmed by our everyday experience); the traumas date back to a preverbal period. It is this absence of image and language that renders thought instable and this limitation that leads to the encounter – and mutual recognition – between psychoanalysis and psychosis.

When a person questions himself radically about the truth of his version of things, we could say, to put it in Foucault's terms, that 'reason' vies with and merges with 'unreason'. At that moment the boundary between construction and delusion becomes unstable and reason is able to take the opportunity to consider its limitations and to accept its inherent fracture – without denying it, as happens in delusion. Freud's reference to the universality of delusion in the form of religion only convinces him further – considering his atheism, it can clearly do nothing to console him – of the radical nature of this break. In this way late Freud communicates and passes on to us both the weight of the drama and the sense of the enigma of human affairs – qualities constantly present along his path.

The writing of *Moses*

Unlike other works by Freud, little is known about the genesis of *Constructions in Analysis*. What little we do know – from Jones (1953–57), Clarke (1980), Gay (1988) – concerns the period when it was published, December 1937, shortly after *Analysis Terminable and Interminable* (1937a). If we know little about its 'material' origin, there is much we can deduce about its 'historical' origin. *Constructions in Analysis* appeared after the publication of the first two essays in *Moses* and is deeply immersed in and interwoven with the same set of problems and, in our view, their lack of solution. In this sense both trace interrupted itineraries – an interruption due not only to Freud's death but also to the limitations of the period and of the *episteme*: 'My interest, after making a lifelong detour through the natural sciences, medicine and psychotherapy, returned to cultural problems which had fascinated me long before, when I was a youth scarcely old enough for thinking.' This is what Freud wrote in the postscript to *An Autobiographical Study* (1925b: 72). Historical, religious and literary problems exercised Freud's thinking during the latter period of his life.

'The debate about psychic transmission that Freud introduced intersected at what he called its nodal points with the threads that make up the fabric of the psychoanalytic work, with the debate on the subject of Freud himself, with his psychic, social, religious and cultural heritage, but also with his position as founder of psychoanalysis' (Kaës 1993: 16). Here Kaës was talking about Freud's entire oeuvre but nothing could be more appropriate as a specific comment on *Moses*. This work met with the approval of very few, and embarrassment and silence on the part of many. Years later it was to be re-examined and subjected to various interpretations.

In this chapter I do not intend to concentrate on the finished work but rather on the effort involved in writing *Moses*, on the doubts that beset Freud during the writing of his 'novel' (which is how he described it to Arnold Zweig), because I think that the doubts are of the same nature as those which propel *Constructions in Analysis*. What interests me are the methodological problems centring on the dilemma: novel or history. I am not driven in this research by a taste for digging through archives or philology but rather by the desire to better contextualise and address certain points of controversy in clinical psychoanalytic theory.

Numerous letters from this period reflect the doubts that hampered the writing of *Moses*, and these are connected to the 'nodal points' of Freud's work. To understand them, in later chapters we shall follow several different paths and then return to *Moses* at the moment of its final draft. Then we shall consider the historical, methodological and analytical limitations of the whole operation and, in turn, open ourselves up to new perspectives.

Moses is one of those works that appear at particular critical moments in history, when the problem of transmission becomes pressing, when there is uncertainty about which bonds, values and knowledge to pass on to the next generation. Written shortly before the outbreak of World War II, a radical crisis, the end of an era, *Moses* bears the tragic mark of 'modernity', that doubt about values and their transmission which characterises the way of living and thinking of a generation, if not an epoch. In this sense it is a work that still has something to say today even though it tellingly defines a specific moment in the life of Freud and the institution of psychoanalysis.

The emergence of the Jewish question, which was to be an integral part of the imminent tragedy, is one of the basic motives behind the writing of *Moses*: 'Faced with the new persecutions, one asks oneself again how the Jews have come to be what they are and why they have attracted this undying hatred. I soon discovered the formula: Moses created the Jews. So I gave my work the title: *The Man Moses, a Historical Novel*'. This is what Freud wrote to Arnold Zweig on 30 September 1934 (Freud and Zweig 1970). Freud was driven by contradictory feelings: about to leave his homeland permanently for Britain, he felt a sense of definitive separation from Judaism. At the same time, however, he wrote an apologia, arguing for its universality, placing it within the continuity of ancient civilisation, praising it for his elevated spirituality at a moment when progress was allied with barbarism. Together with these external circumstances there were also his inner doubts about his investigation – methodological doubts which are reflected in the title itself. In a letter to Jones dated 3 March 1936, he talks about having written a book entitled *The Man Moses, a Historical Novel*, pointing out that the reason it had not been published and was never likely to be was that the essential historical basis was missing.

Freud's thesis is well known: Moses was an Egyptian, a follower of the monotheism of Amenhotep IV, and was killed by the Jews. After his death some local Semitic cults were introduced, promoted by another man who was superimposed on the first Moses. The original monotheism returned in part in the prophetic age and this gave rise to a dualism which has characterised the culture and history of Israel ever since.

The killing of the father, trauma, repression, the double scene, conflict, the return of the repressed – in Moses we find figures and *topoi* typical of Freud's thinking.

The book was supposed to be introduced with a Foreword, never published, which, in view of its importance, we give here in full:

As the sexual union of horse and donkey produces two different hybrids, the mule (Maulthier) and the hinny (Maulesel), so the mixture of historical writing and fiction gives rise to different products which, under the common designation of 'historical novel', sometimes want to be appreciated as history, sometimes as novel. For some of them deal with people and events that are historically familiar and whose characteristics they aim to reproduce faithfully. They derive their interest, in fact, from history, but their intent is that of the novel; they want to affect the emotions. Others among these literary creations function in quite the opposite way. They do not hesitate to invent persons and even events in order to describe the special character of a period, but first and foremost they aspire to historical truth despite the admitted fiction. Others even manage to a large extent in reconciling the demands of artistic creation with those of historical fidelity. How much fiction, contrary to the intentions of the historian, still creeps into his presentation, requires little further comment.

When I, however, who am neither a historian nor an artist, introduce one of my works as a 'historical novel', then this term must allow for yet another definition. I have been trained to the careful scrutiny of a certain domain of phenomena. To me fiction and invention are easily associated with the blemish of error.

My immediate purpose was to gain knowledge of the person of Moses, my more distant goal to contribute thereby to the solution of a problem, still current today, which can only be specified later on.

A character study requires reliable material as its basis, but nothing available concerning Moses can be called trustworthy. It is a tradition coming from one source, not confirmed by any other, fixed in writing only in a later period, in itself contradictory, revised several times and distorted under the influence of new tendencies, while closely interwoven with the religious and national myths of a people.

One would be entitled to curtail the attempt as hopeless, were it not that the grandeur of the figure outweighs its elusiveness and challenges us to renewed effort. Thus, one undertakes to treat each possibility in the text as a clue, and to fill the gap between one fragment and another according to the law, so to speak, of least resistance, that is – to give preference to the assumption that has the greatest probability. That which one can obtain by means of this technique can also be called a kind of 'historical novel', since it has no proven reality, or only an uncomfortable one, for even the greatest probability does not necessarily correspond to the truth. Truth is often very improbable, and factual evidence can only in small measure be replaced by deductions and speculations.

(Yerushalmi 1991: 17)

This passage is shot through with a subtle irony – to be seen in its classification of species and hybrids, a taxonomy whose ordinates and abscissa are on the one hand history and on the other novel and invention. In the end Freud cannot be identified either in the invention of the artist or in the rigour of the historian.

'The historical novel is used in a figurative sense, moderated by a series of observations about the state of the sources' (Bori 1979). The reference to the sources appears every time Freud talks about historical truth. The work is offered as a study of the character of the 'man' Moses. Even though the sources are scanty and contradictory, Freud attempts the enterprise because the 'greatness' of the figure is equal to his 'distance', or rather the *Vatervorbild* (the model, the archetype of the father figure) is great precisely because of its remote origins. When the events are distant and the sources are limited: 'Then,' says G. Duby (in *Il sogno della storia*, 1980), 'we are led to focus rather on the way these events are reported, to study the trace in itself.' Earlier he argues: 'I am convinced of the subjectivity of historical discourse, that this discourse is the product of a dream, a dream which is however not completely free because it is formed by a great backdrop of images that must necessarily be connected to *traces*' (emphasis added). As Freud also says in *Constructions in Analysis*, the events are always more distant in clinical practice and analytic experience since they happen before the acquisition of language.

In many respects the problem of *Moses* is the core problem of psychoanalysis: the problem of events, original events. Faced with the scarcity and ambiguity of the traces, in *Constructions in Analysis* Freud speaks, when referring to the analyst's constructions, of probability, conjectures and hypotheses. In the unpublished preface to *Moses* he talks again about probability. In the end, he says, we will have a kind of 'historical novel' which has no 'proven reality'. The connections between *Moses* and *Constructions in Analysis* are not only methodological but also thematic: the comparison with archaeology, the link between delusion and historical truth, the application of his psychological hypotheses to mankind. When we look carefully, we can see a helicoidal movement in the speculation that runs through *Moses* and *Constructions in Analysis*. When addressing the historical-religious problem of Moses, Freud deploys a theory taken from individual analysis (the theory of the birth of the hero put forward by Rank, who had also used anthropological material). The problems of historiographical method that emerged in *Moses* were posed again in *Constructions in*

Analysis, and at the end of he comes back to historical-religious themes – hence the helicoidal movement. But above all it is the problems of method that are similar. Let us examine the difficulties encountered by Freud in his reconstruction of *Moses*: (a) the source (in the case of *Moses*, the Bible); (b) fixed in writing very late; (c) full of contradictions; (d) re-elaborated and deformed; (e) re-elaborated and deformed to fit the religious and national myths of a people.

Both at the beginning (*Studies on Hysteria*, 1895b) and at the end of his career (*Constructions in Analysis*, 1937b), Freud had to face the problem in his clinical work of (a) sources; (b) transcriptions; (c) contradictions caused by censorship and rewriting; (d) texts and memories re-elaborated and deformed; (e) for the purpose of constructing and maintaining a personal myth. Just as the method of deciphering and reconstruction is uncertain in *Moses*, so is the method of reconstruction in a clinical case.

The relationship between historiography and psychoanalysis, which will be examined in a later chapter, was repeatedly utilised by Freud. Constant in Freud was the comparison between the formation of legends, ancient historiography (which concealed or deformed the true origins of a people) and the defensive constructions of the patient with regard to his past. In clinical practice the analyst must decipher in order to discover the patient's historical truth behind his screen memories and constructions. Similarly the historical truth of a people must be deciphered from the legendary material and from material falsified by analytic historiography. It is necessary to distinguish legend from history. So if this is Freud's programmatic and methodological manifesto, what we see in his practice and theory (instead) is constant slippage, contamination and hybridisation between these two levels.

In *Moses* Freud sets up a game between religious legend (*Sage*) and his *Construction*, between the object to be explained and the discourse that explains it, just as in analysis a game is set up between the patient's mythical construction and the analyst's interpreting and reconstructive language.

In *Constructions in Analysis* Freud is 'seduced' by the comparison between the analyst's construction and the patient's delusion. In *Moses* there is constant slippage between the discourse of the legend and the discourse of the analyst. When talking of his own discourse Freud uses *Darstellung, Konstruktion, Rekonstruktion, Aufbau* (building); to refer to religious legends he uses *Sage, Mythus, Tradition* – but also *Darstellung* and *Konstruktion*, that is, words which describe the production of the analyst. Certain of the 'truth' of his *Moses*, Freud was 'obliged to construct so imposing a statue upon feet of clay, so that any fool could topple it' (letter to Arnold Zweig dated 16 December 1934; Freud and Zweig 1970). The foot of clay is the 'historical method' he adopts. This doubt delayed publication.

He had faced a similar problem of delay in 1914, when he was about to publish *From the History of an Infantile Neurosis.*[1] The question was whether what he had reconstructed was reality or fantasy: 'The old trauma theory of the neuroses [. . .] had suddenly come to the front once more' (1918: 95). That same year, 1914, he contradicted himself when he said: '[the theory of seduction] a mistaken idea [which] had to be overcome which might have been fatal to the young science' (*On the history of the Psycho-analytic Movement*, 1914a: 17). In *Moses* we find the same contradiction as in 1914. Despite his premise of searching for historical truth, in the middle of the text, he once again raises the problem he had started from: 'But no matter whether what we have here is a phantasy or the return of a forgotten reality, in any case the origin of the concept of a hero is to be found at this point' (Freud 1939a: 87). It can justly be argued – and it is a point many, especially historians, have made – that what we see here is a defeat for his method, but I think that precisely this failure leads to a greater specification, delimitation and differentiation both of the method and the analytic space. One might argue that psychoanalysis grows out of and through the 'failure' of history and its limitations, and that only then does the analytic relation become a possibility; a subject in analysis (and the analyst with him) who interrogates himself about his extreme experiences (at the extremes of memory, faithfulness, chronology) interrogates himself at the edges of history about a rupture which however constitutes the very birth of 'his' history.

Freud steadfastly pursued the repressed which escaped him, that unreachable event that cannot be documented. If this is his limitation, we owe to him the intuition, which we have since been able to expand, that the repressed becomes historical truth through the work of analysis, that the novelistic, mythical and at times delusional construction of the analysand is constituted as (historical) truth through his word when there is someone (the analyst) who takes that word as truth. This truth, however, does not live in any defined or definable place. Freud tried obstinately to find that place, to fill a void, a gap in the remote past, to fill it with a possible event. We can readily deduce that the analytic space has its origin in this unfillable original void.

That non-place is at the same time the place that is at the origin of writing (in our case *Moses*) and transference (in the case of psychoanalysis). It is no accident that both writing and transference are described, in Pontalis's (1990) penetrating insight as 'forces of attraction', which underlines the fact that something exists between them which goes beyond simple similarity. Paradoxically, one cannot think outside that non-place, that wound in history. Similarly Balsamo and Napolitano (1994: 24) say that 'in those lacunae [the subject] finds origin, polarity and relationship'. In short 'he finds at that nodal point the engine that propels his actions'. Kaës (1993) states that 'origin is that which escapes us, that from which we are irremediably absent and which eludes our grasp at the moment when we are constituted in and through the desire for another, even more for another that precedes us'. Finally we should also mention Bion, for whom the symbol O indicates both origin and zero. Origin is a crucial problem which brings together Freud's history and that of psychoanalysis, ours and that of the patient.

Departure and debt, dispossession and belonging, 'tradition and rupture' (Russo 1986) are constant themes in the writing of *Moses*. Departure and debt, dispossession and belonging, tradition and rupture are what drive people into analysis and also drive people to become analysts. The vocation and profession of the analyst are founded on such doubt and such uncertainty. The uncertainty we find in *Moses* is not eliminated, and doubt is at the basis of the Freudian 'construction'. The method and the doubt imply each other reciprocally (here again we find Descartes). The individual cannot put his trust in the stability of an ontological place (or an unchanging *cogito, ergo sum*) despite remaining constantly in debt to his genealogical heritage. This loss and this debt, which generate writing, are integral to the transference, where the analyst is 'summoned by the patient to a place where he is not' (Stein 1971). But as analysts we cannot let ourselves be captured by and in that place. 'If everything goes well, the other will never be (re-) found where he was supposed to be or where the other thought he would be found – on pain of the impossibility of analysis' (Chianese 1983).

We have ventured beyond the task we set ourselves at the beginning of the chapter. We leave Freud before the definitive draft of his half novel, half history, before the rejection of the title and the preface. Many controversial themes (repression, trauma, the perception of reality, phantasy), to be found in both *Constructions in Analysis* and

Moses, are part of the clinical and theoretical path Freud set out on and we shall be coming back to them again in the next chapters of the book. Then after this *Umweg* (detour) we shall return to *Moses* at the moment of its final draft and publication.

What drives us along this path? Nietzsche said that the fall of the gods is not so much a drama as an occasion for great laughter. We have yet to hear the gods laugh. The problem of reality, events, origins, the meaning and the arbitrariness of our constructions and reconstructions continues to fascinate and at times torment us. This then is the basic question, the reason for the apparently devious pilgrimage upon which we are now about to invite the reader to embark.

2

Material reality, historical reality, psychic reality

1897–1918

The problem of trauma and the 'reality' of trauma occupy a central place in Freud's thinking in *Moses*. Freud's research in the late 1930s is fuelled by his renewed interest in external reality and the defences employed against it (see in particular *Splitting of the Ego in the Process of Defence*, 1938b). Freud thus returns to what, at the end of the last decade of the nineteenth century, had been the starting point of his vision of pathology and human development as he explored the relationship between reality, memory and imagination (an exploration reflected in his copious correspondence with Wilhelm Fliess; Freud 1897). Of those years, 1897 has gone down in history and in the iconography of psychoanalysis as the year of the '*neurotica* crisis'. But this crisis, linked to the discovery of the Oedipus complex, is only the epilogue of a path which I feel needs to be resumed in order to highlight the specific nature of the Freudian 'discovery' as against discoveries and inventions in other spheres of science or the arts. The fascination of being present at the epiphany of a science is not, however, the only reason that pushes me in this direction.

The question of whether to attribute primacy to the imagination or memory engaged Freud on more than one level: as a scientist dealing with the limitations of his theory, as a physician aware of failures in treatment and as a man facing up to the enigmas of his childhood and destiny. Self-analysis, treatment of patients and theory are all elements within the same knowledge process. In this sense Freud's experience, if we cleanse it of its rhetorical and mythical encrustations, even though specific and unrepeatable, can have the value of a prototypical experience for analysts. The meaning I personally give to this expression will become clear as these pages unfold. Let us now follow this experience as it develops.

In the spring of 1897 Freud still gave credence to the stories of his patients, as is shown by, amongst others, the letters of 6 April, 2 May and Drafts L and M. Phantasies, 'screen' memories and real traumatic events are 'psychical facades constructed in order to bar the way to these memories' (Draft L, p. 248). At the time primary scenes (*Urszene*) were real scenes of seduction. Only later did Freud mean by *Urszene* the scenes of parental coitus, and we have to wait until 1914 before we find the concept of *Urphantasien*, phantasy scenes which, similar to Kantian categories, function as basic and structural organising principles and structures of the unconscious. But already in this period we can find the insights which will be developed later. A process of resignification takes place in phantasies. They contain 'things heard by children at an early age and only understood later' (p. 244). The concept of construction makes its appearance: '[phantasies] are manufactured by means of things that are *heard*, and utilized *subsequently*, and thus combine things experienced and heard, past events (from the history of parents and ancestors), and things that have been seen by oneself' (p. 240). 'Phantasies are constructed by a process of amalgamation and distortion analogous to the decomposition of a chemical body which is compounded with another one' (Draft M, p. 152).

Despite these insights, which will be developed later, the moment of the 'discovery' matures during the summer and is then expressed in a short space of time in the autumn of the same year. The three phases of this development are signalled by the letters to Fliess of 21 September, 3 October and 15 October.

At an early point in his career, after his celebrated announcement – 'I no longer believe in my *neurotica* [theory of the neurosis]' (Freud 1897: 259) – he tried to describe the reasons behind his crisis. As one can see, all three levels we have already mentioned are implicated (self-analysis – theory – therapy):

> So I will begin historically from the question of the origin of my reasons for disbelief. The continual disappointments in my attempts at bringing my analysis to a real conclusion, the running-away of people who had for a time seemed most in my grasp, the absence of the complete successes on which I had reckoned, the possibility of explaining the partial successes in other ways, on ordinary lines – this was the first group. Then came surprise

> at the fact that in every case the father, not excluding my own, had to be blamed as a pervert – the realization of the unexpected frequency of hysteria, in which the same determinant is invariably established, though such a widespread extent of perversity towards children is, after all, not very probable. (The perversity would have to be immeasurably more frequent than the hysteria, since the illness only arises where there has been an accumulation of events and where a factor that weakens defence has supervened.) Then, thirdly, the certain discovery that there are no indications of reality in the unconscious, so that one cannot distinguish between the truth and fiction that is cathected with affect. (Thus, the possibility remained open that sexual phantasy invariably seizes upon the theme of the parents.) Fourthly, the reflection that in the most deep-going psychosis the unconscious memory does not break through, so that the secret of the childhood experiences is not betrayed even in the most confused delirium. If in this way we see that the unconscious never overcomes the resistance of the conscious, then, too, we lose our expectation that in treatment the opposite will happen, to the extent of the unconscious being completely tamed by the conscious.
>
> (Freud 1897: 259–260)

What we have here is what Bachelard (1978) referred to as the 'removal of an epistemological obstacle'. Relieved of the weight of reality, thought is able to range more freely and the various levels implicated in the cognitive process consequently undergo substantial transformations. The first is registered in self-analysis: the transition from material to psychic reality, from memories to phantasies, opens a significant breach in the internal space and offers new tools for investigations, as is shown in the next letter to Fliess of 3 October:

> Very little is still happening to me externally, but internally something most interesting. For the last four days my self-analysis, which I consider indispensable for throwing light upon the whole problem, has proceeded in dreams and has presented me with the most valuable inferences and clues [. . .]. Later (between the ages of two and two-and-a-half) my libido was stirred up towards *matrem*, namely on the occasion of a journey with her from Leipzig to Vienna, during which we must have spent the night together and I must have had an opportunity of seeing her *nudam*.
>
> (Freud 1897: 262–263)

Oedipus is born in Freud's self-analysis. The crisis of the *neurotica* was part of the process of liberating a fragment of psychic reality, but the reality of the event remains hypothetical and conjectural ('during which we must have spent the night together', 'must have had an opportunity'). At most one can say of that event [is] that it will have happened (Laplanche 1987), whereby the future perfect indicates both its conjectural nature and the characteristic of 'living temporality' (Balsamo and Napolitano 1994) inscribed in it. The Oedipus complex is not only supposed and deduced at the moment when Freud (re)constructs it, but there is always a double scene and one cannot be identified without the other. Oedipus is not then a fact in the meaning this word is normally given, as the historian Becker (1958: 48) says: 'the historical fact is in someone's mind or nowhere [. . .] *the real event and the historical fact are two different things.*'

The letter to Fliess of 15 October marks the third period, the last act in the discovery, the final transformation of the process that takes place in the theory:

> One single thought of general value has been revealed to me. I have found, in my own case too, falling in love with the mother and jealousy of the father, and I now regard it as a universal event of early childhood, even if not so early as in children who have been made hysterical. (Similarly with the romance of parentage in paranoia – heroes, founders of religions.) If that is so, we can understand the riveting power of Oedipus Rex, in spite of all the objections raised by reason against its presupposition of destiny.
>
> (Freud 1897: 265)

Oedipus is born in analytic theory. With a process of generalisation typical of Freudian theorising, the Oedipus complex moves from being an individual 'fact' (drawing on his self-analysis) to something universal.

I think that the mutual reference and articulation between (self)-analysis, (re)construction and theory is a specific characteristic of knowledge and analytic treatment. We call such experience 'prototypical' because we find it in the inaugural phase in Freud and again in the inaugural phase of the training of future analysts. As training analysts and supervisors we often come across this circular process. The analyses of trainee analysts are often mobilised, activated, sometimes on a deep level, by the analyses of their first patients (under supervision). Micro- and macro-transformations in those analyses (of trainees) can be used with the mediation of elements of a theory (which itself is in 'training') to open up breaches and previously obstructed cognitive and transformative spaces in the analyses of their patients.

Pontalis (1977: 215–227) calls the impulses of the analyst 'movements'; it is a circular process activated by the patient. These 'movements' are a good omen, the proof that the analysis has started, that the analyst has been touched on a raw nerve. Training analyses and supervisions can have the function of safeguarding this process, of rescuing such 'movements' from denial. In this way the trainee can become familiar with them and, once the training is over, with the help of self-analysis, he can use them in his work.

While the events of 1897 show us this process in its nascent state in the active phase of self-analysis, Freud will offer us later examples of this process in a less transparent but equally significant form when his self-analysis lies in the distant past but is none the less active. The 'Grusha' episode in *From the History of an Infantile Neurosis* (which is sometimes referred to as *The Wolfman*) will provide us with the stimulus to reflect on one of these moments (Freud 1918).

But first let us look briefly at Freud's short but extraordinary paper *Screen Memories* (1899), his first real psychoanalytic text. The starting point is the memory of a scene attributed to 'a man of university education, aged thirty-eight [with a] slight phobia'. Behind this figure hides Freud himself. 'I see a rectangular, rather steeply-sloping piece of meadow-land, green and thickly grown; in the green there are a great number of yellow flowers – evidently common dandelions' (p. 311). It would take too long to go into all the details of this both deconstructive and reconstructive work by Freud. Readers who turn to this paper will have the opportunity to directly benefit from and enjoy its psychoanalytic but also literary sophistication. For our present purposes, suffice it to point out that the remembered scene is a composition made up of several phantasies, connected to traces of significant events from childhood, latency and adolescence (leaving a fondly recalled place from childhood, the father's financial collapse, childhood and adolescent loves, etc.). Chronology is not respected and the events and periods collapse into each other.

The construction thus obtained offers a precious lesson for all analyses and reflects significant turning points in the life and development of the person and hence becomes a paradigm of the subject's unconscious life. The scene, recalled as real, is in fact a phantasy scene arising out of desire which, as we know, does not respect dates and, as

Freud says, passes through past, present and future. Screen memory is thus a construction and, in the conclusion to his work, Freud extends this hypothesis to all memories:

> It may indeed be questioned whether we have any memories at all *from* our childhood: memories *relating to* our childhood may be all that we possess. Our childhood memories show us our earliest years not as they were but as they appeared at the later periods when the memories were aroused. In these periods of arousal, the childhood memories did not, as people are accustomed to say, *emerge*; they were *formed* at that time. And a number of motives, with no concern for historical accuracy, had a part in forming them, as well as in the selection of the memories themselves.
>
> (Freud 1899: 322, original emphasis)

This conclusion anticipates some of Freud's later themes and even outdoes the theses he was to develop in the late 1930s.

In 1899, Freud seems thus to have overcome his wavering between phantasies and memories (of real scenes), a question he was still debating at the beginning of 1897. In this paper there is a decisive stress on phantasy over memory since there is always a 'slipping away of repressed thoughts and wishes into childhood memories' (p. 317).

The relationship between phantasy, memory and reality again presented itself as complex and contradictory, with significant openings and regressions, in 1914, when Freud was writing *From the History of an Infantile Neurosis*.[1] It is well known that Freud's thinking was stimulated and provoked by Jung's criticisms. For Jung the phantasies of neurotics do not come from childhood but are projected retrospectively on to childhood (*zurückphantasieren*) and used by neurotics to elude tasks and difficulties in the present.

In 1914, the concept of *Nachträglichkeit*, already mentioned in the letters to Fliess, became established. The history of the trauma is a story in two acts: the first act is when the traumatic event is perceived and not understood, a moment of semantic negativity; and the second, at a certain distance from the first one, is when an event which is potentially less traumatic than the first receives its traumatic potential from the encounter (*après-coup*) with the first scenes.

Because of this temporal deferral events and experiences do not coincide; the events become experiences not at that moment but at a distance, in memory. So it is extremely reductive to confine psychoanalytic thought within the opposition between external trauma and internal trauma. Freud's thinking, conflict thinking, is a dualistic thinking which cannot be enclosed within oppositions. It is not a question of choosing between external and internal, but rather of joining the two questions. Humphrey Morris (1993) asks: namely, how does the real experience become a psychological trauma and how does a real trauma become a psychological experience? Facts and meaning, events and representations imply each other reciprocally in the dual dimension of *Nachträglichkeit* and cannot be thought of separately. Psychoanalysis can therefore not be reduced to a hermeneutics (which remains in the field of representation) or some form of empiricism (which remains in the field of perception and the fact). Its 'facts' are not 'observable' and its propositions are not 'philosophemes'. Our debt is to a number of French authors (Lacan, Pontalis and, notably, Laplanche) who picked up *Nachträglichkeit* and resignified it, in the true sense of the word, as *après-coup*, and positioned it at the centre of analytic practice, elevating it to an epistemological factor that discriminated between psychoanalysis and other methods, thus going through and beyond Freud. *Nachträglichkeit* is not the weapon Freud used to do battle with Jung. In reality Freud was deeply affected by the criticisms of Jung. Freud's long travail prior to publishing *From the History of an Infantile Neurosis* was the result of his uncertainty as to whether phantasy comes from childhood or is constructed in childhood:

> I admit that this is the most delicate question in the whole domain of psychoanalysis. I did not require the contribution of Adler or Jung to induce me to consider the matter with a critical eye, and to bear in mind the possibility that what analysis puts forward as being forgotten experiences of childhood (and of an improbably early childhood) may on the contrary be based on phantasies created on occasions occurring late in life. According to this view, wherever we seemed in analyses to see traces of the after-effects of an infantile impression of the kind in question, we should rather have to assume that we were faced by the manifestation of some constitutional factor or of some disposition that had been phylogenetically maintained. On the contrary, no doubt has troubled me more; no other uncertainty has been more decisive in holding me back from publishing my conclusions. I was the first – a point to which none of my opponents have referred – to recognize both the part played by phantasies in symptom-formation and also the 'retrospective phantasying' of late impressions into childhood and their sexualization after the event. (See my *Interpretation of Dreams* (1900a), First

> Edition, p.49, and *Notes upon a Case of Obsessional Neurosis,* (1909d) [Standard Ed., 10, 20s ff., footnote].) If, in spite of this, I have held to the more difficult and more improbable view, it has been as a result of arguments such as are forced upon the investigator by the case described in these pages or by any other infantile neurosis – arguments which I once again lay before my readers for their decision.
>
> (Freud 1918: 103)

In 1914 Freud was determined to demonstrate that psychoanalysis was a procedure designed to bring repressed events back to consciousness and, in parallel, to demonstrate the centrality of early sexual experiences in the genesis of neuroses. He had once again managed to create his enemy and generate that atmosphere of tension, battle, love and hate which, as he had said in *The Interpretation of Dreams* (1900), was the climate in which he worked better.

The 'Grusha' episode, which takes up so much space in *From the History of an Infantile Neurosis*, is central to Freud's argument; in it he sought to demonstrate both the possibility of reconstructing past events and that these events always have a sexual content. Spence (1982: 108) used the 'Grusha' episode to demonstrate the historically unfounded nature of Freud's reconstruction and to corroborate his theses of narrative truth as opposed to historical truth. We shall not dwell on the distance that separates us from Spence; our whole argument testifies to it. We want to revisit 'Grusha' for a different reason, to illustrate again the mode of functioning of the analytic 'apparatus', that sort of 'ghost-busting machine' which we saw in action in 1897 at the dawn of the analytic method. Freud's Wolf Man presents the memory of a scene:

> Very soon after this there came the recollection of a scene, incomplete, but, so far as it was preserved, definite. Grusha was kneeling on the floor, and beside her a pail and a short broom made of a bundle of twigs; he was also there, and she was teasing him or scolding him.
>
> (Freud 1918: 91)

At other moments the patient had shown interest in the figure of John Huss, who had been condemned to die at the stake. Freud commented that Huss was often the hero of patients who have suffered from enuresis. (This passage is important because it acts as a bridge to a psychic element in Freud.) Since the patient comes to connect the faggot of kindling used for the bonfire that burned Huss with the governess's broom made of twigs, Freud reconstructed thus:

> This material fitted together spontaneously and served to fill in the gaps in the patient's memory of the scene with Grusha. When he saw the girl scrubbing the floor he had micturated in the room and she had rejoined, no doubt jokingly, with a threat of castration.
>
> (p. 92)

Including his reconstruction in the patient's memory, Freud continues:

> When he saw the girl on the floor engaged in scrubbing it, and kneeling down, with her buttocks projecting and her back horizontal, he was faced once again with the posture which his mother had assumed in the copulation scene. She became his mother to him; he was seized with sexual excitement owing to the activation of the picture; and, like his father (whose action he can only have regarded at the time as micturition), he behaved in a masculine way towards her. His micturition on the floor was in reality an attempt at seduction, and the girl replied to it with a threat of castration, just as though she had understood what he meant.
>
> (pp. 92–93)

Some pages later he comments on the entire reconstruction as follows:

> The Grusha scene was, as I have said, *a spontaneous product of the patient's memory, and no construction or stimulation by the physician played any part in evoking it.* The gaps were filled up by the analysis in a fashion which must be regarded as unexceptional, if any value at all is attached to the analytical method of work.
>
> (p. 112, emphasis added)

It is legitimate to entertain doubts about the 'spontaneity' of the patient's memory of that scene. As for Freud's 'impeccable' reconstruction, it was determined both by the use of theoretical elements (urethral sexuality) and countertransference elements. We know from *The Interpretation of Dreams*, in his associations with the dream of Count Thun, that Freud had suffered in his childhood from enuresis. In one of these episodes the father had exclaimed: 'That boy will never amount to anything.' Freud makes the comment: 'This must have been a terrible affront to my ambition.'

Spence (1982) considers the words of Freud's father a barely concealed castration threat and supposes that he intervenes and inserts himself into the reconstruction of the 'Grusha' episode: Freud made 'Grusha' utter a castration threat because he himself had suffered in childhood. The memory of the Wolf Man is thus deformed by a countertransference element.

But can we ever suppose that we can reconstruct (and reconstruction is precisely what it is) a pure scene without even the slightest countertransferal inference? In my view, countertransference always contributes to giving a meaning to and representing the past in the analytic space. The 'staging' of the analytic situation captures and 'realises' the analytic 'fact'; without that staging, in a sense, that fact does not exist. In one of the next chapters when we speak of the writing up of cases, we will see how truth – and, I would like to add, reality – 'only comes to the surface in the universe of fiction and when it avoids the naturalistic slice-of-life expedient of blind and faithful synchronic recording' (Lavagetto 1985: 198). Nothing is further from analysis than the supposed 'naturalness' which Meltzer (1967) had assumed was a characteristic of the analytic process. Both in writing and in analysis, the 'facts' do not speak unless someone has organised them into a structure that allows them to speak. In both cases what we have are not reproductions but productions, constructions rather than reconstructions.

Later we will have the chance to speak of the organisers and the limits of these 'scenarios'. Here I would simply like to point out that this perspective does not obviate the responsibility and the impact of the analyst. These factors are still brought into play – in writing the plots, setting the scene and directing the characters.

The jigsaw puzzle

Heads I win, tails you lose: the analyst has the game under his control. One can even believe in his good faith, one can be certain that he doesn't cheat, but knowing the rules, experience and expertise have a weight of their own and can decide the result of the game. The 'impact' of the analyst in the analytic situation is one of the many paradoxes of analysis. The patient wants the analysis to have an impact on his suffering and his life but the analyst, to whom this appeal for change is addressed (the operator of this change, so to speak), is supposed to affect the life of the patient without his person, his theory or anything else influencing the internal world of the patient. None of the succession of 'solutions' (starting from neutrality) that have been proposed in the history of psychoanalysis have been either stable or satisfying, and the problem remains open, especially during this historical phase when 'interaction' prevails on the analytic scene.

Psychoanalysis was one of the many sciences at the avant-garde of the great epistemological change that marked the beginning of the twentieth century, However, it has maintained a hard core of resistance and, in my view, has been part of a necessary rearguard action. While during the same period other (often widely differing) disciplines were affirming the ineluctability of the impact of the observer on the observed field, psychoanalysis based itself on two interconnected principles: the objectivity of the observed fact and the neutrality of the observer. This resistance is not to be explained solely by the fact that Freud held a positivist scientific ideal, but also in terms of the specific characteristics of the psychoanalytic object, the disquiet that recognising the impact of the analyst on the patient has always generated: phantasies float and can precipitate realities like moral subjugation, the delusion of influence, the breakdown of individual identity, straying beyond limits and loss of self.

The 'derogatory and unjust' accusation that analytic technique moulded, manipulated and influenced was directed at Freud not only at the beginning but also throughout his career, as is shown by the four 'scenes' we are about to describe. In these scenes we can read both the continuity and the discontinuity of Freud's solutions to this problem and we also can recognise themes and arguments which were later proposed in psychoanalytic literature with less epistemological ingenuousness, with a different language but leaving the ensuing dilemma completely intact.

1896 – *The Aetiology of Hysteria*

Not many years have passed since Freud's translation of Bernhein's book on hypnosis and he is now about to face the unresolved enigmas of his childhood with self-analysis. The talking cure followed on from hypnosis: a transition which is not yet a choice. Freud has only recently stopped laying hands on the heads of hysterics by hypnotic induction. The 'imposition' of hands was followed by the danger of another imposition, much more insidious and tyrannical:

> Other people, too, [. . .] will be tempted, when considering our analytic findings, to ask what degree of certainty the application of psycho-analysis offers. Is it not very possible either that the physician forces such scenes upon his docile patients, alleging that they are memories, or else that the patients tell the physician things which they have deliberately invented?
>
> (Freud 1896b: 204)

Freud is helped out by a child's game:

> Another and stronger proof of this is furnished by the relationship of the infantile scenes to the content of the whole of the rest of the case history. It is exactly like putting together a child's picture-puzzle: after many attempts, we become absolutely certain in the end which piece belongs in the empty gap; for only that one piece fills out the picture and at the same time allows its irregular edges to be fitted into the edges of the other pieces in such a manner as to leave no free space and to entail no overlapping. In the same way, the contents of the infantile scenes turn out to be indispensable supplements to the associative and logical framework of the neurosis, whose insertion makes its course of development for the first time evident, or even, as we might often say, self-evident.
>
> (1896b: 205)

Here we have the first appearance of the jigsaw puzzle.

1918 – *From the History of an Infantile Neurosis*

The years have passed, and psychoanalysis stands on more solid ground. There has been a profound transformation in technique, which has finally freed itself from hypnosis with its suggestion and imposition. But the psychoanalytic movement, only recently founded, is beginning to experience its first splits. Jung has left despite attempts at mediation by wife and friends. As in all self-respecting separations there were temptations and provocations (scientific in this case). One of these continued to tear away at and embitter Freud:

> Scenes from early infancy, such as are brought up by an exhaustive analysis of neuroses [. . .], are not reproductions of real occurrences, to which it is possible to ascribe an influence over the course of the patient's later life and over the formation of his symptoms. It considers them rather as products of the imagination, which find their instigation in mature life, which are intended to serve as some kind of symbolic representation of real wishes and interests, and which owe their origin to a regressive tendency, to a turning-away from the tasks of the present. If that is so, we can of course spare ourselves the necessity of attributing such a surprising amount to the mental life and intellectual capacity of children of the tenderest age.
>
> (p. 49)

Presumably behind these words were the criticisms levelled by Jung. The two accusations – that childhood scenes are invented by the neurotic and that childhood scenes are imposed by the physician – come to overlap and combine:

> And the sense of conviction felt by the person analysed may be the result of suggestion, which is always having new parts assigned to it in the play of forces involved in analytic treatment. The old-fashioned psychotherapist, it might be maintained, used to suggest to his patient that he was cured, that he had overcome his inhibitions, and so on; while the psycho-analyst, on this view, suggests to him that when he was a child he had some experience or other, which he must now recollect in order to be cured. This would be the difference between the two.
>
> Let it be clearly understood that this last attempt at an explanation on the part of those who take the view opposed to mine results in the scenes from infancy being disposed of far more fundamentally than was announced to begin with. What was argued at first was that they were not realities but phantasies. But what is argued now is evidently that they are phantasies not of the patient but of the analyst himself, who forces them upon the person under analysis on account of some complexes of his own. An analyst, indeed, who hears this reproach, will comfort himself by recalling how gradually the construction of this phantasy which he is supposed to have originated came about, and, when all is said and done, how independently of the physician's incentive many points in its development proceeded; how, after a certain phase of the treatment, everything seemed to converge upon it, and how later, in the synthesis, the most various and remarkable results radiated out from it; how not only the large problems but the smallest peculiarities in the history of the case were cleared up by this single assumption.

> And he will disclaim the possession of the amount of ingenuity necessary for the concoction of an occurrence which can fulfil all these demands. But even this plea will be without an effect on an adversary who has not experienced the analysis himself. On the one side there will be a charge of subtle self-deception, and on the other of obtuseness of judgement; it will be impossible to arrive at a decision.
>
> (pp. 52–53)

The jigsaw puzzle reappears.

1923 – *Remarks on the Theory and Practice of Dream-Interpretation*

The 1920s were difficult years, a crisis period for Freud: the death of his beloved Sophie and his favourite nephew. The theme of 'afterlife' pervades the mind and work of Freud, reflecting scepticism about the analytic cure and the nature and destiny of man. The dream itself, the royal road, is called into question; suggestion by the analyst can even penetrate here, reaching the individual's place of truth and authenticity:

> The question of the value to be assigned to dreams is intimately related to the other question of their susceptibility to influence from 'suggestion' by the physician. Analysts may at first be alarmed at the mention of this possibility. But on further reflection this alarm will give place to the realization that the influencing of the patient's dreams is no more a blunder on the part of the analyst or disgrace to him than the guiding of the patient's conscious thoughts.
>
> The fact that the manifest content of dreams is influenced by the analytic treatment stands in no need of proof. It follows from our knowledge that dreams take their start from waking life and work over material derived from it. Occurrences during analytic treatment are of course among the impressions of waking life and soon become some of the most powerful of these. So it is not to be wondered at that the patients should dream of things which the analyst has discussed with them and of which he has aroused expectations in them. At least it is no more to be wondered at than what is implied in the familiar fact of 'experimental' dreams.
>
> But from here our interest proceeds to the question whether the latent dream-thoughts that have to be arrived at by interpretation can also be influenced or suggested by the analyst. And to this the answer must once

more be that they obviously can be. For a portion of these latent dream-thoughts correspond to preconscious thought formations, perfectly capable of being conscious, with which the dreamer might quite well have reacted to the physician's remarks in his waking state too – whether the patient's reactions were in harmony with those remarks or in opposition to them. In fact, if we replace the dream by the dream-thoughts which it contains, the question of how far one can suggest dreams coincides with the more general question of how far a patient in analysis is accessible to suggestion.

If a dream brings up situations that can be interpreted as referring to scenes from the dreamer's past, it seems especially important to ask whether the physician's influence can also play a part in such contents of the dream as these. And this question is most urgent of all in the case of what are called 'corroborative' dreams, dreams which, as it were 'tag along behind' the analysis. With some patients these are the only dreams that one obtains. Such patients reproduce the forgotten experiences of their childhood only after one has constructed them from their symptoms, associations and other signs and has propounded these constructions to them. Then follow the corroborative dreams, concerning which, however, the doubt arises whether they may not be entirely without evidential value, since they may have been imagined in compliance with the physician's words instead of having been brought to light from the dreamer's unconscious. [. . .]

Is it possible, then, that corroborative dreams are really the result of suggestion, that they are 'obliging' dreams? The patients who produce only corroborative dreams are the same patients in whom doubt plays the principal part in resistance. One makes no attempt at shouting down this doubt by means of one's authority or at reducing it by arguments. It must persist until it is brought to an end in the further course of the analysis. The analyst, too, may himself retain a doubt of the same kind in some particular instances. What makes him certain in the end is precisely the complication of the problem before him, which is like the solution of a jig-saw puzzle. A coloured picture, pasted upon a thin sheet of wood and fitting exactly into a wooden frame, is cut into a large number of pieces of the most irregular and crooked shapes. If one succeeds in arranging the confused heap of fragments, each of which bears upon it an unintelligible piece of drawing, so that the picture acquires a meaning, so that there is no gap anywhere in the design and so that the whole fits into the frame – if all these conditions are fulfilled, then one knows that one has solved the puzzle and that there is no alternative solution.

(Freud 1923a: 113–116)

We're back again with the jigsaw puzzle!

1937 – *Constructions in Analysis*

By 1937 psychoanalysis had been acknowledged as one of the key disciplines of the twentieth century. But despite this, according to the 'derogatory and unjust' opinion which we started from and to which we have at various times returned, again the analyst reappears as the great huckster:

> That is to say, if the patient agrees with us, then the interpretation is right; but if he contradicts us, that is only a sign of his resistance, which again shows that we are right. In this way we are always in the right against the poor helpless wretch whom we are analysing, no matter how he may respond to what we put forward.
>
> (Freud 1937b: 257)

In *Constructions in Analysis* Freud does not make reference to the jigsaw puzzle to defend himself. He does not attempt to spatialise time, to keep it in an enclosed space. His faith in the puzzle had already showed signs of strain in *Moses and Monotheism* (1939a: 17): 'Even if all the parts of a problem seem to fit together like the pieces of a jig-saw puzzle, one must reflect that what is probable is not necessarily the truth and that the truth is not always probable.' As we have seen, he tries to address the question by having recourse to the archaeological metaphor. But the excavation remains only 'preliminary labour'; one cannot take a definitive decision. Only the course of analysis can allow us to judge whether our construction is exact; it will all become clear in the course of future events. Freud opens up to the question of the length of the analysis, its potential interminableness. He no longer relies on the childish game of the puzzle as a solution but turns to the game of analysis which is only partly similar to a childhood game: a role play in which Freud assigns the two players different roles and tasks.

But the jigsaw puzzle does not disappear from clinical practice and analytic theory. After Freud we find it expressed in other terms and in forms of various sophistication. From a certain point of view, the narratological perspective in psychoanalysis is a distant relative. Austin (1975) has taught us to take account of the self-referential aspect of every speech act. The reference cannot be reduced to a hypothetical reflection that represents, within language, some empirical extra-linguistic reality. The 'course of development [becomes] for the first time evident, or even [. . .] self-evident', not because the construction refers to an external reality which confirms it but by means of a coherence which is internal to every explicit system, be it narrative, historical or logical.

So reality is the son of *bricolage*? But reality, some might object, offers no discounts to anybody, not even to the most coherent person: sooner or later the iceberg of fact, Bion *docet*, sinks the Titanic of theory. Too often reality demands its 'pound of flesh' and affects the body psychosomatically. It hides in the 'crypt' and family secrets. It is no accident that Abraham and Torok speak of reality topics. No school or movement in psychoanalysis can evade the question of reality and the relationship between mind and reality. Klein, Winnicott, Infant Research and American intersubjectivity all had to take it into account. In Freud the problem of reality and the relationship between mind and reality is not easy to demarcate or reduce to a single dimension. It ranges between the two opposite poles of a mind which functions as a reflection of reality and a mind that has the freedom to create, invent and transform that reality.

Dependent relations and connections to which there is nothing corresponding in reality

In Freud we encounter the problem of reality on various levels: the relationship between the psychic apparatus and reality; reality in relation to clinical practice; the suspension of judgement of reality in analysis; reality in the construction of theory. These levels evolve in Freud's thought and influence each other. In this brief survey we shall start with reality in the construction of theory.

Freud held a positivistic view of science (it would take too long to say whether for reasons of faith, tradition or strategy), but his practice and numerous theoretical and meta-discursive propositions also betray a different position which is a long way from positivism.[2] On the first page of *Instincts and their Vicissitudes*, the most clearly epistemological work in his entire oeuvre, Freud shows a decided predilection for the use of abstract ideas about experience in the construction of a theory:

> Even at the stage of description it is not possible to avoid applying certain abstract ideas to the material in hand, ideas derived from somewhere or other but certainly not from the new observations alone. Such ideas – which will later become the basic concepts of science – are still more indispensable as the material is further worked over. They must at first necessarily possess some degree of indefiniteness; there can be no question of any clear delimitation of their content. So long as they remain in this condition, we come to an understanding about their meaning by making repeated references to the material of observation from which they appear to have been derived, but upon which, in fact, they have been imposed.
>
> (Freud 1915b: 1)

Some time ago this passage led me (Chianese 1988) to draw parallels between the thinking of Freud and Einstein, who at the height of his scientific maturity had hypothesised a speculative leap from experience to theory. Faced with the chaos of experience this leap represents a precious moment of imaginative freedom, the product of 'wonder' in the face of the world, of a 'passion for understanding'. According to Einstein, all concepts, even those closest to experience, are, from a logical point of view, freely chosen conventions. Likewise Freud states: 'Strictly speaking, they are in the nature of conventions' (1915b: 117).

For Einstein this schema not only applies to the way the mind constructs a theory, but can be generalised into a model of thinking *tout court*. In his scientific autobiography, he talks about the constructive nature of scientific thought and calls this way of thinking a groping towards construction, to the point where we are reminded of the famous quotation from Ruchert reported by Freud in *Beyond the Pleasure Principle* (1922): 'What we cannot reach flying we must reach limping.' In short, for Einstein, science is not simply the ordering of empirical material; contrary to what Mach thought, theories are produced by invention and not discovery. The problem of discovery and invention belongs to psychoanalysis, seen both as clinical practice and as theory. In clinical practice discovery and invention perform the function of filling gaps and voids, and at some moments of experience they can become a single and indivisible act.

For Traversa (1981) the specific nature of Freud's research consisted in this particular form of articulation between invention and discovery:

> If I take the succession of stages in Freudian procedure, which I have tried to reconstruct historically, and which suggested the following sequence: invention, discovery, invention and so on, I could argue that, according to traditional epistemology, the first phase of invention has been eliminated. Thus the sequence becomes: discovery, invention, discovery, and so on. In this case the first phase of discovery can be preceded by the presence of a reference scheme (put between parentheses and deduced from the already operating theory) which guides me in my observation of facts, but does so in a context of calm speculation without any of the suffering which is fundamental to the other path.
>
> (Traversa 1981: 10)

According to constructivism, our vision of reality is not a 'true' image of what is to be found outside us; so-called reality is a 'construction' made by those who believe they have discovered it. Here again, more than a discovery it is an 'invention' (Watzlawick 1984)

It would thus seem that psychoanalysis is entitled to claim some paternity for present-day constructivism. On this view the term and concept of 'construction' becomes a general model of analytic thinking and should not be 'restricted [. . .] to the comparatively narrow sense that Freud assigns to it in *Constructions*' (Laplanche and Pontalis 1967). This is the reason that prompted Corrao some time ago to talk of 'Constructionism'.

But it is always difficult to press Freud into a formula. In *Moses* (1934: 108, note 1) he says: 'Our thought has upheld its liberty to discover *dependent relations and connections to which there is nothing corresponding in reality*' (emphasis added). A nice constructivist manifesto, one might say. Perhaps it would be better to quote the passage from the beginning of the note: 'I protest, however, against being misunderstood to say that the world is so complicated that any assertion one may make is bound to hit upon a piece of truth somewhere.' Clearly, any residual enthusiasm is further tempered if we read a passage written the same year as *Moses*. In *An Outline of Psychoanalysis* (1938a), in a chapter with the significant title 'The Psychical Apparatus and the External World', he expresses himself as follows: 'The yield brought to light by scientific work from our primary sense perceptions will consist in an insight into *connections and dependent relations which are present in the external world*, which can somehow be reliably *reproduced or reflected* in the internal world of our thought' (p. 196, emphasis added).

The difference is evident. We find ourselves faced with two different hypotheses of the mind. In one, the internal connections might not correspond to anything in reality; in the other, the connections are in reality and reflected in thought. In his essay 'Negation' (Freud 1925c), the relationship of the mind to reality shows itself in all its complexity. According to Freud (contradicting an old philosophical tradition), the judgement of attribution precedes the judgement of existence. First we judge, on the basis of the pleasure/displeasure principle, what is good and what is bad – we accept the former and repudiate the latter – and on the basis of this we pronounce judgements about the existence of reality. Reality is not simply reproduced in our mind, but is the product of operations of acceptance and rejection. (This point, which will be taken up again and examined in more depth shortly, is fundamental both to clinical practice and to any reflections on the construction of reality made by the infant mind.) But in this revolutionary text we find another theory of the mind:

> It is, we see, once more a question of external and internal. What is *unreal*, merely a presentation and subjective, is only internal; what is *real* is also there outside [. . .] all presentations originate from perceptions and are *repetitions* of them. Thus originally the mere existence of a presentation was a *guarantee of the reality* of what was presented.
>
> (p. 237, emphasis added)

Again we find ourselves faced with two hypotheses about the mind. This is still a very relevant problem. The mind as a reproduction of reality is a theoretical hypothesis which rests on an ancient philosophical tradition: the mind has the function of adequately representing reality, its reliability is fundamental to our approach to the world, to the others, to ourselves. But this vision was seen as inadequate; the active function of the mind that creates, produces objects, resolves problems and transforms reality, began to be affirmed. When we find ourselves in Freud faced with two hypotheses of the mind, the point is not so much to choose between them as to consider them as two functions of the same mental apparatus. It is difficult to keep in mind both functions at the same time: when we work on one level, we lose sight of the other.

This contradiction runs through the analytic method. Green (1995) talks in this context about the principle of psychoanalytic uncertainty. Faced with Freud's 'realist' hypothesis, it is then sterile to set up an opposition between 'conventional' and 'formalist' hypotheses. We would end up with a wearying, endless philosophical debate, but one that excludes precisely psychoanalysis and its specific object.

Another way of focusing on the problem of psychoanalysis is not to talk of reality in the broad sense but rather of reality as dealt with by psychoanalysis. In psychoanalysis we find ourselves in the presence of at least two different concepts of reality: at the time of trauma theory it was the reality of the event, the traumatic event. Freud subscribed implicitly to a corresponding theory of truth (Napolitano 1988): the analytic reconstruction was true if it corresponded to the fact, otherwise it was false; its truth was testified by the disappearance of symptoms. With the fundamental recognition that for the unconscious there is no difference between perception (of reality) and representation permeated with affect, the first concept of reality breaks down. The transition to phantasy theory changes the concept of reality (as well as that of truth). We are no longer dealing with the reality of the event but so-called 'psychic reality'.

This reality has its own depth and 'objectivity'. According to De Renzis (1993), in the transition from theory of trauma to theory of phantasy the subjective, external and accidental elements of the former change into the objective, internal and necessary elements of the latter. In my view this means that although trauma theory can appear more 'realistic', only with the latter does the psyche acquire 'reality' and become the specific object of psychoanalysis. 'Psychic reality is a *particular form of existence* which should not be confused with material reality,' Freud tells us (1900: 620). But in what sense can we talk about psychic reality? Isn't psychic supposed to be 'inside'? And isn't the inside 'subjective', 'purely represented', *not real*, while real is outside? Moreover, is a corresponding theory capable of including and encompassing the 'particular form of existence' that is psychic reality?

The 'semantics of possible worlds' can help us refine the theory of correspondence because in it 'the notion of truth refers to a set of not necessarily real worlds, ontological constraints are loosened and with the loss of the presupposition of existence, the concept of existence is opened up to a much vaster philosophical analysis' (Napolitano 1990).

Possible worlds and real worlds are posited as fundamental dialectical poles within psychoanalysis. Analytical reconstruction, for example, reconstructs the worlds of the past, using the theory which determines the possibility and the limits of such reconstructions.

Starting from the 'premises' of a life which we reconstruct through analysis, as Freud tells us in *Psychogenesis of a Case of Female Homosexuality* (1920), we would have been able to have another 'outcome', other possibilities. We transfer and delimit this dialectic within the 'virtual space' which is created between the analyst, the patient and the theory. At the end of a session a patient holds out her hand to say goodbye to the analyst. The latter (a woman) is aware of a slight undertone of violence in the gesture, the hand is stretched out farther than normal, as if she wanted to reach the uterus (the analyst fantasises). In the following session the episode is recontextualised and interpreted as an intrusive act on the part of the patient looking to harm the creativity of the analyst, to penetrate and deform her fertility. In what 'place' should this aggressive act be located? In the patient's unconscious, wakened by the analyst? Solely in the analyst, in her countertransference and in her adoption of a transparent Kleinian analytic theory? Or perhaps rather in the 'analytic space'? This aggressive act lives and expresses itself in a world that exists parallel to the world we know better, which is therefore more 'real', a world where the act of holding out one's hand is a ritual and consensual act.

Napolitano (1990) argues that we always refer a possible world to a base world, which is often the real world but possibly (as in the case of 'psychic reality' and the 'analytic situation') '*that which is possible is in many respects also real* [. . .]. How then do we centre our system and according to which criteria will we choose the base world if our dominion is bereft of a preferential realist belief?' (emphasis added). We think that this is a central problem of psychoanalysis, perhaps it is what Freud refers to as the 'most delicate question in the whole domain of psycho-analysis', his doubt (1918: 103).

The breakdown of this first concept of reality (trauma theory) has permitted the unfolding of the dimension of the 'other' reality, the psychic reality, which however it has not been possible to anchor, to centre. To resolve this aporia, Freud anchored himself to a theory of realist thought. If the thought reflects reality and reproduces it, then thought becomes the guarantee of the represented reality, but how can it guarantee thinking that he himself, Freud, had radically revolutionised with the concept of the unconscious and psychic reality? This gaping wound is still open, it is part of the Freudian legacy.

Faced with the lack of a centre and the consequent methodological and clinical difficulty of keeping account of and maintaining our specific object (psychic reality), we started searching for fixed points and from time to time they have served as guarantees: the rigidity of a theory, the irremovability of the setting, the formalism of a technique. When these proved to be transient and ephemeral forms, there was still the institution with its power to decide what psychoanalysis was and what it was not. Psychic reality is something of an 'unbearable lightness', unstable and tyrannical, ubiquitous or absent. We perceive its strength when we register the tenacity of the repetition compulsion which manifests itself regardless of the passing of time and historical changes. We perceive the instability of its boundaries, the way it overflows in symbiotic relationships, its absence in autism, its eclipse in so-called 'white psychoses'. Coming from historical reality, in constant interaction with material (and environmental) reality, it does not become confused with it, it is not isomorphic to it; both are transferred and transformed by the fantasy apparatus and the laws of the primary process. In this connection, as Garella (1994) rightly points out, the narratological vision and the vision of Infant Research are at two opposite poles. However, both can elude psychic reality, the former by denying any reference to external reality and looking for confirmation within the narrative puzzle, the latter by seeking a guarantee external to the analytic situation and finding it in the observed reality of development. Considering the particular nature of psychic reality, even today metapsychology appears to us to be the theory best able to reflect and represent the new object of psychoanalysis.

'Psychoanalysis is a form of knowledge that operates in the space of the incomplete. It takes the most effective weapons for thinking of a new object precisely from this Baroque armoury of provisional anatomy, provisional chemistry, provisional chemistry' (Assoun 1981: 209). After Freud, we could add to this list: provisional psychology, provisional infant observation, etc. Psychoanalysis lives in this 'imaginary interval', waiting for this knowledge to include it by cancelling it out. For this reason all attempts, both old and modern (psychology, biology, neurosciences, Infant Research, hermeneutics), to centre it, to give it a centre, actually decentre it. The unconscious, this world of the unrealised, is defined as the impossibility to conceive a centre. Psychoanalysis always risks spilling over – either to 'this side' (towards biology, neuropsychology) or 'that side' (towards anthropology, linguists, philosophy). One must always bear in mind the specific objects of psychoanalysis and its method; among its chosen objects are the unconscious and sexuality. Theorising in psychoanalysis means negotiating between Scylla and Charybdis. There is the danger of thinking of the psychoanalytic field only as a place of intersubjectivity, but there is also the opposite danger of bending our research towards 'that side', or beyond the subject (whether it be the symbolic order, the code or the language).

So do we have to forgo our new knowledge in the creation of theory? Do we have to forgo recognising and distinguishing between historical realities, environment and intersubjective relations in clinical practice? Not at all. It is our duty to pursue both without, however, in the first case abstaining from translating this knowledge, thinking about and dreaming about it in metapsychological terms, and in the second case without thinking that what we gradually discover in terms of environment and intersubjective relations will cover all psychic reality. The position of the analyst we talked about is in many ways (analytic, epistemological, cultural, political) a position which is 'eccentric'. The psychoanalyst operates in the 'virtual space' of the analytic situation, and when he theorises he is positioned in the 'virtual space' between different types of knowledge.

Some might say that all this is only speculation. One seems to hear the 'call to order' which, in our circles, takes the form of the call to clinical practice: as if clinical practice grounded itself and legitimised itself without the thinking which in actual fact conceives and regrounds it. As analysts we find ourselves constantly operating in the space in which thought is systematically in immediate contact with (clinical) concrete experience and it is our duty towards our patients to try to clear up this contact. Speculation forms the foundation and the meaning of our work, and it ought to be our pride.

Freud confided to Hilda Doolittle that his discoveries were the basis of a very serious philosophy that very few understood or were capable of understanding (mentioned in Loch 1977). We need to be clear about the meaning we are giving to the word philosophy. We are referring to a 'practical' philosophy and subscribe to Loch's opinion (1977) that psychoanalysis, by virtue of its intermediate position between medicine and philosophy, can contribute to increasing knowledge which supports existence and can help reply to the question of how one can live, how one ought to live. Freud, Bion, Aulagnier, Abraham and Torok, Loch, to cite only a few, speculate. Their thought, their theories on thought can be reflected in the excellent title of a book by Devereux *From Anxiety to Method* (1967). Their theories come from pain, from anxiety. They are driven by the need to think of what and how the people think who come to us to manifest their suffering, because while that suffering is mixed in with love and hate, it is also made up of a 'less' of knowledge (Bion), a hidden knowledge (Freud), the secret of an Other (Abraham and Torok). Our knowledge, then, is never knowledge of a 'transcendental subject'.

The dichotomy between therapy and knowledge is a false problem. Each time it is necessary to relieve those 'mental cramps', which, to use Wittgenstein's expression, hamper us with non-existent oppositions. I wish to know and I wish to heal by unifying the project of the analyst and the patient to the extent that the latter, most times, comes to ask for 'knowledge which does not represent a purely intellectual good, but a good which allows them to live' (Aulagnier 1970). In this context one can think of how high the stakes are in a delusion:

> The delusions of patients appear to me to be *the equivalents of the constructions which we build up in the course of an analytic treatment – attempts at explanation and cure,* though it is true that these, under the conditions of a psychosis, can do no more than replace the fragment of reality that is being disavowed in the present by another fragment that has already been disavowed in the remote past . . . the delusion owes its convincing power to the element of historical truth which it inserts in the place of the rejected reality.
>
> (Freud 1937b: 268, emphasis added)

This is Freud on the last page of *Constructions in Analysis*, talking about the reality and truth of delusion. The two previous pages revolve around the same subject. Some patients, he notes, when listening to the construction of the analyst, reply not by remembering the reconstructed event but rather with 'abnormally sharp' memories of faces, objects, furnishings, etc., prolegomena of a reconstructed event which would never have taken place on the stage of memory. Freud was tempted to call them hallucinations, but also noted that, under certain conditions, authentic hallucinations can also present themselves in non-psychotic patients. In the hallucination 'something [returns] that the child has seen or heard at a time when he could hardly speak [. . .]' (p. 267). It is not therefore the hallucinations as such that signal withdrawal from reality but 'the delusions' into which we invariably find such hallucinations inserted.

Freud is 'seduced' by the insight that both the delusion and the constructions are narratives which organise fragments and perceptions, which fill the interstices. The delusion organises, with coherence and conviction, a solidly self-referential puzzle, so to speak. Those faces, that furniture, those objects, which come to the surface of memory, are, according to Freud, 'traces' of the repressed, the fruit of a compromise between the 'upward drive' of the repressed and the resistances which oppose it. The construction of the analyst tries to throw a bridge to the repressed and represents a metonymy of forgetfulness.

But another more radical defence mechanism is invoked on the last page of *Constructions in Analysis*: disavowal (*Verleugnung*). There is a double denial at the basis of psychosis. Seen from the perspective of *Verleugnung*, hallucinations and the 'living memories' of non-psychotic patients could be considered as a kind of first pre-narrative registration. While delusions convey a historical truth, hallucinations (with their 'universal character') convey a truth which precedes them, they are 'original registrations' incorporated into old forms of narrative. In the interpretation we owe to the audacity of Morris (1993), traces and fragments (*Stücke*), more than being secondary products of repression, are primary registrations.

In my view, if we follow Morris's hypothesis, we should distinguish between denial (*Verneinung*), disavowal (*Verleugnung*) and repudiation (*Verwerfung*), even though in Freud's work these three mechanisms are not always clearly distinct. Denial address desires and thoughts thus far repressed which the subject denies belong to him. Disavowal is a refusal to recognise the reality of a (traumatising) perception. Repudiation is a rejection of a fundamental signifier (for example, the phallus) outside the symbolic universe. Having made this clear, we think that Morris's argument is valid for *Verneinung* and especially *Verleugnung* (this is in fact the term that appears in the last page of *Constructions in Analysis*).

Laplanche and Pontalis (1967) ask themselves the question: 'does not disavowal – whose consequences *in* reality are so obvious – bear upon a factor which *founds human reality*?' (emphasis added). We may think that denials and disavowals accompany the efforts the child makes 'to establish the primary differences upon which depends the testing of reality: the difference between inside and outside, between perception and memory, between the sexes' (Morris 1993). For Freud these differences are not biological facts but acquisitions made through development.

Disavowals can be present as pre-linguistic opposed 'actions' which at an early age are included in the language through which the child enacts these primitive disavowals, or rather the power of these disavowals to manipulate and at times distort reality is associated with the use of language. One thinks of the well-known game Freud describes in which the action of throwing away and pulling back the wooden spool is accompanied by the expressions *fort* and *da*, whereby both the action and the language are attempts to symbolise the child's acceptance–rejection of the mother's absence. This is an example of the parallel and simultaneous birth of the self and language: there is no self without language and no language without the symbol of denial, so denial and disavowals not only protect but indeed found the self. Primitive disavowals and denials are acts that go to constitute the self, the historical narrative, the story we all create about our origins, the story we construct starting from and around these primary acts of acceptance and registration, rejection and cancellation of reality.

There is no direct translation from perception to memory. Between them intervene first disavowals and then repression – and the stories based on both. Consequently one must accept the existence of something in the original events and in traumatic events in particular which remains radically and irremediably unconscious; and all of this puts a limit on the historicising function of the analysis. Constructions, from this point of view, have the function (one that can never be definitively fulfilled) of bridging the 'referential gaps' opened up by primitive disavowals of reality.

Even if we share the hypothesis put forward by Morris, we still think that reconstructions and resignifications have different effects depending on the prevalence of processes of denial over those of disavowal and repudiation. Because, even if it is true that disavowals protect and found the self, the integrity of the self depends on the intensity of these primitive defence mechanisms through which not only pieces of reality of varying sizes can be deformed and removed but also pieces of self can be deformed and get irremediably lost – and herein lies a difference between neuroses and psychoses. In neuroses, the fabric on which the representations are inscribed is not torn. Traces and fragments are resignified *après-coup* in the course of an analytic treatment, which amplifies and highlights a process of signification that may occur spontaneously (in a non-conscious form) even outside the analysis and can thus shelter the subject from madness.

In psychosis the fabric is torn: the double *Verleugnung* brings the process of resignification up against a hole, a void and as a result it 'runs on empty', as it were. The psychotic is forced to 'replace the fragment of reality that is being disavowed in the present by another fragment that has already been disavowed in the remote past'. The psychotic finds again in reality, in the form of hallucination, what has been repudiated and cannot be symbolised. Early processes of disavowal, with their consequent distortion of the self and the relationship with reality, also occur and arise in the mother-child relationship in relation to the 'unthinkable and unrepresentable' traumatic nuclei of the mother: this is a question we shall return to later. To what extent and how this 'psychotic' tear in the fabric is 'reparable' analytically is a question that lies outside the intentions of this book. However, even in the most fortunate cases, where the fabric holds and the structure of the self is more solid, we must still reflect on the limits (and also the dangers) of psychoanalysis.

Since the first disavowals and first denials constitute the basis of the individual's narrative (mythical, novelistic) constructions which he uses to sustain his identity, analytic work is not only not harmless but is also potentially damaging because it can deconstruct or undermine what had previously performed a defensive but also a structuring function. It is not sufficient in this context to use what Faimberg (1983) calls 'listening to listening', that is, listening to the patient's replies to the analyst's interpretations-constructions. In *Constructions in Analysis* Freud had already instructed us on this point.

We can follow and in part monitor the traces of our words in a patient's dream along certain preconscious paths, but we cannot claim to have complete knowledge about its defensive trajectory in the internal world of the other. This is protected only in part by the sensitivity, empathy and attentiveness of the analyst. The fact is that the patient works unconsciously on his resistance and his defences, even the most primitive, like disavowal. In the most fortunate cases this produces a transformative movement coherent with the identity of the structure. This is the work of *Bearbeitung*, working through. *Construction* and *working through* come to constitute two functions of a single transformative process.

Remembering, constructing, working through

Even though it did not take on the form of a concept until 1937, the term construction, like the closely related concept of working through, was to be found at an early stage and then throughout

Freud's work. It is useful to distinguish the act of constructing (understood as a technique of enquiry and a spontaneous mode of psychic functioning) from the product, the construction in the true sense of the word. The first raises problems of a methodological character, the second epistemological problems. We shall start to address the latter at the end of this section, and they will continue to engage us in the chapters to come. It would be more appropriate to call the method deconstructive-constructive since it operates on the (symptomatic, mythical, delusional, oneiric) 'constructions' of the subject.

At the beginning Freud (see *Studies on Hysteria*, 1895b) used an evidentiary, inductive method. Later, after the 'discovery-invention' of key patterns (e.g. Oedipus, seduction, castration) the method took on a more complex form: in a deductive-inductive movement the facts were subordinated to a partly preconstituted pattern which was the result of experience and the theoretical nuclei that had formed in the meantime:

> The whole spatially-extended mass of pathogenic material is in this way drawn through a narrow cleft and thus arrives in consciousness cut up, as it were, into pieces or strips. It is the psychotherapist's business to put these together once more into the organization which he presumes to have existed.
>
> (Freud 1895b: 291)

Similarly, in *Remarks on the Theory and Practice of Dream-Interpretation*, he states: 'The repressed material is only allowed through bit by bit' (1923a: 115).

To 'put together into the organization which he presumes to have existed' we need to proceed with methodological caution, to follow certain procedures. In the case of Elizabeth von R, the Freud who was interested in 'circumstantial evidence' explains how he 'would begin by getting the patient to tell me what was known to her and I would carefully note the points at which some train of thought remained obscure or some link in the causal chain seemed to be missing' (1895b: 139). Given that the story was incomplete, he made some additions, according to the best models known to him from other analyses, but as 'a conscientious archaeologist' he also indicated where the construction was added to the most authentic part (*Fragment of an Analysis of a Case of Hysteria*, 1905a). Despite the transformation which the method had in the meantime undergone, as late as 1934, in the new preface to *Moses*, Freud's advice was 'to fill the gap between one fragment and another according to the law, so to speak, of least resistance, that is – to give preference to the assumption that has the greatest probability'.

Not only towards the end, as we have seen in *Constructions in Analysis*, did Freud find himself facing a lack of memories and images, with only traces and fragments. In 1918, for example, he declares:

> Scenes [. . .] which date from such an early period and exhibit a similar content, and which further lay claim to such an extraordinary significance for the history of the case, are as a rule not reproduced as recollection, but have to be divined – constructed – gradually and laboriously from an aggregation of indications.
>
> (p. 51)

From the beginning, the concept of construction was linked to that of repression and censorship and this link meant that there was continuity (and consistency) between the analytic method (free association, evenly suspended attention, interpretation, construction) and the metaphysical theory of the unconscious/preconscious, between the reconstructive procedures which seek to recompose the 'organization which he presumes to have existed' and the theory which justifies this procedure.

We mentioned earlier the deconstructive-constructive method and the 'constructions' of the subject, because for Freud dreams, symptoms and memories are the product of 'intentional' constructions of the preconscious and the unconscious; nothing is left to chance. The figures of displacement, condensation, working over and representability, described in Chapter 6 of *The Interpretation of Dreams* (1900) are not only mechanisms of dream work, but general rules of transformation which govern the construction of dreams, symptoms and phantasies. The morphology of these constructions suggests their aetiology. The analytic method follows the reverse path of the construction of a dream, a symptom or a phantasy, using the same rules of transformation: it 'releases' what has been compacted by condensation, it follows the suture lines of the joins, it reduces to elements, it interprets and it reconstructs.

The theory of the psychic apparatus (metapsychology), the theory of symptoms, the theory of dreams, the deconstructive-reconstructive analytic method – together these form a solid and coherent whole.

One may criticise it, but any criticism based on a supposed dichotomy between clinical practice and theory is unfounded. Constructions of the past are made starting from evidence or clues. To compensate for the impossibility of remembering, we construct, often over long periods, the history of the subject. This construction is to be distinguished from interpretation, which is based on the associative material of individual elements. The construction is a necessity for the analyst if he wants to reach the unconscious phantasy, which can only be 're-' constructed since it is itself a construction. A paradigmatic example in this connection can be found in *A Child is Being Beaten* (published in *A Contribution to the Study of Sexual Perversions*, 1919b) where Freud asserts: 'The phantasy "I am being beaten by my father" [. . .] *has never had a real existence*', and later, 'it has never succeeded in becoming conscious. *It is a construction of analysis*' (p. 198, emphasis added).

To put it in the words of Pontalis (1977: 130): 'interpretation is to desire as construction is to fantasy'. The construction addresses the subject that is implied in the phantasy scene. The construction tries to set clarity to work against enigma, order against turbulence. It tries to open up a space in the confinement of time and to the extent to which it unifies periods of time, it shakes off time and ends up being 'anachronistic'. This is yet a further element that brings it close to delusion. Even though the construction throws a bridge to repression, its function is not so much to fill a void as to provoke:

> It is never the aim of discussions like this to create conviction. They are only intended to bring the repressed complexes into consciousness, to set the conflict going in the field of conscious mental activity, and to facilitate the emergence of fresh material from the unconscious.
>
> (Freud 1909: 181)

The memories and dreams that emerge are then put to the test by transference.

The 'analytic method does not tolerate the idea of monumental and edifying constructions' says Russo rightly (1990), and Balsamo and Napolitano (1994), by entitling their book *Constructing and Reconstructing*, point out through the use of the non-finite form of the verbs that constructions are never definitive and global, they are an ongoing activity. Constructions should never be totalising; they meet our need for figures and create reversible and irreversible, destructible figures which have the function of opening a breach in the compactness, stability and 'indestructibility' of the figures of repetition. Constructions play off the distinctive against the compact, the random against the necessity expressed in the symptom and in repetition compulsion. In *Holding and Interpretation: Fragments of an Analysis*, Winnicott (1986) more than once proposes constructions to the patient, corrects them, amplifies them, withdraws them and, with great honesty, explains their limits.

However, analysts have not always treated their constructions as hypotheses. Often they have been transformed into facts which, in a vicious circle, have then been invoked to validate theories, thus transforming conjectures into reality. In recent times analysts have stopped committing such dangerous 'ingenuities' so often (dangerous considering the power which the analyst possesses in the analytic situation), but we find ourselves facing a new misunderstanding, opposite to the first: in the shift from dogmatism to an excess of relativism the analyst and patient combine their efforts in the writing of several stories, 'many different stories'. In my view in this way we confuse the constructions which are reversible and revisitable with the patient's 'stories'.

In Rabant's (1985) brilliant analogy, in the same way as subtitles in silent films relativised and significantly displaced the image, so construction can be considered as a *recitativo* performed by the analyst which allows the analysand to 'recognise' the 'events' which determined a certain number of historical turning points in his life starting from some traces (and from new traces activated by the construction); not an infinite number of events, not all possible, rarely numerous, but at any rate concluded. Since what the patient has to recover is not so much what has been lost by memory but what has been forgotten of his history, it matters little if a construction is not followed by memories. In any case memory, as it is something living, defends itself not only by erasing but in some cases by covering with new (mythical, narrative) forms what it continues to preserve and conceal. Again we should not be deceived and mistake these changeable forms for the many possible stories which analyst and patient combine to narrate; by doing so they feed repression or become allies of denial.

In a supervision, only when the magic flow of the many stories with which the patient had seduced both the analyst and the supervisor had petered out could the traumatic nuclei which had had the function of mythopoeic nuclei be recognised and analysed. The reversible and destructible figures that are constructions have the function of shoring up in the architectural sense. They are scaffolding which makes it possible (argues Rabant) to construct a house floor by floor and which, once the house is finished, is taken away. Keeping to this analogy, just as the scaffolding is not to be confused with the house, so these many constructions are not to be confused with the patient's stories nor even less with the story which they will take away with them at the end of an analytic treatment and which will permit them to keep going after the treatment (Kahn 1978).

Several years after the end of his analysis, a patient visited his analyst and said: 'You know, doctor, if I told someone what we did all those years . . . four times a week . . . what we discovered, I wouldn't know what to say. All those stories . . . Please don't be offended, I've thought about it various times . . . I can remember practically nothing of what we said. And yet I was so keen and it seemed to me so important. . . . My memory of you is positive, I remember that it was quite a special experience, I remember that you helped me and I also know that my life has changed but I don't know why.' Barale (1996) offers us this good example of a successful analysis in which the constructions have performed their function and whose positivity is shown by the fact that they have been forgotten – scaffolding taken down after the analysis is over.

But it is not always like that. There are patients who do not manage to 'forget', and as analysts we can never know with any certainty the effect and the destiny our words will have, what effect our constructions will have in the internal world of the other. This is the reason analysts ask themselves the question: when and how should we communicate our constructions to the patient? Writing about the subject of 'wild psychoanalysis', Freud said:

> Informing the patient of his unconscious regularly results in an intensification of the conflict in him and an exacerbation of his troubles. Since, however, psycho-analysis cannot dispense with this information, it lays down that this shall not be done before two conditions have been fulfilled. First, the patient must, through preparation, himself have reached the neighbourhood of what he has repressed, and secondly, he must have formed a sufficient attachment (transference) to the physician for his emotional relationship to him to make fresh flight impossible.
>
> (1910b: 225)

But Freud seems on various occasions to have forgotten these principles.

The writer Maryse Choisy's analysis with Freud lasted three sessions.[3] She tells us how, after describing a dream, she was faced with a 'wild' reconstruction which Freud, as it were, threw in her face – the secret, at the time unknown to her, and later revealed to be true, of her illegitimate birth: 'In the interpretation of that dream there was something arcane. I didn't go back to Vienna [. . .] [Freud] managed to see through me. I felt transparent like glass. I was frightened. I was so frightened that I did everything possible to avoid analysts. But it took me eight years to get over that panic' (our translation). This happened in 1924. Maryse Choisy fled, just as the young Dora had 24 years previously.

One reason for reflecting on Freud's practice is in order to measure the difference between his technique and ours. He often wavers. If on some occasions he is cautious – 'I ventured to put forward a construction' (1909: 205) – on other occasions he shows his daring and his power. We must, he says, '*oblige* the patient to confirm the analyst's construction' (1920: 18, emphasis added). I do not think that we can recognise the two clearly distinguishable 'phases' of the analysis he describes in *The Psychogenesis of a Case of Female Homosexuality* (1920: 152). In *Beyond the Pleasure Principle* (1922), the role of the patient's resistance was increasingly recognised and this awareness became stabilised in his later writings (1937a: 238; 1938a: 160).

An analysis of the lexis and in particular some of the terms used by Freud in *Constructions in Analysis*[4] can help us understand the way Freud thinks the analyst should propose his constructions to the analysand. Throughout his work he uses an abstract and general designation for this activity: the verb *mitteilen* (*Mitteilung* in the noun form), which means to communicate, to be part of (share) – communication in the active sense of the term. We also find three verbs *vortragen, vorführen* and *vertreten* (noun form *Vertretung*). Neither in French, as Pré-Lavarrière and Rabant have pointed out, nor in Italian can we find equivalents for these verbs. The only verb which could cover all and at the same time underline the coherence of the series is *presentare* (to present). In German these verbs are not to be understood in concrete form and have a strong metaphorical thrust. They imply, for example, an artistic function (to perform a play or piece of music), or a legal function (present, produce witnesses, make a case). Thus these also indicate a style; the term *Ausführung*, used in the third section to refer to the conduct of the treatment, belongs to a set of verbs that is very close to the idea of 'conducting' an orchestra. It is not without importance that *vorstellen* and *Vorstellung* (represent and representation) do not appear in the article. The analyst does not then communicate in neutral objective and 'scientific' form, but in an active, creative 'intentional' form.

This active function of the analyst is also found in the term *Erinnerung* used by Freud when he talks of remembering. Again it is difficult to pin down and translate accurately the nuances of Freud's vocabulary. *Erinnerung* has, in most cases, an active sense which is lost when translated as 'remember' or 'remembering'. To underline the idea of an act, Pré-Lavarrière and Rabant recommend using the French word *rememoration* although this involves a slight deviation from its more common use: *rememorate* normally means to 'remind' someone of something. The common use denotes an action on another person; in the Freudian use, it is the analyst who makes the patient remember (this or that event).

With regard to the objects of memory, that is, the events, in the article we find first of all the characterisation of the past fact as experienced; it is an experience which took place, an *Erlebnis*. This term stresses the subjective dimension of the event. We also find two other terms to refer to the objective dimension of the event: *Geschehen* and *Begebenheit*. *Geschehen* derives from *Geschichte* (history) and adds an extra dimension to *Begebenheit*: the aspect and meaning of the continuity and concatenation of what happens, of events.

When Freud confronts the problem of events it is usually from the perspective of the operations of memory that have them as their object: the event is that which can be forgotten. Both forgetting and remembering imply work; work which takes resistance into account. The destiny of analytic acts and analytic constructions depends on resistance and, in this sense, the working through performs a fundamental function in analytic work. What patients tell us in analysis is always a construction made up of phantasies, perceptions, memories and stories. The past presents itself to us already 'worked through', in the sense that it has been reworked, 'edited', 'constructed' in order to acquire a meaning, a coherence for the subject. The analysis intervenes through deconstructions, constructions and reconstructions. The unconscious construction of the working through can then meet, collude, at times come into conflict with, clash with or rub against the analytical constructions. It is impossible at the beginning of the game to establish what form this complex process will take.

In Bodei's reading (1979) of Freud's text, analysis brings about a revision of beliefs. Opposing transformative knowledge, 'knowledge for change', there is the 'already known', which is fuelled by forces that are opposed to knowledge and change, forces removed from consciousness. Freud (1910b) affirms: 'The pathological factor is not his ignorance in itself, but the root of this ignorance in his *inner resistances*.' Thoughts, representations, unconscious desires disperse energy that can be used for change. It is for this reason that the work on resistance (working through) is such a crucial moment, because it unblocks investments and frees energy that can be used to achieve change and knowledge. Working through and construction define the limits and possibilities of transforming the structure. In the form of concepts, working through and construction express the two souls of psychoanalysis (energetic and hermeneutic). In analysis, working through and construction represent two forms of the same transformative function.

The concept of working through still retains, years later, a certain obscurity although one intuits its extreme importance in analysis. The term appeared very early in Freud's work and was established as a concept in his *Remembering, Repeating, Working-through* (1914b). In *Inhibitions, Symptoms and Anxiety* (1926a), Freud clarified and in part modified his 1914 work, distinguishing between the resistance of the id and that of the ego. This single term (working-through) has been used to translate different German terms, which diversify the concept and give it different shades of meaning. I shall try to explain some of these semantic differences, but basically respect a certain ambiguity which I feel is fertile. The risk of terminological confusion – here I agree with Laplanche and Pontalis – is linked to the actual uncertainty of the concept.

There are at least three forms of working through: psychical working through (*Ver-*, *Be-*, *Aus-*, *Aufarbeitung*); therapeutic working through (*Durcharbeitung*); secondary elaboration (*sekundäre Bearbeitung*).

The concept of work (*Arbeit*) links the three forms of working through. In turn the concept of work implies that of apparatus. A further concept to add to these two is that of transformation, a concept which strictly speaking does not belong to Freud's theories, but which we can include without betraying Freud's thinking. We think this concept fits in since the term apparatus indicates certain characteristics that Freud attributed to the psyche: the capacity to transmit but also to transform a certain energy. We find the term 'work' (*Arbeit*) in many of Freud's key concepts, such as *Traumarbeit* (dream work), *Trauerarbeit* (mourning work). Even drives are defined as 'demand[s] made upon the mind for work' (1905b).

Yet in all these cases, work serves to maintain the internal energy of the apparatus at the lowest level. The differentiation of the apparatus into substructures and the game of investment, counter-investment and super-investment helps us to conceive the ways in which the apparatus 'transforms' energy (the apparatus for Freud is a model or rather a 'fictio'). The various ways in which this function is carried out are defined by the semantic differences between the terms used.

The work in psychic working through (*Ver-*, *Be-*, *Aus-*, *Aufarbeitung*) consists in integrating the excitations into psychic life and in establishing associative connections. It is useful to generalise this point and to make a connection with the work of construction. Working through, which creates associative links, and construction, which bridges gaps, both fulfil a more general function than the psyche, whose function is to restore continuity to the 'discrete' elements of psychic experience. 'Connections' and 'derivations' make it possible to control energy and transform it into a psychic 'quality'.

In *On the Psychical Mechanism of Hysterical Phenomena: Preliminary Communication* from *Studies on Hysteria* (1895b), Freud considers working through both as a spontaneous mode of functioning of the psyche and a therapeutic method. (This mimesis between therapy and psychic functioning we also saw when talking about constructions and indeed it is often to be found in Freud.) The trauma is eliminated, argue Breuer and Freud, either by abreaction or associative working through, that is, by integrating the 'separate psychic group' represented by the trauma into the large complex of associations.

Another 'transformation' that implies working through is the transformation into affect: 'where there is an abundant development [which] cannot be turned into affect by psychical working-over [. . .] sexual tension is transformed into *anxiety*' (Freud 1897: 194).

Therapeutic working through (*Durcharbeitung*) is work which makes the analysand accept interpretations or constructions connected to repressed elements which are thus no longer subject to repetition or the attraction exerted by the unconscious prototypes of the repressed instinctual process. Unconscious formations are 'put in relation with' the personality complex.

There is great affinity between psychic working through, which establishes associative connections, and therapeutic working through, which relates the unconscious to the personality complex. *Durcharbeitung* can be translated as working through to the end, ceaseless, radical elaboration. If we understand the prefix *durch* in the spatial sense, we can translate it as 'through', and in the temporal sense as 'throughout', from beginning to end. Associative work links different and distant times and spaces. Working through is thus a crossing of space and time which potentially has no limits. Working through ranges across scenes of the past, present and transference. During this process, the recovery of the past is only one of the many factors involved (Kris 1956; Greenacre 1981). Both therapeutic working through and psychic working through operate by transforming quantity (energy) into quality, by establishing associative pathways. This latter activity presupposes the first (transformation of quantity into quality) as a preliminary condition.

At this point there is a connection between the energetic and the interpretative-constructive moment. We find ourselves considering that the 'working out might therefore be seen as a frontier-concept between the economic and symbolic dimensions of Freudianism' (Laplanche and Pontalis 1967: 366). Excitations are limited in their discharge, links connect representations in relatively stable forms. The unconscious desire and the organisation of phantasies are regulated by free energy, which is not to be considered a massive discharge of excitations but rather as a circular movement along a chain of representations which presupposes associative links. Creation of meaning and regulation of excitement are closely connected. The trauma which brings with it an increase in excitation is 'put in relation', it enters into a pattern of discourse. At the beginning of psychoanalysis there were three phases: hypnosis, narration of the trauma, abreaction or associative connection. Since then working through has been linked to narration or rather narration has become a privileged form of working through.

We have left *Bearbeitung* to last because it represents the prototype of the working-through function and of the two factors – economic and hermeneutic. At times Freud used *Bearbeitung* to talk about psychic elaboration. However, when associated with secondary elaboration (*sekundäre Bearbeitung*) it refers to a fundamental function of 'dream work'. We shall focus particularly on the term *Bearbeitung* to keep things brief. One tendency of the psyche is to refer the new to the already known – as Bodei (1979) rightly points out – and there is another (the tendency to include the new) which uses the same mechanisms as the first; together these two functions make possible the continuation and integrity of structural identity.

Slow, subterranean work on resistance makes possible a transformative and cognitive movement which is coherent and non-destructive. At work in this process is an unconscious creative activity which is expressed by the term *Bearbeitung*. This can be translated as: working, cultivating, arranging, adaptation or reduction, compilation, reworking, remaking; persuasion (in the figurative sense); (political) manipulation; (musical) arranging; (theatre) adaptation. In psychoanalysis it is impossible to think of 'pure' facts, of memories, for example, which have not been processed, constructed or edited, just as it is impossible to think of 'pure' communications between analyst and patient without considering the transformations which they undergo in passing from one to the other. (After Bion, the concept of transformation has become central to analytic thinking.)

Psychoanalysis is an eminently dialogic science. Its specific nature lies in the intense and prolonged relationship which patient and analyst keep up, and this modality has no equivalent in other scientific or humanistic disciplines. In analysis the history of the patient and that of the analyst intertwine; the words of the one encounter the words of the other, and both are modified as a result. We can follow the traces of a word or construction along the lines of the psychic stratification of the two people who contract the relationship and we can observe their transformation into dreams, symbols and acts; to a certain extent we can follow psychic journeys. In these subterranean territories, working through imposes its own law: not all paths are possible, constraints are determined by structural ties, by the active forces of the structures involved. It is not enough to construct or render explicit our construction to the analysand. Our construction would stand beside that of the unconscious but would not change it. (Freud reminds us of this in *Beyond the Pleasure Principle*, 1922; by then his psychoanalysis was mature and a long way from the intellectual vision of the early days of therapy, a long way, that is, from the time when he believed that it was enough to interpret the unconscious to modify it.)

Working through sets limits but also offers the opportunity for knowledge and change; it determines possible commitments and exchanges. Metaphorically speaking, we could say that it is the *force* which decides the 'tolls'; it is indeed the passions that regulate the exchanges and use the constructions for their unconscious purposes. 'Knowing is working within constraints' (Ceruti 1986) on found materials whose quality and resistance we need to know, and whose recombination (working through) and contamination (construction) can give birth to something new. That something new is primarily the analytic relationship itself: working through and construction do not only indicate two parts of the analytic field (and the work one does) but rather an internal articulation that is necessary to the very existence of the field. We shall be looking at the field and the analytic relationship in another section of the book, so here I only wish to point out that when we talk of relationship we are referring to:

> a complex system whose structure, direction and functions are not simply the sum of the qualities of the two parties (analyst and patient), even if their individual teleonomies, ideologies and stories determine its formation and course. Rather than individual thought, we should talk of thought, of 'collusions' which are not always and not only negative, ideative and emotive formations designed to guarantee a stable system. The relationship can thus be described in terms of its products (rites, myths, constructions) and the transformations can be divided into rapid transformations and long-term transformations.
>
> (Chianese 1990: 56–57)

From this point of view, intra-systemic *Durcharbeitung* uses the energy of the relational field to create links and ties between different parts of the structure, producing new spatial and temporal orders of relationship. The constructions are thus the conscious representations of unconscious *Durcharbeitung* and *Bearbeitung*: formal and narratological representatives of the structural modifications that emerge from time to time, but which, depending on the demands of the system, can also represent 'point-moments' of resistance (Vergine 1981) in the form of ideologies and mythologies, expressions of the relative invariance of the system, point-moments bound to undergo slow transformation which in turn are expressed through constructions.

To the extent to which human beings are autopoietic systems (Maturana and Varela 1980), all their activities and 'structural couplings' (thus also including analysis) must satisfy their autopoiesis. This happens in analysis, as in every social domain, 'through the completion of basic biological preferences (*states of pleasure*) and rejections (*states of displeasure*), which constitute the immediate experimental domain in which human beings as components of a society *realise their individual worlds and contribute to the determination of the individual worlds of others*' (emphasis added). Analysis is then a relationship, possessing an identity which is fostered, specified and maintained, and which, likewise, is expressed through its products. In this sense constructions are not so much important 'for what they discover as for what they bring about' (Rella 1977). Constructions exist to maintain the analytic system for the purpose of creating 'livable' knowledge, to recognise potential despite the network of constraints.

At the end of his analysis, a patient dreamt of an old convent which had previously stood in an isolated position outside the city but which had gradually, with the passing of time, been absorbed into it. There were no monks and it had been completely restructured. The restructuring work had in part respected the old buildings and made them suitable for new functions. The place had become a cultural centre, a place of intense human exchange. At the centre, an effigy of a 'Madonna with child of the fourteenth century' had been preserved over the gate. The place had lost the gloomy, holy atmosphere it once had, the product of its isolation and abandonment. The history of the patient, the course of the analysis, the recourse to now known symbols, made us immediately appreciate the meaning of the dream, which expressed the transformations in the patient's life that had been brought about through analysis.

This necessarily short account may not render the pathos which a dream event of this kind has in an analysis, but it is an emotion all analysts have experienced. The convent made us think of the sense of radical closing off from the world which the patient had expressed at the beginning of his analysis. In this way he expressed not only his own isolation but also that of his whole family. When the patient was four years old, his mother had been admitted to a psychiatric hospital after the onset of catatonic schizophrenia and had died there some years later. Thirty years passed before the patient was to start analysis after having been the terrorised witness to a sudden and 'unpredictable' episode of catatonia that happened to his wife on their wedding night.

The illness and death of the mother deeply affected the family. It was like a mark of shame against which they had defended themselves by entering into deep isolation and had protected themselves with a very rigid religious faith. It is important to focus on the image of the Madonna and child because in it we can read both transformations and limits. To understand that image we need to go back to an old memory which had profoundly affected the patient: the look of his mother staring into nothingness, stunned by the rigidity of catatonia. That particular look was to affect his life profoundly. The gap between the memory and the icon in the dream expresses the change which a fundamental original element had undergone, a change which was realised through an aesthetic transformation.

In interpreting the dream, the patient said that the icon still embodied the distance and the void, but over and above the fixity there was also a sense of maternity – so there was both participation and solitude, death and life. His dwelling, his living in the world, bore that emblem, which represented – so to speak – a 'monument' to a long-lasting memory. The place still bore the same name, the mark of his identity, but that symbol no longer expressed the activities which had once been carried out inside it.

Using not only this dream but also the experience of the analyst, I believe that it is illusory to think that the analyst can either faithfully reconstruct or change the past. The great contribution an analysis can make consists in respecting the constraints of a structure, in deploying working through for the purpose of constructing a 'possible world' to live in. I am convinced, in the words of Jean-Paul Sartre (1964), that 'what is important is not what people make of us but what we ourselves make of what they have made of us'. The constructions in that analysis had had the function of opening up a space in repetition and in the unlivable situation – that is, of opening up the subject at the moment when time collapsed.

One can generalise by saying, as Rabant suggests (1985), that the act of construction, an act of cooperation and co-production by analyst and patient, is propelled by the passion both to transform and sometimes, even if at first sight it may seem paradoxical, to destroy that which appears indestructible, and that this passion is equivalent to the passion to live, the instinct to live. By contrast, the death instinct – the dominion of the indestructible and of immobility – shows itself in the difficulty, sometimes the impossibility of constructing the destructible and the temporary. The analytic adventure is thus no longer a simple reproduction of the neurosis of transference but a 'co-production of the living' (Racamier 1989) which sees the participation of both analyst and patient.

From this perspective, the constructions cannot be easily extrapolated from the complex relationship that becomes established between analyst and patient. The construction frees itself from the usual epistemologists' criteria of verifiability and falsification and it is only in this framework that we will be able to recover its 'instrumental' function. We need at any rate to be very cautious about this instrumental-pragmatic position which has on several occasions come out in psychoanalytic thought and was already present in Freud. We cannot reduce the value of construction merely to therapeutic efficacy, free of any control, thwarting not only every criterion but also every attempt at verification. The danger then is of 'levelling it down to the low profile of pure functionality' (Lavagetto 1985). As analysts we must accept this doubt which obliges us to ask ourselves about the epistemological status not only of analytical constructions but also of analytical practice in general.

So let us return to the questions which emerged out of our reading of *Moses*, a work representative of that line between novel and history, or, if you like, of the ambiguity which runs through Freud's work, which reverberates and is reflected in contemporary psychoanalytic thought. In the next two chapters we shall consider psychoanalysis from the point of view of history and narration, and then come back to *Moses*, our starting point.

3

Psychoanalysis and history
An interminable dispute

Methodenstreit

Case histories are presented in the form of stories; one reconstructs the past, works on traces, gives new meaning to distant events. The parallels between history and psychoanalysis would seem obvious and hardly in need of being pointed out but this comparison is extremely controversial. Analysts have paid little attention to, and at times have shown only superficial knowledge of, historiographical method, while historians have shown caution and distance, if not frank and explicit distrust, towards psychoanalysis. The game might appear to be over, but as the cycle comes back to this subject the relationship between history and psychoanalysis becomes in fact an interminable dispute.

Faced with a problem that is difficult to handle, we prefer to say that it doesn't exist. Spence (1982), for example, has in his own way eliminated the question by setting up an opposition between historical truth and narrative truth, denying psychoanalysis any claim or possibility of access to the former and opting for a rather unclear psychoanalytical narratology. Following on this path, and often with fewer inhibitions, many analysts have recently preferred to talk about narratives and not history in reference to psychoanalysis. But this option, as we shall see in the following chapter, raises an equal number of questions and doubts. The problem of psychoanalysis vis-à-vis history remains unresolved and it is right to keep it open. On the side of the historians Peter Gay did his part some years ago with his book entitled *Freud for Historians* (1985). He argued for the importance of knowledge which is both historical and psychological from the perspective of a project of 'global history' along the lines laid down by Bloch, Febvre and Le Roy Ladurie. Gay inserted the unconscious and the interchange between the psyche and the world into the territory of the historian's research. History and psychoanalysis are both sciences of memory, both connected to scepticism. They would seem to be destined to collaborate in the fraternal search for the truth, but the risks, Gay concluded, are enormous, the prospects of failure terrible, the hope for reward uncertain. However, what ultimately attracts us about this adventurous journey can, after all, reward us for everything: firmer knowledge than ever of the totality of human experience.

Those who follow Gay on this 'adventurous journey' immediately come up against an obstacle which it would be no exaggeration to call foundational. This obstacle takes us back to the historical period when psychoanalysis came into being and was developed, a period at the height of a revolution, a time when a memorable dispute that aroused many passions was raging – the so-called *Methodenstreit*. This dispute started in the scientific field: in 1854 Droysen in his *Grundriss der Historik* had introduced the distinction between explaining and understanding, between natural and human sciences, the former to be investigated using the methods of classical science, the latter needing to adopt methodologies adequate to their object. So historians addressed the question of hermeneutics and elevated it to the special knowledge of the human sciences. The *Methodenstreit* characterised the scientific debate throughout the latter half of the nineteenth century. Wilhelm Dilthey, with his *Introduction to the Human Sciences*, was to institutionalise and give a definite theoretical foundation to the opposition between *Naturwissenschaften* and *Geistewissenschaften*. But it was historians like Heinrich Rickert and Wilhelm Windelband who, according to Assoun (1981), were to elevate 'this pair to the role of a founding division'. Assoun pointed out that Freud started his university studies at a moment when this dispute was already under way and constructed psychoanalysis when it reached its height. Freud, as someone responsive to cultural movements, could not have been unaware of it. However, he proceeded as if for him the question did not pose itself. Psychoanalysis is a *Naturwissenschaft*; for Freud there is no alternative, there can be no science which is not a natural science.

Interpretation was for Freud a variant of explanation (*Erklären*); apparently at least, he placed psychoanalysis outside a strictly hermeneutic dimension. Freud's knowledge rests at most on causality, or, in

Assoun's fitting expression, on a sort of 'semiological causality'. This premise might inhibit any research aimed at highlighting the historiographical side of Freudian research, but it is difficult to encompass psychoanalysis within definite epistemologies, in rigid grids, including those proposed by its own founder. Freud left important traces disseminated throughout his work which reflect a design that delineates the historical aspect of research and analytic practice. This is not an attempt to add Freud the Historian to Freud the Moralist, Freud the Biologist, etc. We are aware of the danger that, as happened with Sulloway's (1979) 'biologisation' of Freud, the process of 'historicising' Freud and psychoanalysis might easily dissolve and distort the specific nature of the borderline science that is psychoanalysis, namely, the quality of newness we mentioned earlier. But if we go back over these traces and follow the contours of that design we realise how simplifying, and in some respects, misleading it is to 'reduce' psychoanalysis to simple narration. Let us now pursue those traces and that design.

In his reconstruction work Freud repeatedly assigned to the analyst the function of a historian. The comparison between psychoanalysis and historiography, between analytic practice and historical practice recurs at many points in his work.[1] Essays such as *Totem and Taboo: Some Points of Agreement between the Mental Lives of Savages and Neurotics* (1913b) and *The Future of an Illusion* (1927) although highly debateable precisely because of their lack of solid sources and a historiographical framework, raise historical and religious questions. The crisis of the 1920s and the essays it produced place the relationship between subject and group, subject and anthropology, subject and history at the centre of the debate. Finally, from the 1930s onwards, the historical problem comes to form the focus of Freud's speculation, as he moves from the question of historical truth to the thinking we find in *Constructions in Analysis* (1937b) and *Moses and Monotheism: Three Essays* (1939a). During that period Freud contradicted his natural-scientific programmatic assumptions and claimed that after a lifelong *Umweg* he had returned to the historical and religious interests of his youth. So was his psychoanalysis a long 'detour', did his 'youthful' interests mark and infiltrate his work more than Freud himself supposed? As we look to delineate that map and that design against the background of his work, we are decidedly in favour of the second hypothesis.

Consistent with the methodological premises of the *Methodenstreit*, my comparison between history and psychoanalysis will focus on method rather than content. The comparison will be between historiographical method and analytical method. From this point of view, even though Gay's book, which centres primarily on content, is very sophisticated and broad-ranging, Edwin R. Wallace's *Historiography and Causation in Psychoanalysis* (1985), while more scholarly and less exciting, offers a good initial methodological framework for my approach. Wallace draws a distinction between Freud the historian and Freud the ahistorian, and in his view the first is principally the Freud of clinical practice.

In *A Reply to Criticisms of my Paper on Anxiety Neuroses* (1895c), Freud distinguished between the categories of 'preconditions', 'specific causes', 'concurrent causes' and 'precipitating or releasing causes' in the genesis of the illness:

> If we accept the idea of an aetiological equation of several terms which must be satisfied if the effect is to take place, then we may characterize as the *precipitating* or releasing cause the one which makes its appearance last in the equation, so that it immediately precedes the emergence of the effect. It is this chronological factor alone which constitutes the essential nature of a precipitating cause. Any of the other causes, too, can in a particular case play the role of precipitating cause; and [the factor playing] this role can change within the same aetiological combination.
>
> The factors which may be described as *preconditions* are those in whose absence the effect would never come about, but which are incapable of producing the effect by themselves alone, no matter in what amount they may be present. For the specific cause is still lacking.
>
> The *specific cause* is the one which is never missing in any case in which the effect takes place, and which moreover suffices, if present in the required quantity or intensity, to achieve the effect, provided only that the preconditions are also fulfilled.
>
> As *concurrent causes* we may regard such factors as are not necessarily present every time, nor able, whatever their amount, to produce the effect by themselves alone, but which operate alongside of the preconditions and the specific cause in satisfying the aetiological equation.
>
> (Freud 1895c: 135–136)

This schema still remains valid and is implicitly used in clinical observation. In the first encounter with a patient it can serve as a general grid of understanding.

In *Studies on Hysteria* (1895b), Freud implicitly follows the earlier schema when he goes through the diachronic account of the symptoms. In the Dora case (*Fragment of an Analysis of a Case of Hysteria*, 1905a: 27) he observes that the adult trauma was 'insufficient to explain or to determine the *particular character* of the symptoms [. . .] we must go back to her childhood and look about there for any influences or impressions which might have had an effect analogous to that of a trauma'. Starting from these findings he asks the patient to tell him the whole story of her life, and he pays attention to the points where a connection is missing and fills in the gaps with hypotheses that fit in as far as possible with the known part. Similarly in the case of the Wolf Man (*From the History of an Infantile Neurosis*, 1918), Freud starts out on the treatment by putting together a detailed anamnesis of the principle disorder, that is, the obsessive ideas of the patient. 'Few historicists, says Wallace (1985), 'could object to such a manifesto.'

> The solution [to the problem of translating obsessional ideas] is effected by bringing the obsessional ideas into temporal relationship with the patient's experiences, that is to say, by enquiring when a particular obsessional idea made its first appearance and in what external circumstances it is apt to recur. When, as so often happens, an obsessional idea has not succeeded in establishing itself permanently, the task of clearing it up is correspondingly simplified. We can easily convince ourselves that, when once the interconnections between an obsessional idea and the patient's experiences have been discovered, there will be no difficulty in obtaining access to whatever else may be puzzling or worth knowing in the pathological structure we are dealing with – its meaning, the mechanism of its origin, and its derivation from the preponderant motive forces of the patient's mind.
>
> (Freud 1909: 186–187)

Wallace's thesis contains an undoubted core of truth, but only providing we recognise that the successions and chronologies that both the historian and the psychoanalyst rely on are a necessity for the latter but also a limit to be overcome. In clinical experience the presumed order is in reality always uncertain and contradictory. When Freud has recourse to chronology, as in the note added to the case of the Wolf Man ('I will once more set out the chronology of the events mentioned in this case history'), he does this to help the reader by giving him an order not directly deducible from the clinical account.

Chronological order is the order of the preconscious but with the concept of the unconscious history, time and chronology must still constantly reckon with their potential cancellation by the atemporality of the unconscious – in other words, both the constant presence of the events and the absence of succession in the events themselves. But the psyche is not only atemporality; temporality is inscribed in the apparatus deriving from the series and succession of inscriptions, transcriptions and translations which, according to Freud, form the repressed. It was this temporality which provoked nostalgia when the transition was made from Freudian psychoanalysis to Kleinian psychoanalysis, which has had to pay the price for a theory that had no time for the undeniable achievements based on the structural and atemporal positions (depressive and schizo-paranoid) which it postulates.

The succession of transcriptions and translations brings about a process of temporalisation whereby the human being 'organises himself according to time, trying to take a new perspective on himself at each new turning in the road' (Laplanche 1991: 210). The analytical process can be understood, then, as an organiser of temporality, activating translations of that which could not be translated and hence was blocked in or out of time, still contemplating the unrepresentable and the untranslatable. This temporality, which is intrinsic to the apparatus and derives from the series of transcriptions and translations, does not in fact coincide with and is certainly not isomorphic with preconscious chronology, and not even the chronology suggested by Wallace (1985), let alone the one proposed by Freud in 1923. These are successions and chronologies which happen, as it were, once there is a fait accompli, useful for giving comprehensibility and intelligibility to the events of a case history. In this form the psychological explanation is first cousin to the historical explanation. In both the idea of determinism is connected to the idea of intelligibility (post-determination) and not predictability (pre-determination) (Von Wright 1969); both present themselves ex-post-facto. In a well-known passage in *The Psychogenesis of a Case of Female Homosexuality* Freud maintains:

> So long as we trace the development from its final stage backwards, the connection appears continuous, and we feel we have gained an insight which is completely satisfactory or even exhaustive. But if we proceed the reverse way, if we start from the premises inferred from the analysis and try

to follow these up to the final result, then we no longer get the impression of an inevitable sequence of events which could not be otherwise determined. We notice at once that there might have been another result, and that we might have been just as well able to understand and explain the latter [. . .] in other words, from a knowledge of the premises we could not have foretold the nature of the result.

(Freud 1920: 145)

We can set up a further comparison between psychoanalysis and history with regard to another aspect of Freud's theory. We have seen how Freud opted for a natural science view and the search for causes. Nevertheless, when he talks about case histories and puts forward interpretations, he does so using terms such as 'intention', 'purpose', 'objective', 'goal', 'function, 'meaning', which must be distinguished from 'causes' as they do not belong to the same order of logic.

In *The Psychopathology of Everyday Life* (1901), Freud, for example, defines as psychic determinism the idea that 'our psychical functioning cannot be explained by purposive ideas' (p. 240). 'Certain shortcomings in our psychical functioning [. . .] and certain seemingly unintentional performances prove, if psycho-analytic methods of investigation are applied to them, to have valid motives and to be determined by motives unknown to consciousness' (p. 239). 'There is sense and purpose behind the minor functional disturbances in the daily life of healthy people' (p. 162).

In *Introductory Lectures on Psychoanalysis* (1916) he states: 'We should then be able to leave all physiological or psycho-physiological factors on one side and devote ourselves to purely psychological investigations into the sense – that is, the meaning or purpose – of parapraxes' (p. 36). 'By "sense" we understand "meaning", "intention", "purpose" ' (p. 61). The type of reading of Freud's clinical practice that we find in Wallace (1985), as in much American psychoanalysis, tends to emphasise the motivational aspect at the expense of instinctual causation. This way of conceiving psychoanalysis, as we shall see, fits into a broader philosophical and historical view which has characterised and continues to characterise Anglo-American thinking and culture.

Finally, the historical current within psychoanalytical thought has taken on board from the Freudian inheritance the clarification of the infantile roots of neurosis, the idea of fixation and, its corollary, regression. The result was to compare the word of the analysand not with his own past, impossibly out of reach, but with objectively observed stages in his individual development. The attempts begun already in Freud's time led to research on childhood, nurseries, etc. This line of research – represented in the last few years by Infant Research – seeks to understand development in its *statu nascendi*, to follow its evolution, levels, crises, changes, to rediscover what subjective and objective messages the analysand's discourse contains.

After describing Freud the historicist, Wallace goes on to sketch a picture of Freud the anti-historicist, embodied in the anthropologist of so-called 'applied psychoanalysis'. As Gay also pointed out, psychic unity, analogical reasoning and the comparative method are the legacy of the cultural evolutionism which Freud the theorist used widely (one thinks, for example, of *Totem and Taboo*, 1913b), and which make his historiography dated and essentially ideologically based. As the American anthropologist Morgan says (1877: 275), the idea of psychic unity assumes that 'the human mind, specifically the same in all individuals in all the tribes and nations of mankind and limited in the range of its powers, works and must work in the same uniform channels and within narrow limits of variation'. Wallace goes on:

> The comparative method is based in the concept of 'survivals' (processes, customs opinions . . . carried on by force of habit into a new state of society different from that in which they had their original home (Tylor, 1874)), the notion that certain contemporary primitive cultures are a faithful reflection of those of prehistoric times, and the conviction that one can rank cultures on a scale of development. This device consisted in extrapolating from known stages in one culture to unknown stages in another. Many of the cultural evolutionists also espoused the idea that psychological processes and memory traces could be transmitted through Lamarckian inheritance, and that the psychological development of each individual bioenergetically recapitulates that of its ancestors.
>
> (Wallace 1985: 30–31)

According to Wallace, Freud's adherence to the concept of psychic unity 'allowed him to ignore history, diffusion, and the role of cultural conditioning in psychology, and hence to feel quite confident in generalizing his discoveries with Viennese neurotics to the members of the exotic cultures he had never visited'. Freud accepted the positivistic schemas of cultural evolutionists without reservation. According to these schemas, civilisations have to follow a regular evolutionary course starting from animism, passing through magic, and finishing up with religion and science. Totemism precedes religion everywhere; structures of matrilineal consanguinity are earlier than patrilinear structures; monogamy comes from group marriage, and so on.

It was Freud's penchant for using analogies, Rieff maintained (1953: 108), that encouraged his cavalier attitude to cultural history: 'The analogy was sufficient to draw the inference. Concrete historical documentation was superfluous. Psychoanalytical analogies were to comprehend all the traditional disciplines of the social sciences.' Rieff also argued (1959) that Freud the social theorist 'so far as he was identical with Freud the natural scientist, showed the traditional positivist eagerness to eliminate the challenge of history by finding lawfulness in nature' (1959: 234–235).

But the relationship between nature and culture in Freud is not so straightforward, nor can it be so easily simplified. A contemporary of Rieff's, Lionel Trilling (1955), proposed a thesis that contradicted Rieff and is in my view more original. He started from the idea that Freud had played a central role in defining the modern concept of culture. Unlike Rieff, and numerous other authors, he extolled Freud's link with biology, which he saw as an aid to the individual threatened by culture, held at one and the same time to be indispensable and suffocating. Trilling argued that Freud's insistence on the incessant search for pleasure on the part of the drives was by no means a reactionary idea. It was a really liberating concept which suggested that culture is by no means omnipotent and that there are some human properties which cannot be put under cultural control. In Trilling's view, the Freudian vision contains a hard core of biological reason which culture cannot reach and which reserves itself the right, which it will sooner or later exercise, to judge culture, to resist it and to change it.

Personally I am of the opinion that in Freud culture and nature do not stand in opposition nor, as Rieff and Wallace would argue, is nature predominant in Freud's theory. We find again the maturity of his thought in his writings during the so-called 1920s crisis, when the problem of the relationship between the individual and culture became more pressing. In *The Ego and the Id* (1923b) the psyche is founded by two organising principles – one biological in nature (bisexuality and *Hilflosigkeit* [helplessness]), the other cultural (Oedipus) – which cooperate to constitute the psychic structures of the ego and the superego. Bodily experience, symbolic experience, intersubjective experience, inextricably connected, are foundation and genesis of the psyche, its aspirations and its structures. It is from them that the psyche takes its form and its model. Biological and cultural organisers interact.[2]

The dichotomy between Freud the historicist (the clinician) and Freud the anti-historicist (the anthropologist) is, in our view, excessively reductive. While he adopts the historical method of deciphering in clinical cases, he also uses theoretical references based on the hereditary nature of instincts. In the case study of the Wolf Man, Freud first gives a meticulous chronological reconstruction of childhood events, starting from the famous dream, and then goes on to say that in the case in question the phylogenetic schema had outdone the real childhood experience of the patient and had thus determined certain fantasies and behaviours. Freud is a historicist (or at least tries to be) in *Moses and Monotheism* (1939a), whereas he is anti-historicist in the Schreber case, where he uses the concept of psychic unity, the comparative method and analogical reasoning.

There is no solution; these dialectical poles continue to alternate right up to the end. Midway through the 1930s the historical problem arose again forcefully, starting from the question of historic truth, to which Freud was to return repeatedly.[3] History and the constraints on the historian are compared with narration and the inventive freedom of the storyteller. This leitmotiv runs through late Freud's speculation until it emerges in the writings that formed our starting point: *Moses and Monotheism* and *Constructions in Analysis*. In *Moses and Monotheism* Freud seems to adhere to a vision at odds with the times. He tries to reconstruct historical and cultural events starting from the story of an individual man, a hero, but his lucidity and awareness are surprising. He says:

> How is it possible for a single man to evolve such extraordinary effectiveness that he can form a people out of random individuals and families, can stamp them with their definitive character and determine their fate for thousands of years? Is not a hypothesis such as this a relapse into the mode of thought which led to myths of a creator and to the worship of heroes, into times in which the writing of history was nothing more than a report of the deeds and destinies of single individuals, of rulers or conquerors? The modern tendency is rather towards tracing back the events of human history to more concealed, general and impersonal factors, to the compelling influence of economic conditions, to alterations in food habits, to advances in the use of materials and tools, to migrations brought about by increases in population

and climatic changes. Individuals have no other part to play in this than as exponents or representatives of group trends, which are bound to find expression and do so in these particular individuals largely by chance.
(Freud 1939a: 107)

This quotation testifies to Freud's knowledge of the new strain of historiography that was becoming established during that period (in 1929 Febvre and Bloch had founded *Annales*). This new historiography had followed on from the idealistic nineteenth-century version which had formed Freud and obviously posed the question of history in a very different way from the 'historical novel' approach which Freud had used when he took on the subject of *Moses and Monotheism*. In 1939 Freud concluded his enterprise. *Moses and Monotheism* and *Constructions in Analysis*, and with them the historical and anti-historical method, trace those interrupted itineraries from which we started our path backwards through Freud's work. The next few pages will take this as a starting point and we will project forwards, following routes which, shortly after Freud's death, were laid down in the field of history and psychoanalysis – opposing and diverging roads.

The year 1942 saw the publication of Hempel's 'The Function of General Laws in History', which started a heated philosophical debate about the foundations of historical investigation. According to Hempel, scientific explanations in history and in other fields (in this way the difference between idiographic and nomotetic sciences was reduced) must appeal both to the particular conditions before the fact to be explained and general laws (which he calls 'covering laws'). The explanation is to be framed in such a way that the *explanandum* (i.e. phenomenon to be explained) is deducible from the *explanans* (i.e. the specific antecedent conditions operating in accordance with an explicitly fixed universal law). Such a law asserts that whenever and wherever circumstances of the kind in question occur, an event of the kind to be explained comes about (Hempel 1962). Psychoanalysts, like historians, often implicitly invoke covering laws. According to Wallace (1985):

An explanation of a particular adult sexual pattern or symptom by invoking the Oedipus complex and citing the specific fantasies, patterns of activity, and memories supporting this hypothesis, could be conceptualized as proceeding through the following covering law: 'any human raised by two

> parenting figures will develop sexual feelings for one of the opposite sex and aggressive feelings toward the one of the same sex.
>
> (p. 49)

Lavagetto makes the acute observation (1985: 218) that unlike the narrator (and this is a significant difference), who is neither guaranteed nor wants to be guaranteed by any covering law, the psychoanalyst has at his disposal explanatory theories and laws which regulate his narrative and 'protect him from arbitrariness'; narratives that can be called analytical only on the basis of those explicit or implicit laws. Analytical constructions, like historical constructions, can thus be placed in the ambit of probabilistic-deductive explanations, which Hempel (1953) distinguishes from the deductive-nomological laws of the exact sciences. For Hempel both explanations have scientific dignity.[4] Considering the particular nature of the psychoanalytic object, general laws in psychoanalysis are expressed in narrative plots, patterns and myths. Hempel's research started an intense debate among scholars and that debate became a anti-metaphysical and empiricist 'research tradition' resulting from the confluence of Hempelian positivism, analytic philosophy and, finally, American pragmatism instrumentalism. We shall try to give a brief description of this debate because it is of particular relevance to any understanding of contemporary psychoanalysis, in particular American psychoanalysis, and its dilemmas and conflicts.

In the 1940s, in the English-speaking world a critique of the speculative philosophy of history developed based on the late Wittgensteinian notion of language as action and meaning as use. The meaning of linguistic expression is not clarified by reconstructing it on a formal level but by understanding its use within specific social contexts. Taking language as central to a critical investigation, the foundations of the historical sciences were examined through an investigation of the terms they use. This produced a strand which diverged from Hempel's positions, despite their shared anti-metaphysical aims.

The difference emerges on the level of explanations. Explanation is no longer only rational, as Hempel suggested, based on laws and principles, but can take on different forms, varying according to the individual authors: it can be intentional, dispositional, probabilistic or situational. In opposition to the formal logic of events proposed by Hempel, there is a 'logic of [human] actions', and concepts such as 'choice', 'decision', 'norm', 'purpose' are introduced. To explain an action means discovering the 'reasons', the 'motives' which have led a person to act in that way. Human reasons, in short, must be distinguished from 'causes': motives, desires and intentions do not belong to the same order of logic as causes.

Dray was one of Hempel's harshest critics and in the 1960s there was a long, intense debate between the two. In short, for Dray explaining a human event did not mean considering it an element in a more general class. It did not mean referring to general laws, as Hempel argued, but finding and using specific explanatory tools designed to investigate human actions. For Dray these tools included 'empathetic understanding', in other words, 'putting yourself in the shoes' of the 'agent'. This terminology and this dispute recall similar terminology and a similar dispute which took place many years later in the psychoanalytic field and saw Kohut and his disciples proposing 'empathy' as a key tool in the analytic investigation and criticising the laws and principles of metapsychology.

To continue this rapid survey: the development of the notion of 'intentionality' proposed by Anscombe and elaborated further by Von Wright deserves especial attention. According to Von Wright, Hempel's declarative logic was inadequate to the concepts that related to man understood as an agent. According to Von Wright, saying that intentionality is characteristic of phenomena connected to human culture means saying in general that these phenomena have a meaning.

In this way he linked intention, action and understanding, justifying the teleological explanation since intentions cannot be considered as logically independent of actions. For reasons of brevity, we have looked at the different positions of Dray and Von Wright, distant from each other in approach and historical period. Our aim has been to point out a protracted and intensely experienced cultural event. The debate started by Hempel emerged in England in the 1940s, reached America and was influenced and in part transformed by American pragmatism and instrumentalism.

During that same period, the strand of so-called 'ego psychology' developed in the field of psychoanalysis, with its roots in the researches of Hartmann. In my opinion, it reflected the cultural climate we have just been describing. This strand of psychoanalysis valorised the centrality of the ego and its functions, autonomous of the unconscious and conflicts, functions which determine specific motives, intentions and purposes towards reality, acts in reality and adaptation to them.

American psychoanalysis, at least as conducted by its leading figures, is 'motivational' psychoanalysis. This tradition continues today. One author who has particularly felt the effect of the cultural climate we have tried to describe, notably the analytic philosophy of language, is Roy Schafer. He makes clear and explicit use of the instrument of language for the purposes of a critical investigation of both the theoretical terms of psychoanalysis and the language adopted in analytic practice (see especially *Aspects of Internalization*, 1968 and *Language and Insight*, 1978). Schafer's very terminology, with his adoption of terms such as 'agent' and 'language of action', reflects analytical philosophy and the criticism of metapsychology fits very well into the anti-metaphysical programme of that philosophy.

One may not share the approach of American psychoanalysis but it is at least founded on a heritage of complex and detailed ideas. The research tradition we have been sketching here developed at the same time as the other, but was to have very little relationship with it. Starting in France, it was to profoundly affect the human sciences in European culture. We would like to start again from this point to speak of another 'story', one that is better known to us and which involves history and psychoanalysis in equal measure.

In 1947, the publication of Lévi-Strauss's *The Elementary Structures of Kinship* sparked a wide debate which was to become the research tradition known as structuralism and involved many fields of knowledge (linguistics, anthropology, history, psychoanalysis) Pomian (1981) states:

> The most important change among those which in the twentieth century have affected the human and social sciences as a whole is the doubling each of them underwent (with rare exceptions) in theory and history or, if you like, the appearance of theories hinging on objects which at first were addressed only from an historical point of view.

Here we have the opposition, which some see as crucial, between history and structure. Lévi-Strauss's critique is directed in particular against those who put too high a value on historical interpretation. In Lévi-Strauss's view, the temporal dimension unjustly enjoys special prestige, as if diachrony founded a type of intelligibility not only superior to that contributed by synchrony but above all a specifically human order. Lévi-Strauss (1964) states:

> In fact history is tied neither to man nor to any particular object. It consists entirely in its method, which experience proves to be indispensable for cataloguing the elements of any structure whatever, human or non-human, in their entirety. It is therefore far from being the case that the search for intelligibility comes to an end in history as though this were its terminus. Rather, it is history that serves as the point of departure in any quest for intelligibility. As we say of certain careers, history may lead to anything, provided you get out of it.

Starting from these assumptions a heated debate developed over several decades between Lévi-Strauss and historians. Notwithstanding this dispute, structuralism has had a deep influence on the historians of *Annales*.

We shall dwell briefly on this school of historians, which has profoundly changed historical thought, because its research is now part of our common cultural heritage. The event, 'structure' and 'long duration' are terms/concepts also widely known outside the field of historical studies. In fact, one of the peculiar phenomena brought about by structuralism was a kind of methodological, conceptual and lexical osmosis between the various fields involved: anthropology, history and psychoanalysis. In this last field, Lacan is the researcher who has most notably felt the influence of and at the same time represented this cultural tradition: 'the unconscious is structured like a language', 'the Ego is a symptom'. Lacan radicalised later Freud's concept of the split Ego. For him the subject is irremediably divided. 'Beyond' the subject, structure and language found subjectivity which thus does not find its centre in intentions, motives or purposes of the Ego.

After Freud then, we can identify two broad currents in psychoanalysis: historical and structural. Earlier we pointed out how central the notions of fixation and regression are to the historical strand in its investigations (with the help in some sectors of the direct observation of the child) into the varying degrees of subjectivity and objectivity in the analysand's discourse. In the structuralist approach, on the other hand, the patient's words count at the moment he pronounces them in synchrony, jointly with the transference which connects him to the analyst. Starting from free association and evenly hovering attention, the attempt is made to recover the latent meaning of the discourse, to establish the substitutions and the relations between the signifiers of the moment since the structure is not explained so much by an investigation into meaning as by the 'non-casual' way the meanings are articulated. By valorising the synchronic aspect, in analytic treatment the same value is given, independent of their diachrony, to the events of the past, desires, dreams, links to the present and fantasies. On the question of 'the observation of childhood', for the structuralists we have no other eyes than our adult eyes. It is not the child that explains the adult, it is the adult that explains the child, that speaks in the adult we are listening to. Hence it is illusory either to consider our constructions as real or to believe that we can understand the reality of the past by means of 'objective' study. The analyst's work translates from the latent to the manifest through the mediation of the laws of the symbolic, of which linguistics is only one particular application.

Two examples of structure in psychoanalysis are represented by the 'original phantasies' and the Oedipus complex. The former represent for Freud 'categories', organisers which form the 'core of the unconscious'. They pre-date experience, they are constituted by it and in part they guide and determine it.[5] In the interpretation put forward by Laplanche and Pontalis, who accepted and extended Freud's heritage, primal scene, castration scene and seduction scene are structural organisers: 'in the primal scene [. . .] it is the origin of the individual that is figured; in seduction fantasies, on the other hand, the origin, the source of sexuality; in castration phantasies, the origin of the difference between the sexes' (Laplanche and Pontalis 1985: 70). In the 1985 postscript, they clearly express the structuralist derivation of their reading of Freud. It is to their credit that they knew how to articulate individual history and structure without negating either.

The Oedipus complex is also a structure. In *The Ego and the Id* Freud wrote:

> For one gets the impression that the simple Oedipus complex is by no means its commonest form, but rather represents a simplification or schematization which, to be sure, is often enough justified for practical purposes. Closer study usually discloses the more complete Oedipus complex, which is twofold, positive and negative, and is due to the bisexuality originally present in children: that is to say, a boy has not merely an ambivalent attitude towards his father and an affectionate object-choice towards his mother, but at the same time he also behaves like a girl and displays an affectionate feminine attitude to his father and a corresponding jealousy and hostility towards his mother. It is this complicating element introduced by bisexuality that makes it so difficult to obtain a clear view of the facts in connection with the earliest

> object-choices and identifications, and still more difficult to describe them intelligibly. It may even be that the ambivalence displayed in the relations to the parents should be attributed entirely to bisexuality and that it is not, as I have represented above, developed out of identification in consequence of rivalry.
>
> In my opinion it is advisable in general, and quite especially where neurotics are concerned, to assume the existence of the complete Oedipus complex. Analytic experience then shows that in a number of cases one or the other constituent disappears, except for barely distinguishable traces; so that the result is a series with the normal positive Oedipus complex at one end and the inverted negative one at the other, while its intermediate members exhibit the complete form with one or other of its two components preponderating.
>
> (Freud 1923b: 33–34)

One must foresee all possibilities, including those which are virtual and without a present manifestation – this is the point made by Hjelmslev (1943) à propos language, a comment which is valid for all structures.

In *The Ego and the Id*, Freud identifies the meanings derived from kinship ties and articulates them along the axes of desire and identification, love and hate, bisexuality and *Hilflosigkeit*. We can thus speak of structure – according to Green – because Freud introduces us to a very rich combinatory game which generates a field of both normal and pathological situations and constellations. Since Freud gives these structures a properly human calling, this is not conceivable, as we shall see later, beyond the relationship which the subject has with his progenitors. This calls into play the historical dimension. History is not conceivable beyond structure and vice versa.

There is a radical difference between the languages, methodologies and ideologies expressed through structuralist-based European psychoanalysis, on the one hand, and American psychoanalysis, on the other. Starting from Freud, two strands were formed which rested on and were nurtured by two different research traditions. One privileged and expanded the Freudian concept of the ego, its autonomy, its motivations, its functions. The other tradition took the Freudian concept of the unconscious structure to its extreme consequences.

Analytic reconstructions have thus had two differing destinies: on the one hand, construction has taken the form of the reconstruction of motives, interests, contexts, the present and past of the subject (or the agent, as Roy Schafer would put it); on the other, construction is structured like the reconstruction of the phantasy which runs through history, a phantasy which does not find its organising principle only in history itself but also in a pre-individual structure.

One problem remains unresolved: it is a problem we have not addressed in this section because of its methodological intent. Where is the analytic reconstruction located, where is the analytical space which founds, delimits and justifies the whole reconstructive and, if one prefers, constructive operation? We shall talk about this space later in the book, but for the moment we would only like to point out that Italian psychoanalysis has made and continues to make a significant contribution to this subject, dedicated as it has been, ever since the 1980 Conference on Analytical Relationships, to examining and trying to describe this space, albeit in divergent and contradictory ways depending on the approach taken.

It is probably here that we can find a meeting point, despite the cultural differences that separate us from much of American psychoanalysis. It is no accident that starting precisely from the critique of the claimed historicism of analytical reconstruction (Spence), using contributions from contemporary philosophy (Schafer), these authors, but also others, have questioned the analytical couple itself and its operation, following a critique of some assumptions of the theory of a technique that is held to be ideological, rhetorical and essentially false. Whether or nor we share their conclusions, which we shall return to later, the critical starting point is the one which in Italy has brought about a fresh problematisation and reflection on the analytical situation.

I talked about different conclusions because, starting from their common critiques, the solutions outlined, especially by Spence, and Wallace's theoretical-clinical formulations, make us realise that there is a basic difference between some positions expressed by European psychoanalysis. It is impossible not to agree with Schafer when he says that in psychoanalysis the traditional distinctions between subject and object, between observation and theory, between past and present no longer hold. But we do not think that Spence's so-called 'naturalisation' is the way to reach a faithful and unambiguous reproduction of the analytical session. Starting from some shared assumptions (breaking the concept of linear causality, the end of the division between object and subject, the crisis of ingenuous historicism), we can think of the analytic relationship as an auto-poietic system, recovering operationally for this purpose two fundamental concepts of Freudian psychoanalysis: repetition compulsion and deferred action. They can be thought of as joint agents, thus assuming the form of the key figure in a psychoanalytically based constructivism.

Here I have briefly anticipated my proposal, or rather model, of the analytic field, which I intend to illustrate and develop more fully in later chapters. The great Freudian innovation on the question of history lies in these two notions which break with the classic vision of time – time as linear and irreversible. Freud offers a reflection not on 'time' but on different 'kinds of time' operating in a structure. This is a cognitive provocation launched by psychoanalysis into the arena of the human sciences. These are the reasons why we do not agree with Wallace's reductive criticism of repetition compulsion and the absence of the concept of deferred action in his treatment (as indeed in much of North American psychoanalysis).

'That which is fundamental to psychoanalysis can only be so if it is in harmony *a posteriori* with that which is fundamental to the human being' (Laplanche 1987). Accordingly, the various schools and theories of psychoanalysis assume different and divergent 'foundations' of man. The differences in psychoanalysis are therefore never solely clinical or theoretical. What we are dealing with are different conceptions of man, his relationship with the past, the chances of understanding it, treating and being treated through its recovery. The presence (or absence) and the centrality of the notion of *après-coup* in a theory of man and treatment is by no means unimportant since it subverts dominant models. According to Kaës (1933: 30): 'Time, memory and the relationship of the individual with his own psychic history are modified: psychoanalysis, the experience of re-inscription, is not affiliated with any other psychotherapy.'

Après-coup implies that there is always dissymmetry between the here and now and the 'repressed': a gap (despite our interpretive efforts) between the event and the meaning, between what determines us and the grasp we might have on it; a difference between what we are possessed by (through genealogical heredity) and what we possess. The unity of the person remains a myth, his fundamental dimensions are absence and difference. We agree with Freud that the temporal unity of the subject is an illusion and the mirror image of our varying degrees of possession of the past.

Schafer's 'agent', in contrast, seems to seek to master his history. His 'treatment' of language (of the patient, the analyst, theory) seeks to eliminate that which is impersonal in the linguistic expressions used in psychoanalysis. This may be a useful way of reviving an over-stereotypical language that has been reduced to a lifeless jargon, but by doing so it also removes the language of the unconscious, of the id, that third person that speaks to us, which is the language of a decentred subject. In various places Kohut and his followers suggest that a non-cohesive self is only the pathological consequence of an original empathetic 'failure'. 'Good' empathy in an analytic cure can compensate for this (biological) tendency towards cohesion. The re-emergence of an idea (or perhaps it would be better to say, of an illusion) that psychoanalysis had shattered over its hundred years of history is proposed as new. Indeed the concept of a 'unifying and united subject' is a pre-analytical one, to put it in Pontalis's (1977) terms, one which can be recognised and which thus eludes the 'irreducibility of the conflict', the 'irreconcilability of representations', the 'otherness of the unconscious' and the 'disparate multiplicity of identifications'. In my view, the otherness of the unconscious and the multiplicity of identifications are two sides of the same coin.

The work of re-inscription, a translation marked by the timeframe of *après-coup* allows us to annex to our psychic territory (though never totally or definitively) a history which before being ours is the story of another, others, a desire of theirs which precedes us and inside which we must be born. Awaiting the newborn child are parents, relatives, their stories and their plots: 'the world is already there for man', as Merleau-Ponty suggests.

The story of another, the story of others

Any reflection about history and the connection between history and structure must start from a preliminary distinction between the pre-subjective, intersubjective and subjective dimensions. This distinction separates and disarticulates a whole which in fact acts in an inseparable way. The process of subjectivisation (the subject is not a given but a process) means the assimilation of structures and pre-subjective symbolic orders which are mediated by extremely significant intersubjective relations. Lacan (1978) says:

> Freud discovered in man the weight and axis of a subjectivity exceeding individual organization conceived as the sum of individual experiences,

> and even as the individual line of development [. . .] a possible definition of subjectivity [can be formulated] as an organized system of symbols, pretending to cover the totality of an experience, to animate it, to give it its meaning/direction.

This previously existing structure which grounds the subject's history acts, in Balsamo and Napolitano's apt metaphor (1994: 144) as a 'fund' which, at one and the same moment ensures 'points of certainty' and gives the subject a place in the kinship system, providing it with a fantasy 'capital'. The analogy is with a financial fund which potentially can be spent, used or wasted. Kinship systems, starting from the name we are given, organise identificatory processes in the succession of generations, in the sphere of possible and impossible relations, exchanges and prohibitions that 'end up penetrating the body of every member of society and mould him according to their order' (Godelier 1990).

By having *Urphantasien* revolve around the taboo of incest, Freud anticipated what in the thinking of Lévi-Strauss was to become the fundamental anthropological law organising symbols, language and human exchange. According to Bonomi (1968), structure is 'that set of rules which (*even if they do not fall into the field of knowledge and the observable*) none the less function as regulating principles of the founding activity of interacting agents' (emphasis added). The Oedipus complex is a structure that links the biological and the cultural, and is important in the 'founding activity' of subjects. Yet it is not 'observable', and this marks a major limitation on 'empirical observation' in psychoanalysis. Intersubjective relations which are potentially observable (I refer mainly to the mother–child relation studied by Infant Research) have undoubted importance although they do not cover the whole field of research and analytical experience. It is through these highly significant intersubjective relations that the 'fund', the heritage, the pre-subjective order is transmitted to us.

Traditions, ethnic groups, family ideologies, the characteristics of parents and their possible pathologies function as mediators, regulators of these pre-subjective orders and laws. Their style and key features become the seal of this transition. Here a 'new' type of research enters into play – transgenerational research – which in my view is the continuation of something 'ancient'.

The problem of the other in relation to the subject, its foundation and its alienation was at the centre of philosophical, literary and anthropological debate in the twentieth century. As early as 1897, Freud said, phantasies 'combine things that have been experienced and things that have been heard, past events (from the history of parents and ancestors) and things that have been seen by oneself' (Draft L, 2 May). Since then the psyche has presented itself as an amalgam, where it is difficult to distinguish between what strictly speaking belongs to the subject and what derives from the other, from his words and his mythology. This thought runs through Freud's work and emerges clearly in some key texts such as *Mourning and Melancholia* (1917). The theme is taken up dramatically in the writings of the 1920s. During that period both Freud and Pirandello saw the individual as animated and 'experienced' by many subjects: 'Each individual is a component part of numerous groups, he is bound by ties of identification in many directions, and he has built up his ego ideal upon the most various models' (*Group Psychology and the Analysis of the Ego*, Freud 1921: 129). Today's transgenerational research can thus be understood as a 'return' which we trust will lead to a healthy new awareness. It can only be a source of pleasure that many analysts have now finally stuck their heads out of the nursery. Having interrupted the holding of their patient–child and still confused by an excessively long *rêverie*, they are discovering that the patient is not a child, that he has a first name, a last name, kinship relations.

At times this rapid shift arouses suspicion and I hope that Italy will not be invaded, as France was some years ago, by a swarm of newly ordained discoverers of 'crypts' and that the transgenerational approach will be more than a symptom of a fin-de-siècle, end-of-millennium malaise or, even worse, a fashion. To avoid this fate, I think it is useful to look at the transgenerational approach in the light of the theory of the psychic apparatus and its topography.

In the last few years there has been a broad and widespread rejection of metapsychology, seen as a useless and outdated theoretical apparatus. But the so-called transgenerational approach, if one wants to avoid reducing it to a more or less detailed anamnesis of one's ancestors, and to avoid transforming it into the umpteenth wrong that parents and grandparents have visited upon their children and grandchildren, means a return to metapsychology, to the theory of the psychic apparatus and to a revision which includes the other as a permanent condition in its structure. Laplanche moved in this direction with his hypothesis of 'original seduction'. So too did Lacan and Winnicott with their models – even though, as Baranes justly points out (1993: 208), in Lacan the problem becomes emotion and instinct, in Winnicott sexuality and the father.

The reference to metapsychology is constant in Abraham and Torok (1987), who launched the theme of the transgenerational and still today are the authors who have investigated it mostly profoundly and rigorously. They talk about the 'topography of reality' when referring to the psychic reality not worked through by an other, which is located in the psyche of the subject. They also use the metapsychology of incorporation and introjection, along lines set down by Ferenczi, and of mourning, following Freud. Metapsychology is a constant point of reference for other authors (Kaës, Baranes, Faimberg) who deal with transgenerational transmission. This does not mean forsaking research into and clinical use of primary relations – on the contrary. The maternal relation can be enriched and enhanced as a result, its function expanded; for too long it has been restricted by an atemporal and potentially alienating cliché.

Originary immaturity obliges us to be dependent on the other, on his treatment of us, a dependence which with the advent of the Oedipus complex, as Freud says in *The Ego and the Id*, is transformed into the dependence of the ego on the superego and the ego-ideal; dependence on the speech and words of the other, potential 'violence', but also a necessity, a question of quantity, duration and sensibility. Aulagnier writes:

> The ego can ignore everything except that other ego which it needs in order to be able to think about itself and hence to conceive its desire. Only in this way can the ego invest narcissistically in the image of its self it thinks conforms to what it is for him and what it is for the other. Only if the ego can internalise the image of a self which at a certain moment was the object of parental desire, only on this condition can it be sure that whatever happens it will be able to find its origin in the desire of those who have given birth to it.
>
> (Aulagnier 1975: 392)

How many times have we had to listen to a defect in this desire, listen to people who have suffered because they were not 'desired' and who came to find themselves outside any kind of stabilising inscription, outside their head. How many times has the excess of that desire dispossessed the individual of his own story: 'for in this labour which he undertakes to reconstruct *for another*, he rediscovers the fundamental alienation that made him construct it *like another* and has always destined it to be taken *by another*' (Lacan 1966).

In his excellent introduction to Aulagnier's (1975) book, Luchetti says: 'The ego . . . is always in search of meaning, it is a historian of itself, an untiring constructor of its own history, but precisely for this reason it depends fundamentally on the discourse and thought of the other [in particular] for the first chapters of its history, its pre-history.' The individual can thus be compared to something the mother has been unable to 'conceive' and has been enacted in the relationship between the mother and the child. At this point the primary mechanisms of defence such as disavowal and denial (which we talked about earlier) are set in motion, with the consequence at times of serious mutilations of the ego and the exclusion, the negation of pieces of reality of varying sizes. But because getting an idea of one's own origin is vital, when the 'parental gap' is too wide, delusions can emerge in which the subject looks to find his origin in religion (the delusion of the Messiah and of founders of new religions) or in the genesis of the cosmos.

In the process of historicisation a fundamental function is performed not only by the father, as is commonly argued, but also by the mother; I would say 'primarily' the mother. I think that the full value of the historicising function which, starting as long ago as 1964 Aulagnier assigned to the mother and her discourse, should be recognised. The maternal discourse which locates the child in the chain of generations defines the 'reality' of kinship relations and in this way allows the child to start to construct the story of his own origin. The lack or distortion of this discourse leads to the 'primary delusional theory' which Micheline Enriquez writes about (1988). This maternal function does not exclude and indeed comes to complete the better known function of *rêverie* and holding. In this framework one should reflect whether Winnicott's 'good enough' mother is such when it is good for symbolisation (as J. L. Donnet suggests, quoted in Baranes 1993: 215).

The analogy between mother and analyst has been abused all too often but, in my view, it is more (and I would add more realistically) applicable if we extend the maternal function to symbolisation and historicisation. In transference the analyst does in fact try to facilitate the processes of historicising and transforming the events of the past, including transgenerational events. Since Abraham and Torok, all authors have been using constructions for these genealogical stories which operate and work over the long term. The temporality of the constructions is set in opposition to the *kairos*[6] (as Rabant 1985 suggests) of the interpretation: not the timeframe of experience but the timeframe of destiny. We could say that interpretation is to experience what construction is to destiny.

For Lacan the question of the subject concerns his history as something he misrecognises and which, despite himself, he expresses in his whole behaviour when obscurely he tries to recognise it: 'His life is guided by a problem *which is not the problem of his experience but that of his destiny* – that is, the question: what does his history mean?' (Lacan 1978: 55, emphasis added). Destiny is a complex theme and the analyst is forced to address it because he encounters it in his practice. The individual is a 'link in a chain which he serves against his will,' says Freud. 'No generation is able to conceal any of its more important processes from its successor' (*Totem and Taboo*, 1913b: 159). Destiny, like myth, to which it is closely akin, runs through us. It lives in us independent of our 'will'.

Working through and construction in analysis can remove elements of our destiny from unconsciousness, distinguishing between what we have received and the use we have made of it; a process of historicisation understood as the appropriation by the subject of his genealogical inheritance, a subject who takes his thought and narrative from that inheritance. But this is not always immediately possible, it cannot always be transformed. Some patients are profoundly marked by the 'negativity of transmission' which deprives them of their own history, alienating them even from their consciousness of self. Some patients do not know the story of their own life and appear thus as people 'without history'. In the course of these analyses long preliminary work is necessary to weave the torn canvas we spoke of earlier, to construct the framework, the scenic space on which to project, live and represent the story of that analysis and that life. It is no accident that we mention analysis before life, because only after the construction of the analytic relation and the development of his history, only starting from that point, will the patient manage to recover the plot and story of his life.

'The analysis must work on the constitution of a space that is missing,' says Aulagnier. 'It must primarily be concerned with establishing a relationship with the other which is not there from the start. And this obliges us [. . .] to work on the construction of something that has not actually happened for the ego.' Green talks of 'tertiarity', an area between inside and outside, analyst and patient. The analytic adventure in these cases becomes not only a question of transference and countertransference but also 'co-production of the living' (Racamier 1989), an activity that involves analyst and patient alike. By taking another route we have once again come back to the analytical relationship whose formation and function we will talk about at length later.

4

Psychoanalysis and narrative
A controversial relationship

Should the case histories we write read like short stories?

For the psychoanalyst, writing is not a superstructure but part of his or her work and experience. Psychoanalysis and writing meet in manifold forms – from the simplest to the most complex and abstract. During his training and professional career the psychoanalyst writes session reports and then case histories in order to become an associate or an ordinary professor. Once his training is finished he still continues to write. His works may contain brief clinical suggestions but it is increasingly rare that he writes extensively about an analytical treatment, which is a point worthy of more in-depth reflection.

We can speak only briefly of the other levels on which psychoanalysis and writing meet. Transcriptions, translations: from *Project for a Scientific Psychology* (Freud 1895a) to *A Note upon the 'Mystic Writing Pad'* (Freud 1925a), the 'scene of writing' runs through metapsychology. In this context Derrida (1967) has written an exemplary essay. Literature, psychoanalysis, writing 'and others' have been the object of in-depth research by Lavagetto (1985), an author to whom these pages are greatly indebted. For Pontalis (1990) writing, together with transference and dreams, is a 'force of attraction'. Lionel Trilling (1950) defined psychoanalysis as a 'science of tropes'. It seems superfluous to cite Lacan who equated condensation with metaphor and displacement with metonymy. Benveniste (1956) defined *The Interpretation of Dreams* (1900) as a compendium and inventory of figures of style.

The complexity of the relationship between psychoanalysis and writing, previously the object of research for a small number of analysts, has recently been evident on a broader scale and become a more general problem. Following changes in Italian training regulations, teachers on the judging commissions now have their first contact not directly with the candidates (associate members, ordinary members, teachers) but with their written papers on their clinical-theoretical experiences. It is well known that problems, disagreements and contestations have arisen. It is essential that the psychoanalytical institution should not close itself off by devising primarily pragmatic solutions, identifying, for example, typical forms of writing appropriate to institutional purposes. I think instead that this is a valuable occasion for starting to think about writing about psychoanalytic clinical practice. The problem does not simply concern the passage of analysts through the various stages of training; it relates to the question of the transmission of psychoanalysis and above all its communicability. This is a cultural problem of great topicality given that the hotly debated 'crisis' of psychoanalysis also involves the problem of communicability.

The aim of these pages is only to offer some ideas and these notes can only be the start of a wider and more complex debate on a problem that came into being with psychoanalysis itself and which every generation of analysts has had to confront.

In *From the History of an Infantile Neurosis*, Freud wrote:

> I am unable to give a purely historical or a purely thematic account of my patient's story; I can write a history neither of the treatment nor of the illness, but I shall find myself obliged to combine the two methods of presentation. It is well known that no means has been found of in any way introducing into the reproduction of an analysis the sense of conviction which results from the analysis itself. Exhaustive verbatim reports of the proceedings during the hours of analysis would certainly be of no help at all.
>
> (1918:13)

The difficulty, according to Freud, was how to nail down a multidimensional formation on the surface level. Freud distinguishes chronology from themes, the history of the illness from the history of the treatment. These elements do not coincide and their different articulation generates various styles and narrative forms through which to transmit the experience of an analysis. This differentiation implies that there is no precise, seamless equivalence between the analyst who day by day is immersed in experience, and the writer-analyst, the narrator of that experience. We need to take this difference, this gap into account when we judge the former (the therapist) through the latter (the writer).

Let us start with the former, the analyst-therapist who day after day goes through the experience of analysis. In his work of recording and decoding the patient's production he has often been compared to the reader of a text. However, 'people are not words'; this was the indignant complaint of the young son of a psychoanalyst talking to his brother about their father's work. Everything speaks against the analogy between analysing and reading a text. Even though Lotman (1973) extends the concept of text (he explains that text means in the broadest sense any communication recorded in a given sign system), the original form underlying the extensive use of the concept is the written text. The reading of a text, given the fixity of writing and the primacy of sight, is far from the mobility of the analytical situation and the dominant role played by listening (De Micco 1996). It is no accident that analysts are enjoined not only to keep their attention evenly suspended, but also not to takes notes during the session, not to lower the capacity and breadth of listening and not to fix and prematurely translate what they hear into sign traces, not to transform into information what is in the broadest and richest sense of the term a communication.

Another analogy, this time based completely on listening, is between the analyst who gathers stories and experiences narrated by the patient and the 'oral historian' who listens directly to the voices of witnesses to historical events and traditions. However, whereas the historian learns about things not known to him and the knowledge belongs to the witness, the analyst is the one who is the authority, as Lavagetto suggests. But in analysis this is only partly true because the analyst, by virtue of his competence and impelled by the 'practice of suspicion', can learn from the words of the other more than he knows consciously. The analyst who possesses knowledge and authority has the task of transforming the figure of the 'subject supposed knowledge' of the analyst and certainly he is never a neutral listener. What an analyst listens to in the first sessions is the history of the patient.

Is there a correspondence between the history of the patient and the 'history of the illness', as suggested by Freud (1913c: 134)? On this point we feel that a brief digression is in order. In the tradition of western medicine the 'history of the illness' corresponds and flows into the notion of 'course' – a development and natural process which can be studied independently of the patient. Illnesses are classified as nosographic entities; they are seen in formal rather than substantive terms. The history of the patient is thus annulled and comes to correspond to the history of the illness. In the field of mental illness nosography freed the patient from the moral chains dictated by the equation between mental illness and moral illness and shackled him instead with the chains of medicine. What continued to be accepted was that the history of the illness could be the history of the subject, of his life and his suffering. Freud broke with this tradition: he looked at content and not only at forms of illness, at the patient more than the illness, he listened to the patient. He gave credence to the words of those who were not entitled to speak because official medicine forbade them to do so. The story of the patient was not annulled by the illness and consequently did not correspond to 'course' and 'treatment'.

However, in our view, the concept of the history of the illness as course and natural process partly remains even in this changed framework. There is a development of the neurosis which the doctor must facilitate. If he becomes a 'screen' for the patient, making himself opaque as a person (let us leave aside the question of how little this applied to Charcot, Breuer and Freud), he allows the illness to develop through the artificial form of the transference neurosis which owes its characteristics to the underlying illness. So the development, the 'natural' history of the treatment is dictated by the illness. The extent to which, despite appearances (behind the surface of a theory that rapidly became more complex), this vision maintains its force is demonstrated by the success which the formula 'natural process' (Meltzer's gift to analytic treatment) has had in times that are recent but which appear distant looked at from our present profoundly changed perspective.[1]

To see how analysis was experienced and depicted before the 1950s (before the concept of countertransference was fully taken on board), we can learn much from reading some treatments described by Bouvet, in our view a unjustly neglected writer of great value. In them the analyst makes himself actively responsible for mobilising the neurosis of transference. His presence permits the development of the neurosis of the 'ill person', as Bouvet calls him, and thus the history of the treatment and the history of the illness come to correspond in a development and following a sufficiently predictable direction, if we know the nature of the illness, its ethiopathogenesis and its course.

The introduction of the 'variable' analyst in the early 1950s did not change things very rapidly. The outstanding ground-breaking work of Heimann (1950) still forms part of a tradition that sees the analyst functioning 'as a mirror who reflects the patient'. Countertransference is a further fundamental function which can be used to avoid impeding the development of the transference neurosis and to avoid opposing it with obstacles coming from the internal world of the analyst: 'This will protect him from entering as a co-actor on the scene which the patient *re-enacts* in the analytic relationship' (p. 84, emphasis added).

With the broadening of the concept of countertransference and the advent of the model of the bi-personal field it has become increasingly difficult to find a correspondence between the history of the illness and the history of the treatment and to consider the latter as a simple consequence or 'repetition' of the former. The history of the illness is no longer the sole and main factor to impress its style on both the treatment and its narration. At present it is increasingly hard to maintain Heimann's reservations vis-à-vis the analyst as co-actor and we cannot avoid considering him as the co-author of the 'analytic novel' which Ferrari and Garroni (1979) have written about with great rigour.

The whole business of analysis, a multidimensional formation, has grown increasingly complex, but I believe that likewise our awareness of complexity – something which has been present since the beginning and which Freud's comments in 1914 reflect – has also grown. In order to reflect on this complexity we shall thus continue to use the quotation of Freud as a starting point for the moment of transition from the direct experience of analysis to its written translation. To introduce 'into the reproduction of an analysis the sense of conviction which results from the analysis itself [. . .] exhaustive verbatim reports of the proceedings during the hours of analysis would certainly be of no help at all' (Freud 1918: 13).

Even today trainees are told not to take notes during the session, not to write reports at the end of sessions and when writing up cases not to re-read the protocols in mere chronological order but to process them first. Lavagetto, in a chapter of his book on Sadger, talks about the pedantic analyst of the early days of psychoanalysis who would slavishly transcribe everything that happened during the session in a boring and confused form. On this point, Freud had the attitude of a master and advised Sadger to abandon at least part of his technique and above all not to take verbatim note of what the patient says. Many ideas, he said, were false connections, secondary elaborations and treating them the same way as important things would easily suggest a lack of critical spirit. At the culturally lively Wednesday meetings, where tensions and passions broke out, Stekel criticised Sadger and recommended that he 'present things in an artistic way'. Freud shared this opinion, arguing that case histories are completely indigestible if they are not manipulated. The only possibility left was scrupulous but artistic presentation as in the case of Dora (1905a).

In an official text *Recommendations to Physicians Practising Psychoanalysis* (1912b) Freud came back to this subject. He said that taking notes during the session could:

> be justified by an intention of publishing a scientific study of the case. On general grounds this can scarcely be denied. Nevertheless it must be borne in mind that exact reports of analytic case histories are of less value than might be expected. Strictly speaking, they only possess the *ostensible* exactness of which 'modern' psychiatry affords us some striking examples. They are, as a rule, fatiguing to the reader and yet do not succeed in being a substitute for his actual presence at an analysis. Experience invariably shows that if readers are willing to believe an analyst they will have confidence in any slight revision to which he has submitted his material; if, on the other hand, they are unwilling to take analysis and the analyst seriously, they will pay no attention to accurate verbatim records of the treatment either. This is not the way, it seems, to remedy the lack of convincing evidence to be found in psychoanalytic reports.
>
> (p. 114)

Freud only wrote up cases in the form of a clinical diary at the beginning of his career; some cases in Freud's various *Studies on Hysteria* (1895b take this form. We shall see that it will be used again in the first part of the draft of *Notes Upon a Case of Obsessional Neurosis* (1909). The diary corresponds to a stage in his theory when the repressed was conceived as layered on concentric levels which move in from the periphery to the centre and these levels can be traced in the stratigraphy of an archaeological 'excavation' and reported in writing through a linear chronological narrative which reconnects the suppressed or hidden links of repression, going on to close the gap in the continuity of conscious events.

But the tear in the fabric that Freud talks about in *Totem and Taboo* (1913b) soon became the norm; temporal collapse and complex temporality, like *après-coup*, were the constant object of his experience. He broke with the linearity of his early career and the clinical diary was replaced by a new form of writing which corresponded to a different stage in his theory, in particular the theory of the repressed: theory and technique influenced and modified writing.

The 'thematic point of view' came to prevail over the chronological viewpoint. The themes ordered the events in a hierarchy dictated by meaning rather than time. The chronology Freud reports in the case of the Rat Man (in *Notes Upon a Case of Obsessional Neurosis*) and the Wolf Man (in *From the History of an Infantile Neurosis*) serves to help the reader, providing an order not directly deducible from the clinical report, which reworks events, connects them to other events, independently of their temporal sequence. The events circle around key scenes and plots, as in the case of the dream and the primary scene of the Wolf Man, which means that when he or she reads the case histories the reader may have the impression of reading a fascinating tale.

De Micco points to a further element which transforms Freud's clinical cases into tales. Following the structuralist current of Propp and Feimas, she says:

> For a text to be called a tale it must stage a reversal of the original situation following a well-established system of values which the entire unfolding of tales tends to confirm. This is what provokes the effect of meaning in the narrative development (the transformation of the original situation) and the final satisfaction (the re-establishment of a system of values with a powerful persuasive effect). The original situation, as it is a situation of 'imbalance', tends to drive the narrative development, so that a situation of 'balance' is re-established; in every narrative an implicit axiological and evaluative level is at work. And it is precisely this effect of meaning that stimulates the participation of the interpreter, activating a state of waiting, and that determines in him an emotional experience.
>
> (De Micco 1996: 16)

It is this sense of initial 'imbalance' and final 're-balance' which we find in Freud's clinical cases starting from the paradigmatic case in *Studies on Hysteria* (1895b).

If this produces an equation between case histories and tales, we must remember however that the plots and key scenes in Freud's 'tales' are the outcome of the theoretical models which he was constructing. His tales were often interspersed, as Lavagetto suggests, with meta-narrative propositions, explanatory schemes present more often than in a normal tale and also differently (because mostly they are theoretical propositions), which interrupt the linearity of the tale and serve to explain the rules of transformation, those covering laws which function as organisers. In this sense, contrary to the radical devaluation of metapsychology brought about precisely by the narratological trend, I think that metapsychology represents a coherent set of rules of transformation, an instrument which generates analytical novels. The question becomes a serious problem in contemporary psychoanalysis where many different metapsychologies, acting according to different and sometimes incomparable rules of transformations, generate Kleinian, Winnicottian, Bionian, etc. novels. In the case of the Wolf Man there is an evident transition from the writing up of the case in the form of a clinical diary to the report organised according to at times implicit, but often explicit, theoretical rules. When Freud started writing he faithfully used the verbatim reports of the first eight sessions with the patient. Then, before moving on to the subsequent exposition, he marked the transition by pointing out: 'This is as much of the present case history as I am able to report in a detailed and consecutive manner' (1909: 186).

In writing up the rest of the treatment, instead of following this consecutive order he assembled the events, grouping them together along lines dictated by his experience and his theory. As we have copies of the session protocols after the first eight, we can read all the protocols before the theoretical-clinical conclusions Freud came to. Thus we can note (as I argued in the seminar I held on 'The Ratman: From the Diary to the Construction of the Case' which deployed this method) that other theories and rules of transformation could suggest different conclusions that diverged greatly from Freud's.

Reflecting on the context and theory of Freud at the time would be a way of delimiting the field of interpretations and avoiding a kind of drift, but if we generalise and look at the field of contemporary psychoanalysis, we must recognise that there is a danger of endless hermeneutics and a narratological drift due also to a plethora of theories. If more than one translation is possible, where does it lie and how can one express in narrative form that specificity and uniqueness which many attribute justly to psychoanalysis? Fortunately the dichotomy is not as unbridgeable as it might appear. To this end let us turn again to the case of the Rat Man, which we have used as a pretext for a general point.

Freud's view that the matter dictates the style is highly relevant to the Rat Man. When we move on from the reading of the session reports to the account of that analysis (Lavagetto 1985), we note that the rhythm, the pauses, the openings, the periods of waiting which had characterised the analysis and been reported day after day in the protocols are present in the account but that it fails to reproduce them faithfully. The succession of those moments does not correspond to this, but the 'artistic' presentation captures those moments, events, states of mind, transforming, translating and at the same time representing that reality and thus allowing the reader to enter into the analysis and to live through those moments, events, periods of waiting and suspense.

I believe that this communicative concentration and tension (which is the product in this case of Freud's great storytelling ability) is what we should expect not only from trainees but also from the few analysts who write clinical cases. They should, that is, not just illustrate a working method and scientific ability to apply clinical and theoretical content within the basic framework of our discipline. The term we use is tension rather than capacity or even less training because the attempt is always bound to fail to some extent. Writing, telling stories is an attempt to semiotise an experience which can never be totally semiotised. When the work is complete, we have to reflect on the nature of our account, on a whole that is made up of 'history of illness' and 'history of treatment'.

The expression I have borrowed to head this section, inspired by Freud's famous remark: 'it still strikes me myself as strange that the case histories I write should read like short stories' (1895b: 160), points to the fact that the question about the nature of our productions remains open and topical. It is a question which one can delimit within the compass of the debate which animates this book by saying that one of the key dilemmas remains the narrative-history pair-opposition. Narrating means explaining and in some contexts the narrative is a special form of explanation. Forster's famous example – 'the king died and then the queen died' – cited in books about narrative not only indicates a temporal succession but the reason for the sequence. It is an explanation of it; it does not only point out that the queen dies after the king but also the reason for her death. *Post hoc propter hoc*: the milestone of *The Interpretation of Dreams*.

Stories are told on the basis of a temporal principle, according to the structure beginning-middle-end (Chatman 1978). In this sense a narrative is always historical but at the same time the relation and the difference between narrative and history are never transparent and evident, their borders are not clear-cut. Gallie (1955) is of the opinion that historical discourse has strong analogies with the literary genre of the story, coinciding with a narrative which presents itself as 'a complete whole' in reference to which it is only possible to understand the sequence of actions, thoughts and feelings which constitute it. The 'complete whole' is reminiscent of Freud's use of the word 'self-evident' when he tries to scientifically accredit his narrative puzzles. We saw earlier how Freud's clinical stories centre around plots and key scenes connected to theoretical nuclei. We find something similar in the field of historiography. According to Walsh (1951) a story is not made up of single actions but complexes of actions and events which form a unit recognisable as a whole whose distinguishing characteristic is represented by a leading idea which gives meaning to events and differentiates one historical process from another. Leading ideas are to be understood as 'real' forces in historical process, but once identified they take on the function of explanatory methodological tools.

There is still a lack of symmetry between the respective referential tendencies of history and literary fiction, a difference Freud was always interested in. In the fields of literary theory the reference is more an effect of language than its epistemological 'anchor'; each language act is self-referential. The reference to language is never simply the reflection inside language of an empirical extra-linguistic reality. According to Ricoeur (1984), the history and the story can, however, mediate each other reciprocally, each attaining its objective only thanks to that of the other. The considerable transforming power of fiction lies in its ability to 'unrealise' the constraints of time and knowledge through traces. Due to its almost historical character, fiction can perform a liberating function from the 'hidden possibilities' of the real world. 'That which might have happened', which for Aristotle is the subject of poetry as opposed to history, creates a fusion between the potential of the real past and the unreal possibilities of pure fiction. There is profound kinship between the quasi-past of fiction and the unrealised potential of the historical past.

In an interview Marguerite Yourcenar once said that for history as for everything else nothing is possible and everything is possible. There will never be a completely exact description of a moment in life and at the same time we can come close to infinity, as the mathematicians say. We argued earlier that constructions should not be totalising but reversible and revisitable. We must always be aware that they are the fruit of reduction, which takes some events (but not all) into account, especially those that have remained on the level of potential ('hidden possibilities') but have contributed to the determinism of those that are evident. It is precisely these 'non-real' or 'non-realised' events (the unconscious is the realm of the unrealised, says Lacan) which are or at least should be the specific object of the psychoanalytic investigation and reconstruction.

In investigating these subterranean territories which are hidden behind the apparent din of conscious history, poetic translation and reconstruction can become a single indivisible act, a substantial part of analytic method. This is what emanates from a reading of some authors, such as Nicolas Abraham. As Derrida says, in Nicolas Abraham one cannot dissociate the analyst from the theorist of arché-psychoanalysis from the poet translator. Poetic translation and psychoanalytical interpretation open up new mutual perspectives, they orientate each other, beyond any privilege of unilateralness. Poetic translation is not an application, a test, a conclusion; it belongs to the process of analytic deciphering in its active and initial phase. Nicolas Abraham and Marie Torok (1987) ask whether the analyst has an ear for all the 'poems' and all the 'poets'. Their answer is: certainly not. Those whose message we have not managed to understand, those whose mutilated, gap-filled text we have heard so often, the puzzles without a key, those who have left it without having revealed the distinguished work of their life, those that always come back to mind, ghosts of their incomplete destiny, obsession of that lacuna. Which one of us is not grappling with some ghost who claims the sky owed to it and who is in debt to our heath?

Poetic translation does not mean that each analytic couple can produce its truth; many analyses, many truths, many 'poems' are possible. Nor does it mean that every analyst is able to capture the secret, the truth, the poem of that individual, the life he analyses; and this independently of his 'blindspots' and the supplements of analysis he subjects himself to. One must accept and recognise these limits. Poetic translation, for Abraham and Torok (and it should be the same for all analysts), is not pure fiction, not 'bark' (to use their term). Psychoanalysis must make it possible to touch the concrete foundation of the human. Psychoanalysis is not dogmatic, nor is it a sort of recovering but, by putting into practice its rigorous methods, it can progress along the path of theory and the path of practice as a living and ever renewed science.

All hermeneutics has its constraints; in psychoanalysis these are represented by theory, the fruit of our research and experience, which guides us in our work and in that minimum of prediction which we must have in our practice. Finally, within theory, we cannot give up the determinism which is the fundamental and definitive discriminating factor between literary fiction and analytical reconstruction. A reflection on determinism starting from Freud would take us too far away from the purposes of this book. Determinism still remains a principle that can be interpreted and reinterpreted but which we cannot give up without rendering vain the very possibility that we can understand and treat our patients.

Theory and determinism can limit stories and delineate the field of real events and 'hidden possibilities', but rarely can they give psychoanalysts' accounts the persuasive force which emanates from the analysis itself. Rarely do therapist and storyteller combine harmoniously. Those stories acquire the value of 'reality' and especially 'truth' inside that special device which is the analytic setting. It is there that the discourse becomes a 'living discourse' and knowledge a knowledge which 'supports existence'. According to Loch (1977), this is the type of knowledge an analysis must move towards. In a number of highly rigorous essays Loch, among the most authoritative of theorists of psychoanalysis, considers the setting a 'form of life', in Wittgenstein's meaning of the term. In this form of 'shared' life between analyst and analysand, the stories, which are always self-referential, take on truth and life because they are determined and generated by the emotional investment (transference and countertransference) which nourishes and supports the analytic relationship.

The development of the analytical novel (in the sense of the term as used by Ferrari and Garroni) and treatment are able to coincide because inside that form of life they are inseparable, as we have already pointed out when we spoke of working out, the hermeneutic moment (interpretations and constructions) and the energetic moment (the level of investment). It is this area of instinctual investment which can never be completely semiotised. 'Transference is a passion, not a "saying" and this is what makes it difficult for both patient and analyst to talk about it' (Pontalis 1990: 58). There cannot be a total and complete reflection in language. So once again we come into contact with that limit of language which we encountered at the beginning when we started talking of *Constructions in Analysis*, and we also touch an opposition which is renewed cyclically in the history of psychoanalysis.

On the one hand, we have the narratological strand which by excluding metapsychology and especially the 'energetic' can be heading towards an endless and ultimately meaningless drift. On the other, there is the strand which we can trace back to Groddeck, Rank and especially Ferenczi, which gives little value to language, which it considers the same as a surface effect, and follows instead empathy, direct contact with the patient beyond words, thus over-valuing the level of investment. The outcome is an opposition between a linguistics without emotion and a mystics without language (Green 1973). By proposing an articulation between construction and working through, we gave a central position in treatment and analytical knowledge to the concept of work; work which inside that special device we call the setting can 'generate knowledge which', according to Aulagnier, 'is not a pure intellectual good, but a good which enables patients to live'.

Freud invented and inaugurated that singular form of life whose importance he was unable to fully grasp. He did not understand that that particular 'scenic' device not only amplified and made it possible to highlight certain phenomena but in part also generated them. He sought validation beyond the setting, urging analysts to escape from the 'therapeutic prison', convinced that the scientific value of psychoanalysis went beyond treatment in the strict sense of the word.[2] This instruction and this invitation still remain valid, although they are in fact rarely followed. Faced with the new nature of his clinical experience, he sought to understand it through literature. But since he was both 'seduced' by and sceptical about literature from the very beginning, at the same time he also took recourse in the metaphor of archaeological excavation, driven by the urge to find a kind of 'materiality' in the traces of the past ('monuments' rather than 'documents'), to search for a more direct contact with the unconscious that was captured in the indirect and metaphorical form of literary fiction.

If we follow the parallels and the evolution of the two metaphors of archaeology and literature, through their play of light and backlighting, we can gain a special vision of the different stages and theoretical layers of Freud's speculation.

Writing and excavating

'I have been trained to the careful scrutiny of a certain domain of phenomena. To me fiction and invention are easily associated with the blemish of error.' This is what Freud wrote in the unpublished introduction to *Moses and Monotheism*. Forty years earlier, writing about the case of Elizabeth von R, he had felt the same unease and the same need to apologise and to distance himself from literature by taking refuge in his identity as a physician:

> I have not always been a psychotherapist. Like other neuropathologists, I was trained to employ local diagnoses and electro-prognosis, and it still strikes me myself as strange that the case histories I write should read like short stories and that, as one might say, they lack the serious stamp of science. I must console myself with the reflection that *the nature of the subject* is evidently responsible for this, rather than any preference of my own. The fact is that local diagnosis and electrical reactions lead nowhere in the study of hysteria, whereas a *detailed description* of mental processes as we are accustomed to find in the works of imaginative writers enables me, with the use of a *few psychological formulas*, to obtain at least some kind of insight into the course of that affection.
>
> (Freud 1895b: 160–161, emphasis added)

Despite the justifications and the distancing, the repeated reappearance of literature at key moments separated by such a great distance of time justifies the suspicion that the recourse to literature was anything but superfluous in the birth and development of psychoanalysis. At the beginning of this development it was not a superstructure. Literature not only performed a descriptive function, but was better suited to the nature of the subject as it offered a better explicative structure ('few formulas'): schemas, emplotment, key scenes are both descriptive and explicative.

Literature was not superimposed on nascent psychoanalysis but came to form a supporting structure. Freud's writing ability was at the service of research, discovery and initial theoretical frameworks.

At this stage, literature functioned as a container and for this function the classical literature in which he was formed was sufficient. It was the moment of the discovery of the unconscious, the moment when there was division between layer and layer, between conscious and unconscious, between reason and unreason. Its stories were not only to be read but would also explain and in some way teach and educate, like the short stories and naturalistic novels of the mid-nineteenth century: emblematic of this narrative style is the beginning of the case of Katharina (Freud 1895b). The style was not in question at that moment, nor was the classical reason that informed it. As the writing unfolded it was reason that made the case history 'self-evident' for the first time.

But if we want to better capture the state of nascent psychoanalysis we must turn to the other great metaphor and interrogate it – the archaeological metaphor, which started in parallel to the literary metaphor. Let us follow its path and development with an intra- and inter-metaphorical reading. Through this 'archaeology of knowledge' we will find connections and intra- and inter-metaphorical transformations which are independent of Freud's conscious will. These will also be valuable for a reflection on the status to assign to the patient and the analyst in the analytical experience. In *The Aetiology of Hysteria* Freud wrote:

> Imagine that an explorer arrives in a little-known region where his interest is aroused by an expanse of ruins [. . .]. He may content himself with inspecting what lies exposed to view, with questioning the inhabitants – perhaps semi-barbaric people – who live in the vicinity, about what tradition tells them of the history and meaning of these archaeological remains, and with noting down what they tell him – and he may then proceed on his journey. But he may act differently. He may have brought picks, shovels and spades with him, and he may set the inhabitants to work with these implements. Together with them he may start upon the ruins, clear away the rubbish, and, beginning from the visible remains, uncover what is buried. If his work is crowned with success, *the discoveries are self-explanatory . . . Saxa loquuntur*!
>
> (Freud 1896b: 192, emphasis added)

We are some way from the problems of construction, reconstruction and even restoration: the finds talk alone, independently of our conjectures, constructions and restoration work. We find ourselves faced with Freud's perennial need to bear witness to the non-interference of the analyst, to affirm the reality of 'events'.

While literature is used as a descriptive-explicative structure, from now on archaeology will always be used as a methodological metaphor. 'Instruments' (hoes, spades) are given to the 'semi-barbarian' (to the patient), instructions about method are given, but between archaeology and the semi-barbarian there is an unbridgeable asymmetry; we cannot trust his stories. What 'tradition tells them of the history and meaning of these archaeological remains' belongs to legend and ancient hagiographic and hidden historiography; the truth is not there. As we have already pointed out, psychoanalytic practice cannot be compared to 'oral history'. The semi-barbarian is basically not conscious of his past: this is the first idea of the unconscious. The archaeological method corresponds perfectly and fully to the analytic method. At this theoretical stage of psychoanalysis, the morphology and topography of the psychic terrain express aetiology independently of the speaker: so stop digging!

If, despite their descriptive-explicative utility, 'fiction and invention are easily associated with the blemish of error', archaeology as a method offers Freud the guarantee of that objectivity without speculation which is the illusion he pursues. But the status of archaeology was very different: already in 1854 Evans (*Dictionary of Architecture*) argued that restoring a building was not only a question of maintaining it and repairing it, but involved re-establishing in a complete state that which might never have existed at a given moment. This is a valuable comment that is relevant to the constructivist point we are trying to make: for Evans it is not only a question of speaking stones but the reconstruction of a world, a possible and not necessarily real world. This vision, this philosophy is one which Freud, as we shall see, will come close to but ultimately avoid. The road was more tortuous; a fundamental stage along this path was the case of Dora. With Dora literary 'beauty' is marred and the archaeological 'stones' start to need someone to give them a voice.

Let us once again examine the two metaphors – literary and archaeological – both of which we can find in the case of Dora (*Fragment of an Analysis of a Case of Hystoria*, Freud 1905a):

> In face of the incompleteness of my analytic results, I had no choice but to follow the example of those discoverers whose good fortune it is to bring to the light of day after their long burial the priceless though mutilated relics of antiquity: I have restored what is missing, taking the best models known to me from other analyses; but, like a conscientious archaeologist, I have not omitted to mention in each case where the authentic parts end and my constructions begin.
>
> (p. 12)

The stones no longer speak on their own, but nevertheless we are still a long way from the problems of construction Freud referred to (1937b); the talk is mostly of restoration. Freud is forced to allow the interpreter to intervene by making 'additions' that are essential to understanding the find, but these are treated as a foreign body to the 'authentic part'.

Let us come back to the literary metaphor in the Dora case. Freud argues polemically: 'There are many physicians who [. . .] choose to read a case history of this kind not as a contribution to the psychopathology of the neuroses, but as a *roman à clef* designed for their private delectation' (p. 12). Later he states:

> I must now turn to consider a further complication to which I should certainly give no space if I were a man of letters engaged upon the creation of a mental state like this for a short story, instead of being a medical man engaged upon its dissection. The element to which I must now allude can only serve to obscure and efface the outlines of the fine poetic conflict which we have been able to ascribe to Dora. This element would rightly fall sacrifice to the censorship of a *writer*, for he, after all, *simplifies* and *abstracts* when he appears in the character of a psychologist. But in the world of reality, which I am trying to depict here, a complication of motives, an accumulation and conjunction of mental activities – in a word, overdetermination – is the rule.
>
> (pp. 59–60, emphasis added)

I am convinced that Freud was totally unaware of his changed attitude towards literature. While in 1895 the 'few psychological formulas' and the 'detailed descriptions' of the poet were useful in attempting to reach a 'vision of the whole' (case of Elizabeth von R, *Studies on Hysteria*), in 1901 the simplification and abstraction of the poet were insufficient in the face of complex psychic reality. In psychoanalysis overdetermination is the norm, with it the explicative structure of literature begins to fall apart, writing is no longer adequate to the new discoveries of psychoanalysis. We should not forget that Dora is the story of a humiliating defeat, a failure of early psychoanalysis. The element that had not been taken into due account was the analyst himself and the role he plays in the dynamics of the treatment.

It is no accident that Segre (1984) considers the case history of Dora an important moment in the birth of the modern novel, because in it the author is called into play; he enters the field and is to be found in the very fabric of the work.[3]

Notwithstanding Freud's 'traditionalist' choices in the literary and artistic fields, the Dora case history marks the transition from tradition to modernity. 'Archaeology', 'writing' and classical 'reason' are inadequate to take account of the multiple meanings and stratification of psychic events; there is a need for new writing. Reason does not abdicate its rights, but transforms into the reason of modernity, our reason, the reason which, parallel to the complex events it investigates and the multiple meanings it pursues, manifests itself as 'multi-layered and netlike' (Lavagetto 1985). The two extended archaeological metaphors – one in *Civilization and its Discontents* (1930) and the other in *Constructions in Analysis* (1937b) – are different in terms of content and style and are both conceptually distant from the previous metaphors. In 1930 the psychic apparatus is compared to the ruins of the republic of Rome:

> Now let us, by a flight of imagination, suppose that Rome is not a human habitation but a psychical entity with a similarly long and copious past – an entity, that is to say, in which nothing that has come into existence will have passed away and all the earlier phases of development continue to exist alongside the latest one. This would mean that in Rome the palaces of the Caesars and the Septizonium of Septimius Severus would still be rising to their old height on the Palatine and that the castle of S. Angelo would still be carrying on its battlements the beautiful statues which graced it until the siege by the Goths, and so on. But more than this. In the place occupied by the Palazzo Caffarelli would once more stand – without the Palazzo having to be removed – the Temple of Jupiter Capitolinus; and this not only in its latest shape, as the Romans of the Empire saw it, but also in its earlier one, when it still showed Etruscan forms and was ornamented with terracotta antefixes. Where the Coliseum now stands we could at the same time admire Nero's vanished Golden House. On the Piazza of the Pantheon we should find not only the Pantheon of today, as it was bequeathed to us by Hadrian, but, on the same site, the original edifice erected by Agrippa; indeed the same piece of ground would be supporting the church of Santa Maria sopra Minerva and the ancient temple over which it was built. And the observer would perhaps only have to change the direction of his glance or his position in order to call up the one view or the other.
>
> There is clearly no point in spinning our phantasy any further, for it leads to things that are unimaginable and even absurd.
>
> (p. 70)

The analogy takes over and Freud is captured by the fascination of the metaphor which he has to interrupt voluntarily since it risks becoming 'absurd'. Just as in construction, Freud follows what can become another mythology: total preservation of the psychic and in particular of the past. But if nothing is lost, almost nothing is in its original state; the structure of the original must be deduced. We are not in the presence of stones that speak by themselves, but 're-makings'. Distant ages collapse into each other, 'finds' are used in subsequent ages for new constructions, new buildings; Evans was right when he said that restoration meant bringing back to a state which might never have existed at any given moment.

The psychoanalytic theory of the psychic apparatus is very distant from the linear elegance of the beginnings; 'complexity' has long since taken up residence in the idea that Freud had of the human mind. We have now reached *Constructions in Analysis* (1937b) and its extended archaeological metaphor:

> His work of construction, or, if it is preferred, of reconstruction, resembles to a great extent an archaeologist's excavation of some dwelling-place that has been destroyed and buried or of some ancient edifice. The two processes are in fact identical, except that the analyst works under better conditions and has more material at his command to assist him, since what he is dealing with is not something destroyed but something that is still alive – and perhaps for another reason as well. But just as the archaeologist builds up the walls of the building from the foundations that have remained standing, determines the number and position of the columns from depressions in the floor and reconstructs the mural decorations and paintings from the remains found in the débris, so does the analyst proceed when he draws his inferences from the fragments of memories, from the associations and from the behaviour of the subject of the analysis. Both of them have the undisputed right to reconstruct by means of supplementing and combining the surviving remains. Both of them, moreover, are subject to many of the same difficulties and sources in error. One of the ticklish problems that confronts the archaeologist is notoriously the determination of the relative age of his finds; and if an object makes its appearance in some particular level, it often remains to be decided whether it belongs to that level or whether it was carried down to that level owing to some subsequent disturbance. It is easy to imagine the corresponding doubts that arise in the case of analytic constructions.
>
> The analyst, as we have said, works under more favourable conditions than the archaeologist since he has at his disposal material which can have no counterpart in excavations, such as the repetitions of reactions dating

> from infancy and all that is indicated by the transference in connection with these repetitions. But in addition to this it must be borne in mind that the excavator is dealing with destroyed objects of which large and important portions have quite certainly been lost, by mechanical violence, by fire and by plundering. No amount of effort can result in their discovery and lead to their being united with the surviving remains. The one and only course open is that of reconstruction, which for this reason can often reach only a certain degree of probability. But it is different with the psychical object whose early history the analyst is seeking to recover. Here we are regularly met by a situation which with the archaeological object occurs only in such rare circumstances as those of Pompeii or of the tomb of Tut'ankhamun. All of the essentials are preserved; even things that seem completely forgotten are present somehow and somewhere, and have merely been buried and made inaccessible to the subject. Indeed, it may, as we know, be doubted whether any psychical structure can really be the victim of total destruction. It depends only upon analytic technique whether we shall succeed in bringing what is concealed completely to light.
>
> (pp. 259–260)

In describing similarities and differences from archaeology, Freud tries to carve out a space for a new form of work, namely psychoanalysis. I think, however, that Freud the archaeologist and Freud the psychoanalyst live side by side, and hence there is a different relationship with time, with things past, with their recovery and their 'immortalisation'; in short, an open dialectic takes shape with regard to 'loss' and its negation. In *Constructions in Analysis*, even though it reflects a crisis of the image and the word, Freud still pursued the illusion that 'all of the essentials' would be 'preserved', that it 'depends only upon analytic technique'. This was a last-ditch attempt because immediately afterwards there was to be a different conclusion, a turning point if not an actual break: 'But our comparison between the two forms of work can go no further than this; for the main difference between them lies in the fact that for the archaeologist the reconstruction is the aim and end of his endeavours while for analysis the construction is only a preliminary labour' (p. 260).

Excavation, which first had coincided with the analytic method, has now become only a part of it – 'preliminary work'. What we discover through excavation only has the 'value of a hypothesis'. We await its 'effects' [. . .] 'we claim no authority for it' (p. 265). In short, it is a 'conjecture' awaiting replies from the patient. In *Constructions in*

Analysis, excavation is followed in the text by a description of a technique to decipher the replies of the patient and produce an 'assured conviction': a substantial change in Freud's science. By this we do not want to say that only then does the patient enter the field. The person who 'resists' the analyst's constructions makes an early appearance on the scene of psychoanalysis, and, as we have seen, Freud always had to defend himself against the accusation of moral subjugation.

I am convinced that a merely diachronic reading fails to do justice to thinking of such structural complexity as Freud's. When I say that *Constructions in Analysis* points to a change in method, I am saying that there is more awareness of this change. Where previously it had been hinted at and had to be deduced, now it is part of the theory. Freud's writings on technique (1912b, 1914b) and the descriptions of method which can be deduced from his subsequent writings, testify to the continuation – in the theory – of the illusion of an objective method. Only slowly did it become necessary to include the patient consistently in the very fabric of the method, in that he or she starts to become what he or she now is for us: 'a dynamic term which continually interferes with the competence of the analyst and obliges him to re-shape himself continually according to his behaviour' (Ferrari and Garroni 1979). With *Constructions in Analysis* and with the limitation that Freud puts on 'archaeology', psychoanalysis defines itself as an *Erfahrung* (movement of the subject in contact with the object, in contact with the movement of the object).[4] There was 'resistance' by Freud to accept this theoretically – but it was the resistance of an age, of an episteme.

But what is the deep-seated need that sustains Freud's 'archaeology'? We think it is the same need as that which set in motion and developed metapsychology. It is the same reason that was behind the spirit which created topography, stratification and geology, both in the archaeological metaphor and in the topographical version of the metapsychological metaphor: the need to spatialise time, to hold it, to force it into a space (which can be extensive but is still limited), a closed space (*Civilization and its Discontents*) (1930: 70): 'If we want to represent historical sequence in spatial terms we can only do it by juxtaposition in space: the same space cannot have two different contents.' It is the same demand for 'closure' which on the level of clinical theory leads to the metaphor of the jigsaw puzzle: the idea of finding, as in the case of the Wolf Man, the piece which, put in the right place, serves to explain everything, which leads to a solution.

This thesis stands in opposition to the infinity of time, the interminability of the analysis and the multiplicity of interpretations. Again we would not be doing justice to Freud if we read him only diachronically and argued that infinity and interminability only appear at the end (*Analysis Terminable and Interminable*, 1937a).

The awareness of infinity and interminability, although less theorised, parallels the attempt to spatialise and contain time. Let us consider the valuable intuition which appeared in a 1900 letter to Ferenczi, some years before he developed the theory of transference and 38 years before *Analysis Terminable and Interminable*, when he talked about beginning to see the interminability of treatment as a characteristic which regularly presents itself and is linked to transference.

Let us leave excavation, which remains as a great methodological myth, and turn again to 'literature'. There is no lack of changes on this territory either. However, they need to be discovered; they are substantial but not evident. Earlier we quoted Segre's view that the case of Dora was one of the first examples of the modern 'novel'. In a similar paradox, Freud's 'conservatism' meant that he was unable to exploit the break and innovation which other writers, literary figures and artists exploited and drew on. Much has been said about Freud's conservatism but little emphasis has been put on the fact that, in the mid-1930s, the classically trained Freud enjoyed a great deal of contact with a literary avant-garde which, although it had absorbed the lessons of the nineteenth-century novel, had at the same time passed beyond it.

The historical novel (Feuchtwanger, Stefan Zweig, Anton Zweig, Ludwig, Mann) was an essential feature of the literary scene in the 1930s, and, appearing as it did at a dark moment in the history of mankind, testifies to the 'democratic humanism' that Lukács talks about.

We started from *The Man Moses, a Historical Novel*, and our 'devious route' which led 'us first to something unexpected and incomprehensible' is now coming to an end and leading us back to it. It is difficult not to mention that a transition, a transformation took place between the introduction to the case of Katharina and *Moses*. But this does not absolve us from asking critical questions about the specificity of that form (the historical novel) and to point out that, despite everything, the 'advanced formula' was in implicit contrast with the explicative demands both of (Febvre's and Bloch's) 'new history' (which was coming to the fore precisely at that time) and of psychoanalysis itself on account of its borderline position as a science.

On the other hand, the critical interrogative imposes itself even more forcefully, as we shall see as the book continues, when we examine the alternative hypotheses to history and the historical novel identified by Wittgenstein in the 1930s in his comments on Frazer (Wittgenstein 1967), an important source for Freud's anthropological studies. Let us take a step back and return to the solutions which Freud tried to provide to the perennial problem of events and origins with the historical novel. At the time Arnold Zweig was his confidante and guide but his favourite conversation partner was Thomas Mann, who at the time was looking at the link between the writing of history and the writing of novels.

5

The crisis of history and the creation of 'analytical space'

'Historical plots are not my forte, let's leave them to Thomas Mann'

> On what authority can a poet be the orator at a ceremony in honour of a great scientist? [. . .] Literature and psychoanalysis have both been conscious of the close relations between them for some time. But the solemnity of this moment lies, in my view at least, in what is the first public meeting between these two spheres, in the open acknowledgement of that consciousness of affinity. As I said, for a long time both sides were unaware of these connections, these deep-lying sympathies.
>
> (Mann 1956)

With these words, Thomas Mann introduced his speech 'Freud and the Future' on the occasion of Freud's eightieth birthday in 1936, a speech Freud himself was very pleased with. In a letter dated 17 June 1936, Freud wrote to Arnold Zweig about Mann: 'a noble *goy*. It's good to know that there are still some around. Sometimes one doubts it' (quoted in Schur 1972). Mann had already offered his opinion in his paper 'My Relation to Psychoanalysis' in 1926. 'Freud's Position in the History of Modern Thought' is the title of a speech he gave at the Club of Democratic Students in 1929. On that occasion Freud talked with gratitude of Mann as one of the elected spokesmen of the German people, who gave him a place in the modern history of the mind with benevolent and significant words (Jones 1953–57).

Direct relations between the two had begun with Mann's visit to Freud in March 1932. *The Tales of Jacob* was published in 1933. As with many other relationships, Freud's relationship with Mann was ambivalent. While it became ever more evident that he saw Mann as the source of inspiration for *Moses*, in 1934, in a moment of dejection about his novel Freud wrote (with a mixture of irony and admiration): 'Historical plots are not my forte, let's leave them to Thomas Mann' (quoted in Bori 1979: 14). On this point Robert (1974) suggests that Freud was 'jealous' of Mann for *Joseph and his Brothers* and this is confirmed by a letter dated 29 November 1936 where he seems to be competing with Mann over the story of Joseph.

Of the various speeches and essays dedicated to psychoanalysis, 'Freud and the Future' (Mann 1968) is of particular importance because of the comparison Mann makes between literature and psychoanalysis. He almost seems to be pointing out, albeit in a friendly manner, some examples of Freudian 'crypto-amnesia' when he says:

> Sigmund Freud, the founder of psychoanalysis as a therapy and general research method, trod the hard path of knowledge as a doctor and natural scientist in absolute solitude and independence, unaware of the consolation and strength that great literature would have offered him. He did not know Nietzsche, whose work contains anticipations of many Freudian insights; Novalis, whose romantic, biological dreams and inspirations came so amazingly close to analytic ideas; Kierkegaard, whose Christian courage to go to psychological extremes would have impressed and encouraged him deeply; and certainly not Schopenhauer, the melancholic symphonist of a philosophy of drives that sought return and redemption.

The essay contains some acute insights into the profound nature of psychoanalysis:

> The union of subject and object, their flowing into one another, their identity, the insight into the secret unity of world and ego, destiny and character, occurrence and action, the secret of reality as the work of the soul – precisely this would have been the essential basis of any initiation into psychoanalysis.

But the central theme of the essay is myth: 'While I was speaking to you I found myself wondering whether I might not have led you into error about the true content of my talk and whether, considering everything I say, especially towards the end, it might not have been better to entitle it *Freud and Myth*.' The question of myth is the most interesting aspect of the essay because it allows us to compare the positions of the writer and the psychoanalyst. Mann (1968) introduces the subject by talking about his novel *Joseph and his Brothers*, and soon sets up a comparison with psychoanalysis:

> However, the only later discovered involuntary concord [between the novel *Joseph and his Brothers* and psychoanalysis] is something very exciting. Can this be called influence? It is more like sympathy, a certain intellectual proximity which psychoanalysis, for obvious reasons, was aware of before me and which has given rise to the literary attention for which I have long been grateful to it. The last example was the sending of an offprint from the journal *Imago*, an article by a Viennese Freudian scholar entitled 'On the Psychology of Ancient Biography' – a rather arid title which gives no idea of the strange things to come in the article. The author shows how older, more naive life descriptions based on legend and folk culture, in other words, the artist's biography, pick up established, schematic and typical characteristics and events, conventional biographical formulas about the history of its hero, as a way of acquiring legitimisation, showing how genuine they are, how they are right – right in the sense of 'how things always were' and 'how it is written'. For people like to recognise things, to find the old in the new, the typical in the individual. Our whole feeling of the familiarity of life.

Mann goes on to ask whether it is possible to distinguish clearly between the typical and the individual:

> Life is truly a mixture of formal and individual elements, a tangle of numbers in which the individual imprint can hardly distinguish itself in the impersonal formula. Many extra-personal elements, many unconscious identifications, many conventional and schematic forms have a decisive importance in the life not only of the artist but also of man in general.

Psychological interest turns into mythical interest to the extent that the typical is already mythical, so that instead of talking about 'lived life' we can talk about 'lived myth':

> The lived myth is the epic idea of my novel, and I see that since as a story teller I made the step from the bourgeois and the individual to the mythical-typical, my secret relationship with the analytic sphere has, so to speak, entered its acute phase. An interest in myth is innate to psychoanalysis in precisely the same way as an interest in psychology is innate to poetry.

The 'continual atemporal presence' of the myth is embodied in historical figures that have been barely identified, repetitions of the primitive *Urbild*. As Bori (1979) rightly points out, in Thomas Mann's vision 'there is an abundance of historical detail, both essential and incidental at the same time'.

'Lived myth' – the myths think and live through us. On this point Mann recognised a parallel between the historical novel and psychoanalysis, but equally here lies their substantial distance. Freud's position was in fact radically different: it was different at the time of his rift with Jung (which, it is well to remember, was partly caused by their divisions on the question of myth) and continued to be so in the 1930s. His constantly repeated formula was that religion contains a core of 'historical' but not 'material' truth.

Crisis of history

In the novel that he used as a medium, Freud wanted to reach the promised land of history and historical truth. The project behind *Moses and Monotheism* (1939a) was different, and in some ways stood at the opposite extreme to Mann's historical novel and the kind of 'anthropological novel' we find in *Totem and Taboo* (1913b). It is not a question of the *Urvater* killed by the primordial horde (a kind of myth in which 'history is narrated in extremely condensed form, as if what has in fact gone on for ages had happened only once'), but rather of identifying the historical truth of the selected case, reconstructing the historically given event – unique and unrepeatable – of one man, Moses. While the time in which events unfold in myths is enclosed within the myth itself, in *Moses and Monotheism* we are dealing with an event that is neither mythical nor historical.

But the state of the sources was desperate. The storm of doubt is reflected in numerous letters sent to Jones and the two Zweigs: he talked of his story lacking an indispensable historical basis and having to considerably curtail the rigour appropriate to an historical-psychological investigation. Yet the great effort he has to make reveals valuable traces that point to the development of his thought, and it is this tested and then interrupted development which we are trying to pick up again and explore. He tries obstinately to find a gap, a hole in the remote past. In the field of analysis the equivalent of this hole is the 'value' of transference in the sense in which Marx talked about 'exchange value'. So we can infer that this original unbridgeable void is where analytical space originates. The effort ends, the premise is repudiated and in the published book the 'factor of doubt' remains, as well as the difference between truth and probability. However, the book presents itself as a purely historical study. This is the view taken by Bori (1979) and repeated (1989). Bori is a historian who is by no means hostile to psychoanalysis and to Freud the historian. He says:

> As they are without any solid historical-exegetical support, his theses remain extremely conjectural and, regarding the death of Moses, improbable. They should not be read as illustrations of the theoretical achievements of *Totem and Taboo*. We need to try to understand the core of objective and permanent truth, the point the author valued so highly. They should also not be read only as autobiographical testimony to internal paths taken by the author.
>
> (Bori 1979: 10)

Unlike Bori (the historian), I believe that if we want to understand his position – although for different ends and purposes (analytical and not historiographical) – it is worth thinking afresh about some of Freud's 'internal paths' in order to understand his position: he (the analyst) was faced with the man Moses, and his theory of reference suggested a possible model of polyvalent space unfolding between the analyst (his self-analysis), theory and the patient with his history to decipher and reconstruct. What then must *Moses and Monotheism* reveal (if understood as construction) and also cover up (if understood as legend)?

According to Bakan (1958), Freud remits Moses' wrongdoing and cancels his parricide because he is a foreigner. For Robert (1974), *Moses and Monotheism* was the last stirring of rebellion against the fate of lineage, 'a rejection of blood ties', the rejection of Jacob: 'The hero is the man who rebels against the father and in one way or another kills him.'

So it is repression, the return of the repressed, that is the driving force behind *Moses*, and repression is the 'historical' (and not 'material') truth Freud refers to – the basis of his profound conviction of truth. Despite the fragility of the documentation, this is, as in every authentic psychoanalysis, an experience of truth, the felt conviction of truth.

Moses and Monotheism brings together all Freud's basic ideas about repression. That repression was once again in Freud's thoughts is reflected in the wonderful literary text entitled *A Disturbance of Memory on the Acropolis*, sent to Romain Rolland in 1936 (further proof that writers were his favourite conversation partners at that time.) This work contains one of the most vital and fascinating expressions of the return of the repressed. It is no accident that in that very same year he expressed the view to Rolland that repression is 'the starting point of the whole of our deeper understanding of psychopathology'. The particular rhythm and structure of *Moses and Monotheism* are based then on repression, understood as historical truth. These characteristics are what differentiate the historian from the psychoanalyst, writing history from practising psychoanalysis.

The Jew and the Egyptian are superimposed one on top of the other: this is an 'analytic' and not an historical 'truth', and certainly not one that can be backed up with historical documents. History distinguishes between places, distances the past from the present, distinguishes between ethnic and geographic identities; in this sense the separation from the Egyptian is the founding gesture of the Jew.

For Freud and psychoanalysis things are different: we have reunification (Moses and Egypt) and likewise internal fracture within the subject. Freud does away with identity as something given – canonically, psychologically and historically – and sets up an analytic truth, the truth of repression: identity is not one but two, the one and the other, the Jew and the Egyptian.

De Renzis (1993) points out: 'Originally no "one person" contained within himself all the elements of the later difference, but rather difference itself, absence.' Likewise, De Certeau (1975) states: 'We shall see that the "one and the other" is inverted in the game and in the un-known of "neither one nor the other".' The Freudian construction does not lend itself to the spatial distinctions of classic historiography, where there is a subject who wants to know who is in the present place, separated from his object and from the place where his object is located: the past. The past and the present operate within the same polyvalent place.

Towards a psychoanalytic constructivism

On several occasions I have mentioned possible itineraries that start from Freud. I have tried (and am continuing to try) to throw light on something within Freud that was in the background, hinted at, at times glimpsed and feared. Let us look again at the passage already quoted: 'No, our thought has upheld its liberty to discover dependent relations and connections to which there is nothing corresponding in reality; and it clearly sets a very high value on this, since it makes such copious use of it both inside and outside of science' (1939a: 108).

Let us not be mistaken: Freud does not always maintain this position; he stops awhile and then comes back. Let us compare this passage with two others where he talks about fiction: in *The Question of Lay Analysis* (1926b) he makes the point:

> It is a hypothesis like so many others in the sciences: the very earliest ones have always been rather rough. 'Open to revision' we can say in such cases. It seems to me unnecessary for me to appeal here to the 'as if' which has become so popular. The value of a 'fiction' of this kind (as the philosopher Vaihinger would call it) depends on how much one can achieve with its help.
>
> (p. 194)

But hardly a year later (in *The Future of an Illusion*, 1927) he says:

> But I think the demand made by the 'As If' argument is one only a philosopher could put forward. A man whose thinking is not influenced by the artifices of philosophy will never be able to accept it; in such a man's view, the admission that something is absurd or contrary to reason, leaves no more to be said.
>
> (p. 29)

Freud tells the story here of 'one of my children who was distinguished at an early age by a peculiarly marked matter-of-factness. When the children were being told a fairy-story and were listening to it with rapt attention, he would come up and ask: "Is that a true story?" When he was told it was not, he would turn away with a look of disdain' (p. 29). Freud's position on this wavers. He resembles a 'dancer in delicate balance on the tips of her feet'.

There is no definitive, decisive shift into the field of mental experience or fictional experiments that might point to a parallel between Freud's thinking and that of Einstein; at least not on the evidence of their correspondence – where both give the impression of being tired, scholastic and bored. But the Freud of the 1910s – the years of invention (Pauletta 1983; Chianese 1988) – is different. Freud cannot be placed definitively among the ranks of those whom Musil (1932) described as 'possible' as opposed to 'real' men:

> Anyone possessing [a sense of possibility] does not say, for instance: Here this or that has happened, will happen, must happen. He uses his imagination and says: Here such and such might, should or ought to happen. And if he is told that something *is* the way it is, then he thinks: Well, it could probably just as easily be some other way. So the sense of possibility might be defined outright as the capacity to think how everything could 'just as easily' be, and to attach no more importance to what is than to what is not.

These are the words of Musil, a pupil of Mach (the link between Freud, Einstein and Mach was the subject of the first work quoted above). We are already beginning to sketch the possible outlines of that 'auxiliary scientific philosophy' which, according to Gargani (1985), Freud complained was missing from psychoanalysis. In fact, in his *Introduction to Psycho-Analysis and the War Neuroses* (1917–19), in the passage quoted by Gargani, Freud argued that it was medicine which was without an 'auxiliary scientific philosophy' and psychoanalysis had one. However, this is not the point.

Gargani's argument is of extreme interest to psychoanalysis. He describes the way in which Wittgenstein, in the 1930s, tried to outline an analytical conceptual methodology which might constitute an auxiliary philosophical discipline for psychoanalysis. Whether or not we agree with Wittgenstein's position, the interconnection is intriguing. In the 1930s Freud was trying to follow the path of history and Wittgenstein, starting with his criticism of Frazer, reaffirmed his scepticism about the value to be attributed to historical interpretation: the origin and genesis that could reveal the deep meaning of the events under examination need not be real or simply plausible. Wittgenstein thought that the right and interesting thing to say is not that that arose out of this but that that could have arisen like that (Wittgenstein 1967). Consider how close this is to what Musil was saying: here the questioning of nineteenth-century certainties and all the knowledge that produced them is at its height.

'But I can also see the evolutionary hypothesis as nothing more, as the clothing of a formal connection states' Wittgenstein (1967). This work on Frazer's *Golden Bough* by Wittgenstein can be usefully compared with Freud's theses in *Moses and Monotheism*. Wittgenstein argues that it is a mistake to suppose that the reason an account of the Beltane celebration makes such an impression on us is that it has developed from a celebration where a *real man* was burned. This was his criticism of Frazer's hypothesis. Consider Freud's insistence on the material reality of the primordial killing of the father. Commenting on Wittgenstein's thesis, Bouveresse says: 'When a celebration, a ceremony or a rite makes an impression on us, its presumed origin is not sufficient to explain its meaning externally: *it is the evident internal meaning that makes evident the idea of a definite origin*' (1975: 71, emphasis added). We could also say that analytical truths must be assumed to be an internal experience, to have the felt conviction of truth.

Accordingly, we need to look again, also in the wake of the hypotheses advanced by Laplanche and Pontalis (1985), at the whole problem intrinsic to the primal scene. According to the linear causal model, what happens first (the primal scene) determines what happens later through the repetition compulsion. But if we look closely, Freud does not say that it is the repetition compulsion that makes us do the same thing. There is no content within the primal scene that is separate from its repetition: the primal scene, we could say, is the body of its repetitions.

From this perspective, *après-coup* becomes the retrospective working through of meanings which come to constitute the meaning of the primal scene. Repetition compulsion would then refer to the activity of a 'deferred thought which digs into the depths of distant time because of the meaning which the deferral attaches to the theme of its own analysis' (Gargani 1985). In this way repetition compulsion and *après-coup*, which can be thought of as agents acting together, represent key figures (forms) for the constructivist way of thinking in the field of psychoanalysis.

The return of the repressed and repetition compulsion should not be understood as demonic entities, as Freud himself led us to think, but as ways in which the psychic apparatus functions and as forms of knowledge. Repetition compulsion seeks to bring on to the scene of transference that which has been repressed, *après-coup* to give meaning to what has happened in the past but also to what happens again in analysis. Both act together, sometimes in synergy, to construct analytic knowledge. Since, starting from the *Project*, memory traces are to be understood as particular forms of facilitations, they should always be considered in relation to other traces (chronological relations, continuity, causality, spatiality, etc.) with which they combine to create systems. For these reasons traces can be re-actualised in certain contexts (an association or a relation) and remain silent in others. In this sense we cannot talk about their 'reality' independently of the context that activates them. We can then talk about constructivism because the transference–countertransference system creates the premises and generates the space for the future of those traces. The analyst's self-analysis (of which countertransference is an expression) and analytic reconstruction thus combine to construct the very reality they are investigating.[1]

Analytic space

To come now to *Moses and Monotheism*: we can say that historical reconstruction, self-analysis and theory represent mutually referring poles of reference. This is the same scheme we deduced from the 'discovery/invention' of Oedipus in 1897 and the Grusha episode in 1918[2] and which we have generalised as the model of the analytic field. We can isolate three referential poles in the analytic system: the analyst, the patient and the theory (referents or regulating principles). One might be tempted to privilege one of these points of reference, making the other two part of the one we choose: self-analysis and the history of the patient translated into the referential language of theory; or theory and the history of the patient understood through self-analytical referentiality. Any attempt in one of these directions cancels out the virtual space which is created between these poles and which we can call the analytic field. The poles or referents move within the same 'place', which is therefore a polyvalent place. This is the 'place' or 'non-place' that Freud had consistently tried to fill with an event. None of the poles can be the only reference point, the code for the others, while each is a metaphor of the others, and, as a metaphor, is a system of reciprocal relations. There is therefore no stable element (self-analysis, patient's history, analytic theory) which stops this reciprocal reference and which 'by attributing truth value to one pole assigns to the others a function of image, substitute or effect' (De Certeau 1975).

In defining the analytic field as a virtual space, we are thinking about a 'fantastic' image taken from optics. Let us imagine the analytic relation as an optical instrument: patient–theory–analyst form the reflecting lenses, the analytic space is 'virtual' because it corresponds to a place inside this apparatus. As in all optical instruments (including the human eye), it is a notional and not a material place, but nonetheless essential to sight. The analytic space is the background against which we see events and the worlds of the analysis unfolding – events and worlds which would otherwise be invisible. The analytic situation thus allows psychic reality to represent a reality which, both in its original form and in the form of its revelation, is not limited in the analytic space to an individual psyche because from the very beginning it is constructed and continues to develop in a relational space.

By taking some Freudian premises to their extreme consequences we have come to the point of proposing a model of analytic space that requires some clarification. When we talk of self-analysis we do not want to emphasise the solipsistic aspect of the analyst's mental work. We are distrustful of the complacent expression of the analyst's feelings which can be found in some corners of recent literature. This emphasis on the intimate life of the analyst hinders rather than helps listening to the patient and, to use Green's vivid expression, generates 'ventriloquistic' interpretation.

We start from the assumption that countertransference is not 'contra' transference but is something that accompanies transference and shadows its movements. While the patient needs the analyst to experience his transference, the analyst needs the patient for his countertransference. We link together self-analysis and countertransference because we think that self-analysis should not be considered an 'irregularity' of Freud's, the product of an obvious, particular historical contingency: the fact, namely, that he needed self-analysis because there was no other analyst. We believe that self-analysis must be interpreted as a basic characteristic that is 'prototypical' of the analytic experience. We agree with Bollas (1988) when he sees 'the contemplation of countertransference as a systematic re-integration into the psychoanalytical movement of a psychoanalytical function (self-analysis) that had been exiled'. A function which makes the analyst a 'constant surprise to himself'. John Klauber has put this point very well:

> The analyst also *needs the patient* in order to crystallize and communicate his own thoughts, including some his inmost thoughts on intimate human problems which can only grow organically in the context of this relationship. They cannot be shared and experienced in the same immediate way with a colleague, or even with a husband or wife. It is also in his relationship with his patients that the analyst *refreshes his own analysis*. From this mutual participation in analytic comprehension the patient takes the essential part of the treatment and the analyst the deepest trust and satisfaction.
>
> (Klauber 1976: 283, emphasis added).

Placing theory as the third 'subject' in the analytic field may arouse some puzzlement in analysts who consider theory as a defence, a superstructure that is added on last of all. But theory does not come along at the end and arrive from outside; it is at the origin of the process and internal to it. We could speak of a theory that starts from below and from above. It finds itself at the two ends of a chain, both at the point closest to, and furthest away from, the logic of the unconscious.

'Theoretical work,' says Pontalis (1988: 131) 'should be nothing but the recovery of strength through thought operating in the psyche, where we already work and theorise what excites it.' From this perspective, it is difficult to avoid theorising; man is a 'theorising animal' from childhood on. It is no accident that Freud talks about infantile sexual theories.

When we speak of theory in the analytic field, we refer to a theory that comes from below. Atomic theories, following unconscious and preconscious impulses, shape an interpretation, predispose the analyst towards a certain way of listening (which, like all other ways of listening, is selective), mediate between analyst and patient, avoid collusion and symbiotic systems. Aulagnier talks of 'fluctuating theorisation', which she sees as an unavoidable dimension of analysis: 'Psychoanalysis is a *praxis* which has always been and can only ever be theoretical and clinical.' Theory must be capable of fluctuating in the sense of accepting movements, crises, accelerations in the analysis: a theory which does not allow the analysis a defensive 'theoretical tranquillity'.[3]

We talked earlier of the balance between analyst, patient and theory. As in Calder's mobiles not only the balance of the system but also its lightness and elegance are determined by the proportions of forces, the weight of the single elements. Variation in the effect of one or other of the components distinguishes psychotherapy from analysis and characterises different analytic styles. Creating and maintaining the analytic space requires constant discipline on the part of the analyst, who must seek that balance without going too far in objectivising the patient or being too invasive in his countertransference. This does not always happen. In many analyses there are often long periods of 'psychotherapy', 'support' and other things which are fruitful from a therapeutic point of view. Only at certain privileged moments do the three field vectors meet: we might use the much abused designation *hic et nunc* to refer to these point-moments.

We think that Enriquez is referring to such moments when she speaks (1988: 173) of special moments when patient and analyst 'find themselves on the same wavelength, thinking the same thing at the same moment, and these are recognised as great moments of analytic happiness and psychic fecundity which permit the subject to find his own words with which he will be able to write his own version of a story he had been forbidden to know and remember'.

The model of the field I have expounded here has not been taken exclusively from a reading of Freud. It is the fruit of my clinical experience and contact with various analytic cultures. These cultures and experiences have informed my way of reading Freud; I too have looked at the past through the eyes of the present. While my research into Freud's work has allowed me to trace an albeit erratic path of successions, it is difficult for me to tell the story of an experiential and cultural event which I am still participating in, a development, a journey of uncertain destination which involves large sections of contemporary psychoanalysis. The lines I shall try to trace in the latter part of the book are suggested by the fruitful analogy I have discovered between analytic and scenic space, by the view that present developments in the model of the analytic field derive from the extension and expansion of the model of countertransference and finally by the conviction that the concepts of relation and analytic field, which have helped delineate the present landscape of Italian psychoanalysis, need to be more broadly debated between different research traditions if we are to have a clearer definition of a shared conceptual model. The latter part of the book is intended as a contribution in this direction.

6

The analytical field: scenarios of multiple entrances

A scenario of multiple entrances, in which nothing says that the subject will find itself in the first place.

(J. Laplanche and J.-B. Pontalis)

The stage – a stage which accepts the fantastic reality of the six characters – is no fixed, immutable datum. Nothing in this play exists as given and preconceived. Everything is in the making, is in motion, is a sudden experiment: even the place in which this unformed life, reaching after its own form, changes and changes again contrives to shift position organically.

(Pirandello)

It is on stage that the unity of thought, gesture and action is reconstituted.

(A. Artaud)

Virtual space, scenic space

'At this point we are reminded that the work of analysis consists of two quite different portions, that it is carried on in two separate localities (*Schauplätze*), that it involves two people, to each of whom a distinct task is assigned.' Thus states Freud in *Constructions in Analysis* (1937b: 258). We shall have occasion to come back to these words and to ask ourselves the question: who is the addressee, who is used by us to introduce the subject of the spaces and scenes that characterise psychoanalysis in its genesis and its development?

Talking of the articulation made up of analyst, patient and theory is a way of trying to describe a device for the creation of a ('virtual') space. In this way we delineate a scene ('locality') and not the objects and figures that occupy it on different occasions. The creation of that space is the premise that allows the psychic reality to be represented in the analytical situation.

Taking 'psychic reality' as the specific object of the analytic investigation is in itself a choice which differentiates our position from others in contemporary psychoanalysis. Accordingly, the 'analytic field' is for us a field of phantasies and 'representations' more than 'interactions'. Analytic 'objects' are 'absent' objects (Bion 1962). It is misleading to call them 'ineffable', as people often do, because even though they may be unconscious, they produce real effects, and profoundly determine the life of the subject. They need a device, a scenic apparatus which makes them 'visible' and, in a certain way, also 'liveable'.

The methodological transformations imposed on clinical psychoanalysis throughout its long history have expanded the possibilities of representing psychic reality in the analytic situation. For this reason the title we have taken for this chapter talks about scenarios or scenes (in the plural) with several entrances and exits. At present, analytic scenes can be entered through the mind of the patient but also through the imaginary and the 'phantasmatic' of the analyst. The model of the 'analytic field' can thus be seen as an extension and an enrichment of the analytic situation, a broadening of its space.

Spaces, scenes, actors: psychoanalysis originated in a scene that was in many ways theatrical. The young Freud's journey to Paris to see Charcot was an encounter with a theatrical universe, a theatrical space. The actor, in part the director, but also the overlooked victim of Charcot's *mise-en-scène* of his hysteric patients was Charcot himself – a man famous for his highly histrionic temperament. In the painting *Clinical Lesson at the Salpêtrière*, André Brouillet places Charcot and a patient in the classic arched posture typical of a hysteric crisis centre stage, surrounded by the gazes of students. Clearly visible in the left-hand corner is a drawing showing a patient in the contortion phase adopting the very same position as Charcot's real patient; one body imitating another, one scene reproducing another. Everything takes place on the level of visibility, the gaze, ostension, theatricality. The space is 'full', as Pontalis rightly points out (1977: 14) when commenting on these scenes and this painting. The big absentee from this space is psychic space. Starting from this over-full space and these completely visible scenes, Freud went on to constitute another space and another scene. In the creation of the analytic situation, he soon eluded the gaze. He shifted from the theatre of the body to the theatre of the mind. Only as he moved away from that space was he able to construct the space of the psychic apparatus and the space of the analytic situation. Since then therapeutic scene and the scene of the mental apparatus have determined each other reciprocally. If we distinguish between these two scenes it is in order to better understand and define its intersections, the reciprocal effects and the transformations of the subject generated by such interactions. If we set off and venture into the 'private theatre' (as Anna O calls it), we come across dream scenes, plots with several figures (as described by Freud in *The Ego and the Id*, 1923b), the patterns of original phantasies. What forms the background to these places and, despite their typicality, what unites them is the Freudian conception of the psyche as space, a conception that first emerged in the *Project for a Scientific Psychology* (1895a) and was to accompany Freud throughout his journey. Late Freud (1938c: 299–300) states: 'Space may be the extension of the psychical apparatus. No other derivation is probable. Instead of Kant's a priori determinants of our psychical apparatus. Psyche is extended; knows nothing about it.' The most important point here is the last ('knows nothing about it').

The importance of this fundamental space is something we become aware of when it is distorted. We register the presence of the backdrop when it is torn. Things invisible or absent become present in the dream because there is a 'dream screen' (Lewin 1953): every representation presupposes a space where representation can take place. Without a canvas there is no painting, without a stage there is no play, no performance – no 'representation'. Beyond representation, which in the case of the dream coincides with 'figuration', we meet the death drive which is fixed to 'real' representations which become actual either in compulsive acting or in a destiny that compulsion leads to repeat.

We know the importance Bion attributes to what he calls the α function – which separates the internal from the external, the conscious from the unconscious, waking from sleeping. And we know that when the screen is missing, the tear in the canvas prevents those people we label as borderline and psychotic from finding a scene other than the external world, and what cannot be symbolised on the 'stage' of the mind is re-found 'not-symbolised' in reality. Internal 'characters' are thus confused with external people; characters, or people, are without an author. Many patients thus do not have the chance to 'leave the stage', haunted as they are by their ghosts. In the same way as there can be an excess of 'theatricalisation' (e.g. in hysteria), its lack (a kind of 'de-theatricalisation') characterises other states such as psychosomatics. The psychic can only live if there is a kind of doubling or duplication whereby the body is represented in the mind, the external world in the internal world. That 'other stage' is needed – the stage Fechner referred to and which Freud (1900: 48) mentioned when describing mental space in Chapter 7 of *The Interpretation of Dreams*. According to Fechner, the stage of dreams (as Freud reminds us) is different from that of representative waking life. Dream work is the work required to produce on this 'stage' sequences and manifestations starting from a text which is unknown to the subject and which we deduce from scenic sequences and manifestations. In dreams we are directors, actors and spectators. For the dreamer (the spectator) dream scenes represent his double and at the same time 'alterity', something visible that cannot be approached. So there is identification and distance, differentiation and participation. At moments of great anxiety one can always say: after all it's only a dream. What is thus represented and 'realised' in the dream is also 'exorcised' (Petrella 1985). For me to be represented in the dream, I must keep the annulment and dissolution of the subject at a distance. The dream enables me to follow my many characters, my many selves without getting lost.

'The stage accepts the fantastic reality of the characters,' wrote Pirandello in the introduction to *Six Characters in Search of an Author* (1921). It was during that decisive period of crisis that Freud conceived of the psyche as a stage on which several characters moved. As Laplanche and Pontalis write, as a result of the secondary topography the Freudian model of the psyche is

> shot through with anthropomorphism: the intersubjective field tends to be conceived of after the fashion of intersubjective relations, and the systems are pictured as relatively autonomous persons-within-the person (the super-ego, for instance, is said to behave in a sadistic way towards the ego). To this extent then, the scientific theory of the psychical apparatus tends to

> resemble the way the subject comprehends and perhaps even constructs himself in his phantasy-life.
>
> (Laplanche and Pontalis 1967: 452)

The subject is doubled, multiplied, the various characters which animate it and battle it out to hold the stage are represented and precipitated by multiple, complex and at times contradictory identifications: they describe, they dramatise the history of the subject and his crises. But it is not only 'history' which writes the texts and casts the roles; there are plots which precede history, merge with it and fuel it: the original phantasies are rich sources of texts and stages.

In the phantasy scene the subject does not aim at the object; he depicts himself as being captured in the sequences of images, he participates in the scene without 'being given a place; *hence the danger in the treatment of interpretations which claim to reach that place*' (Laplanche and Pontalis 1985: 87, emphasis added). In this context the primal scene is a 'scenario of multiple entrances, in which nothing says that the subject will find itself in the first place' (p. 78).

Drawing on Laplanche and Pontalis, we have given this section the title 'The analytic field: scenarios of multiple entrances'. This is not to argue that the primal scene is the key scene in analysis; we are opposed to any vision which privileges, circumscribes and limits the analytic situation in some kind of privileged scenario.

The point of the quotation – which we have transformed and expanded – is to show that the analytic situation is one of several scenes and several entrances and exits, which allows the patient to cross the field of representations. He does not have to find his place at once ('in the first place') and we should not make him find his 'place' at once. If he did, he would repeat and we would reinforce the environmental action which has forced him to find precisely that place. In the analytic situation he will thus not be able to misconstrue the force of those scenarios and also those unconscious parental injunctions which have fixed him in that role and that position. For all this to happen, the analyst too must give up his fixed place; he cannot be a subject with a strong status and fixed role.

The device of the setting transforms psychic 'writings' into scenic plots, 'transcriptions' into texts, unconscious traces into transferences. It has already been said, but it is well to repeat it, that the truth 'only comes to the surface in the universe of fiction and when it avoids the naturalistic slice-of-life expedient of blind and faithful synchronic recording' (Lavagetto 1985). I do not think that we can ever capture the truth and the reality itself of the analytic situation through audio-visual recordings of analytic sessions; nothing is further from the sort of 'realism' into which the analytic condition is forced.

The objection might be raised, however, that the analytic situation is nothing like theatre. There is no special place in it for the actions typical of the theatre; it is enlivened by discourse and words that convey feelings. But here we use theatre to refer not so much to the form and content as to the 'representational device', to take the simile used by Petrella in the preface to his (1985) volume. In the theatre, action, forbidden in analysis, is prescribed, but it is also, as Petrella points out, 'limited to representation', used for the purpose of representation. In this sense, theatre and the analytic situation, for all their differences, are devices for representing, 'artificial' devices whose duration, beginning and end are regulated. The representation (or performance) can be put on within a binding spatial-temporal framework.

Every breach of this framework ('acting'), either by the analyst or the patient, which breaks down the boundaries between life and scene, also infringes against the possibility of representation. It is only by virtue of these limits and borders that the ego of the actor-patient can take on the role of spectator and create the necessary distance between spectator and actor. Only when there is a beginning and an end, limits and borders, can one 'leave the stage'; for the purposes of representation (performance) it is as important to 'leave the stage' as it is to stay on stage.

These borders and limits of the analytic situation bring about *epokè*, that suspension of judgement about reality which has the function of 'unmasking reality' (Leclaire 1971), revealing the phantasies that pervade. Within these limits and borders, pain, suffering, neurosis and mourning can enter the world of representation although on occasions the strength of the pain and mourning is so intense as to prevent representation.

As a device the setting works – as does the theatrical device – because of the basic awareness that it is a game, a fiction, but at the same time it is constantly ensnared by it. It is well known that some people are unable to maintain this illusion, this fiction. They want more reality in the relationship; they demand, to put it in Pontalis's words (1990: 56) their 'pound of flesh', 'to be paid in kind and personally without an exchange currency'.

Winnicott has taught us the importance we should assign to illusion and play. In *Playing and Reality* (1971: 51) he argues: 'Psychotherapy takes place in the overlap of two areas of playing, that of the patient and that of the therapist. Psychotherapy has to do with two people playing together.' The ability to live the illusion corresponds to the ability to play and the ability to play is an index of a person's sanity: 'The corollary of this is that where playing is not possible then the work done by the therapist is directed towards bringing the patient from a state of not being able to play into a state of being able to play.' For Winnicott the area of play needs a place and a 'time'. This place 'is not inside by any use of the word [. . .] Nor is it outside, that is to say, it is not part of the repudiated world, the not-me, that which the individual has decided to recognize [. . .] as truly external' (p. 55).

We become aware of this 'place' and this 'time' not so much when we are immersed in it, when we are, so to speak, 'engrossed in the game', as when we move along its margins. Later we shall be describing the events that can happen both to analyst and patient in the moments just before the analytic session begins. At that time and in that place the rules and hierarchy of levels (between action and thought) of the analytic session are not yet in force but equally the rules and levels that govern the 'everyday' are no longer applicable. Since the setting acts as an attractor, the actions can mime a discourse, the objects stand for words and symbols.

These events on the margins of the session help us understand the extent to which living, representing in life and in the session, and storytelling are continuous 'moments of being' (to use the words of Virginia Woolf) which the caesura of the setting make contiguous. As Petrella (1985: 33) justly points out: 'What varies are the position of the subject, his point of view, the position also regulates his awareness.' Artaud (1958) asserts that 'it is on stage that the unity of thought, gesture and act are reconstructed'.

Considering the importance of the analytic device, just as I have never adhered to the obsessive, defensive ritualisation to which setting has been subjected in recent years, I likewise do not share the often acritical proposals to modify the situation of the setting in order to cope with the so-called 'crisis' of psychoanalysis which are supposedly imposed by this crisis. In recent times there has also been a tendency towards an excessive simplification which reduces the whole business of analysis, largely though not solely, to the interactive dimension between two subjects: analyst and patient. This approach fails to take into sufficient account the complexity of transference and countertransference and consequently also the multidimensionality of the figures of the analyst and the patient.

Transference shows us the difference on a daily basis and enables us to measure the distance that exists between real person and 'psychic' person, between person and character, between the analyst as 'vehicle' and as 'addressee' (Pontalis 1990) of the transference feelings of the patient. Transference allows us to experience the richness and the limits of analysis as 'scene'.

In this context *Observations on Transference Love* (1915a) remains one of Freud's most courageous books. On 4 March 1915 he wrote to Abraham about it, saying that he felt it was the best and most useful of the whole series, but also that he was sure it would be resolutely rejected. According to Musatti, there was one point in the essay that might have caused a scandal (and Freud was aware of this), namely the sudden shift where he remarks that the reasons given by the doctor to illustrate the unreal character of transference love correspond to the peculiar characteristics of any 'authentic' act of falling in love.

Transference presents itself as real and unreal, repetition and 'first time' (Pontalis 1990), representation and crisis of representation, scene and rupture of scene.

The most widely known and most often cited aspect is repetition. In analysis acts, phrases, scenes of the repressed past are repeated, not to separate oneself from them but to re-enact them as faithfully as possible. The impossibility of being faithful to the original perpetuates repetition. The relationship with the original is what makes the job of both director and actor so hard in performances ('repetitions') on stage. As in the theatre, repetition in analysis, instead of producing monotony and stereotypes, can be transformed into a living representation. Peter Brook (1980; quoted in Petrella 1985: 2) sees this as the fundamental function of the *assistance* offered by the director and the audience: assistance given by the eyes, the focus, desires, pleasure and concentration. Brook recently made the point that director, author, actor and spectator all have the same importance. Hence, talking only makes sense if the speaker is sustained by the nature of the other's listening. Similarly, in the analytic situation, the assistance given by 'the eyes, the focus' of the analyst and the patient can free repetition from unconscious stereotype and give it back life and meaning.

But transference does not always present itself in the form of faithful repetition, and it does more: Freud also speaks about 'revised and corrected editions'. Here too we remain in the field of representation. But transference is not only representation, word and scene; in transference the patient 'seeks to put his passions into action without taking any account of the real situation' – so writes Freud in *The Dynamics of Transference* (1912a: 108). Previously in *The Interpretation of Dreams* he recalled: 'If we look at unconscious wishes reduced to their most fundamental and truest shape, we shall have to conclude, no doubt, that psychical reality is a particular form of existence not to be confused with material reality' (1900: 620). It is this (psychical) reality that makes its claim in transference. And this never realised reality (the unconscious is the realm of the unrealised) seeks and claims to be realised in the transference. In this sense the transference is both repetition and 'first time', scene and its rupture: 'There is a complete change of scene; it is as though some piece of make-believe had been stopped by the sudden irruption of reality – as when, for instance, a cry of fire is raised during a theatrical performance' (Freud 1915a: 162). As Pontalis (1990) rightly comments: 'If we insisted on the theatrical metaphor, we would come up against the following paradox: repetition, "true" repetition, in the Freudian sense, is that which provokes transference and what eludes representation, the represented and figured scene and the series of "repetitions" which preceded and allowed it. [. . .] Tonight is improvisation night' ('*si recita a soggetto*').

At that moment, to quote Pirandello (1921): 'Nothing [. . .] exists as given and preconceived. Everything is in the making, is in motion, is a sudden experiment.' Faced with that 'fire', the irruption of psychic reality into the therapeutic situation, Breuer had fled and on various occasions Freud had mentioned his companion and master's lack of courage and equally had seen that moment (and the thoughts that followed from it) as the moment the analytic method was born. He had constructed a device which kept analysis sufficiently sheltered from and equipped to fight that possible 'fire', making a separation between the role and function of the analyst and that of the patient. So towards the end of his life he continued to make the point: 'We are reminded that the work of analysis consists of two quite different portions, that it is carried on in two separate localities, that it involves two people, to each of whom a distinct task is assigned.' He went on:

> It may for a moment seem strange that such a fundamental fact should not have been pointed out long ago; but it will immediately be perceived that

> there was nothing being kept back in this, that it is a fact which is universally known and, as it were, self-evident and is merely being brought into relief here and separately examined for a particular purpose.
>
> (1937b: 258)

Why was Freud so insistent? What explains his barely hidden embarrassment about an event that was supposed to be 'universally known'? Who was he addressing? One readily thinks of Ferenczi – who at the time was participating almost too actively in the analytic situation, who failed to respect the roles and the two separate scenarios and united both patient and analyst in one scene. His warning was probably addressed to Ferenczi at that period:

> Don't love your patients beyond the rules prescribed by neutrality. Show your benevolence by listening to them and deducing what has been repressed. And if the primitive traumas have annihilated them to the point of abolishing in them every memory, every trace of that catastrophe, express your love by constructing what has happened to them. That's it.
>
> (quoted in Green 1990: 303–304)

By moving away from Charcot, away from that collusive space in which the physician was an unconscious accomplice in capturing the patient, Freud had gradually constructed another space in which both collusion and capture were avoided, thus occasionally putting even drastic limits on the function of the analyst (consider the short, sharp 'that's it' in the passage quoted above). It was up to those who came after him to investigate in more depth the role and the unconscious of the analyst who had always been, since the days of Charcot, a character on the analytic scene who was both an essential and a burdensome presence.

7

On the traces of countertransference

In a letter to Jung written in 1911 Freud says:

> I deduce that you and Pfister have not yet acquired the necessary coldness in carrying out the profession, seeking yet to impose yourselves and give much of yourselves, in order to obtain something in exchange. As a venerated old master am I allowed to warn you that this technique regularly leads to miscalculations, and that it is better to stay inaccessible and to insist on the aspect of receptivity? We must never permit our poor neurotics to make us mad. The article on 'countertransference', which I think is necessary, should not be printed but copies should be circulated among ourselves.
>
> (quoted in Turillazzi Manfredi 1994: 105, our translation)

The few times that Freud touched upon the question of countertransference he did so with great reticence and caution – at odds with the 'love of truth' which, as he said in *Analysis Terminable and Interminable* (1937a), 'precludes any type of sham or deceit' (p. 248). The fact is that the history of countertransference started post Freud. Our aim here is not to trace the stages of this history, as this is a task others have already taken. Our reading will be short and synchronic: we shall compare texts and authors from different periods, because it is our opinion that on the subject of countertransference certain themes and problems continue to be debated that have been acute since the very beginning. We agree with Turillazzi Manfredi when she argues that countertransference is an open problem and one that is difficult to position in analytic thought.

The 1950s were the heyday of countertransference. This period saw a long succession of works on the subject, but from the beginning open criticism was loud, reflecting widespread resistance in analytic circles. Here are some examples: 'countertransference is the same as transference – it is then immediately obvious that countertransference is undesirable and a hindrance' (Fliess 1953, quoted in Tower 1955). 'The [countertransference mistake] should be admitted, to allow the patient to express his anger, and he is entitled to some expression of regret from the analyst' (Little 1951). 'It is not safe to let even subtle manifestations of the countertransference creep inadvertently into the inter-personal climate. The analyst must recognize and control these reactions' (Alexander 1954, quoted in Tower 1955). 'Countertransference,' Sharpe had already asserted in 1947, 'must be healthy.' These criticisms are quoted in a work by L. E. Tower (1955). Not as well known as others (e.g. Paula Heimann), in our view she is a writer of great acuteness and clarity of expression. This is how she replies to these criticisms of countertransference:

> All of these – and similar attitudes – presuppose an ability in the analyst *consciously to control his own unconscious.* Such a supposition is in violation of the basic premise of our science – namely, that human beings are possessed of *an unconscious which is not subject to conscious control,* but which is (fortunately) subject to investigation.
>
> (Tower 1955, emphasis added)

Since countertransference, just like transference, has its roots in the unconscious, it does not manifest itself in an open and obvious way; it needs to be 'investigated', its 'traces' need to be interpreted. The traces Tower points to include: 'anxiety in the treatment situation'; 'disturbing feelings toward patients', or the opposite, 'stereotypy in feelings'; 'love and hate responses'; 'erotic pre-occupations, especially ideas of falling in love with a patient'; 'dreams about patients and acting-out episodes', etc. We mention Tower because of the centrality she gives to the unconscious. The points we shall be making about countertransference revolve around the centrality of the unconscious which should always be kept in focus.

Thus Turillazzi Manfredi's shrewd and provocative question (1994: 133) – 'Where is the countertransference going?' – corresponds to the question 'Where is the unconscious going?', or if you like 'Where has the unconscious gone?' To start this search, let us for the time being leave the 1950s, Tower and analysts' defences against countertransference and the unconscious.

Cut, dissolve, change of scene: contrast through editing. The landscape before us now looks profoundly different. The analyst talks a lot about himself, sometimes more about himself than about the patient. The unconscious does not seem to be accessible through gaps or 'traces', but it is there visible, ready to be narrated, ready for use. This is another form of defence against countertransference and the unconscious – negation on display. When we engage in this sort of public self-analysis, we see our own true blind spots, we realise the deep-seated reason for our own loves and hates, we understand, sometimes with surprising speed, our own unconscious fantasies and those of the analytic pair – in short we are conscious of our own unconscious.

Another form of defence against the (unconscious) countertransference takes the form of the opposition between empathy and countertransference. Starting from Kohut (1971, 1984),[1] who considered countertransference as essentially an interference in the work of analysis, countertransference begins to be seen as the negative version of empathy. Where we have the former the latter is missing, or at least it is seriously obstructed. The opposition between empathy and countertransference can in fact be found early on in the literature. Tower (1955) proposes it in a way which is the opposite of what we have recently become used to:

> It is not enough to talk just about dedication, empathy and rapport, important as these are. I have brought the analyst's libidinal responses into this discussion because they evoke so much countercathexis among analysts; I feel that this countercathexis belongs to the category of rigidity defenses of the analytic group.

At that time, the question was addressed, using a different vocabulary, by Racker (1953), who distinguished between concordant and complementary identifications, which determine concordant countertransference and complementary countertransference. For Racker concordant countertransference was based on introjections and projections, 'on the discovery of something which belongs to others as if it were one's own ("this part of you is me") and on the equation between what is one's own and what is the other's ("this part of me is you")' (p. 95). Complementary identification, on the other hand, comes about when the patient treats the analyst as an internal object, with the result that the analyst feels treated as such and identifies unconsciously with this object. 'In general,' Racker says, 'excluded from the concept of countertransference are concordant identifications, which occur in the analyst and are the reason for the *empathy* with the patient. He goes on: 'We need to consider the fact that the tendency towards *empathy*, that is, concordant identification ("understanding"), largely originates from positive and sublimated countertransference; this places *empathy* in relation to countertransference in the broad sense' (p. 96, emphasis added).

Empathy ('concordant countertransference', as Racker sees it) is accepted and recognised because it is positive and sublimated countertransference. We are prepared to recognise in us ('this part of you is in me') something or rather someone which is familiar (*heimliche*) to us; countertransference proper brings with it the difficulty of recognising in ourselves the non-familiar (*Un-heimliche*), the foreigner, the 'other person' that Freud spoke of in *The Unconscious*:

> Psychoanalysis demands nothing more than that we should apply this process of inference to ourselves also – *a proceeding to which, it is true, we are not constitutionally inclined*. If we do this, we must say: all the acts and manifestations which I notice in myself and do not know how to link up with the rest of my mental life must be judged as if they belonged to *someone else: they are to be explained by a mental life ascribed to this other person*.
> (1915c: 169, emphasis added)

This passage helps us understand some points made by Pontalis. He uses the word 'movements' to talk about the feelings triggered in the analyst by the contact with the patient:

> No analysis works, that is, operates directly on the subject, unless the wounds which re-awaken our sores, those sudden infiltrations which pervade and animate our psyche, are lived by the analyst. But this is a good omen, telling proof that the patient has become my patient (on occasions this takes time) and, symmetrically, his analyst has been embodied for him.
> (Pontalis 1990: 67)

He goes on, even more audaciously, to say: 'Then we are touched to the quick, and this is good. This reminds us, if it were necessary, that we are not similar to our patient but *we are ourselves a patient*' (emphasis added). Countertransference is thus 'transference into us of the stranger, of that which is most strange to the patient'.

This is the movement towards, the heading towards *another person* that Freud talks about – the 'patient' we were and continue to be. Each analysis that properly gets going involves a revisitation of the analyst's analysis: 'In the relationship with the patient, the analyst reactivates his own analysis' (Klauber 1981). Seen in this light countertransference is not 'counter' transference, nor is it a simple response to transference according to the stimulus–response model. Talking about the word *Gegen-übertragung*, Gribinski pointed out that the preposition *gegen* not only meant 'against' but also 'nearby'; that is, being near the transference of the patient, following his 'movements'. Psychoanalysis, as has been pointed out several times, is *Erfahrung*: the movement of the subject that shadows the movement of the object.

To connect the countertransference to the unconscious of the analyst leads to contact, though not similarity, between the countertransference with the self-analytic process of the analyst. The contiguity of transference to countertransference, in its broadest sense, brings the model of the countertransference close to that of the 'analytic field'. Let us start from self-analysis, which in our model constitutes one of the poles, one of the three principle organisers of the analytic space. Tower makes the point with typical clarity:

> It does take time to analyze anyone, including oneself, and a busy analyst, spending most of his day with patients, naturally pushes aside much potentially illuminating material about himself [. . .] After all one goes through to become an analyst, to have to become aware of the pervasiveness of countertransference phenomena is a threat and a letdown. [. . .] The preliminary personal analysis is often regarded by the practicing analyst, remote in time, forced on him, and related to former problems, as having no connection with present operations, about which there may thus be a bolstering of defenses and rationalizations. The analysis (or observations) of the functioning analyst may be a most important 'royal road' toward understanding the treatment process.
>
> (Tower 1955: 229–230).

According to Turillazzi Manfredi, the countertransference:

> ought above all to promote self-analytic work. This is an intent that has fallen

> into disuse for several reasons: on account of the idealisation of the training analysis, perhaps because of the necessity, already dictated by Freud, not to entrust oneself only to the self-analytical structure, and finally perhaps because of the easier comfort of taking other paths of technical use which are undoubtedly also profitable.
>
> (Turillazzi Manfredi 1994: 13)

We have already pointed out that for Bollas (1988) the contemplation of countertransference represents 'the systematic re-integration into the psychoanalytic movement of that psychoanalytic function (self-analysis) which had been exiled'.

This interplay between transference and countertransference brings the model of countertransference, in its enlarged vision, close to the model of the 'field'. As long ago as 1965 Kernberg wrote: 'The totalistic conception of countertransference is coherent with a concept of the analytic situation as an interactive process in which the past and the present of both participants as well as their precise reactions to the past are fused into a single emotional position which involves both.'

Taking her cue from Neyraut (1974), Turillazzi Manfredi writes: 'The firm assumption now is that transference and countertransference have the same roots, as if they were a single phenomenon, which only changes its name depending on whether it flows towards the armchair or towards the sofa' (1994: 133). And finally, there is Bion (1975a) who recommended: 'Investigate the caesura; not the analyst; not the analysand; not the unconscious; not the conscious; not sanity; not insanity. But the caesura, the link, the synapse, the (counter-trans)-ference, the transitive-intransitive mood.'

Everything that has thus far been said about countertransference is, so to speak, a countertransference of 'representations', not an inhibiting countertransference but one which promotes and feeds the field of representations, the virtual space. But countertransference is more than this: it can also present itself as an obstacle, resistance, obstruction and inhibition of the analytical space and its formation both in forms that are sensational and strong and in ones that are silent and closed.

Searles (1959), with the clinical courage that is his hallmark, in two papers ('The Schizophrenic's Vulnerability to the Therapist's Unconscious Processes' and 'The Effort to Drive the Other Person Crazy – an Element in the Aetiology and Psychotherapy of Schizophrenia'), talks about two-directional influences, which move from the mother to the psychotic child, from the analyst to the psychotic patient and vice versa. In the former he describes how unconscious parts of the therapist are transformed into hallucinations or even into parts of the patient's personality. One psychical apparatus directly influences the psychical apparatus of the other: there are blatant forms of psychical transmigration. This is not interaction but rather a hard-fought battle to fulfil the subterranean *Diktat* of the schizophrenic mother: either you exist through me or you don't exist at all. The space between the two is completely erased, it is non-existent, it does not come into being.

Other countertransference phenomena (described by numerous other authors, including Pontalis) are less blatant. They work on the mind and the body, they make us realise that like the transference also the countertransference is not only representation but has somatic effects. In some analyses, we feel stuck in our thinking and our body, we are unable to analyse. Psychosomatic phenomena arise which vary according to the characteristics of the analyst, but the effect is identical: these countertransference events, with their varied phenomenology, produce the same effect – the obstruction of the analytic space.

This is a fragile space to which the analyst must devote constant care. It can be threatened by excessive realism on the part of the patient or analyst (in his theories); or by maintaining the analyst in a fixed position and role forced by the complementary identifications (Racker 1953) activated by the patient; or finally by those phenomena, some manifest (Searles 1959) and some more hidden and physical, which we are describing.

One or more of these elements, by attacking the analytic space, attacks one function of this space: developing (occasionally bringing into being) the psychic space. These two spaces are connected on a very deep level. But these phenomena (we are referring especially to those registered by the psychosomatics of the analyst) can show us not directly but in 'negative' form (that is, like the negative of a photograph) what is at the root of the various types of countertransference we experience, what feeds them.

This is a kind of 'originary' countertransference which we do not perceive when empathy flows or when the painful movements of the analyst contribute to activating the field of symbols and memory. The moments when we are touched, as Pontalis puts it (1977), 'to the death', when our activity as an analyst is inhibited, we perceive and take up contact again with those 'fundamental questions that are typical of every analyst' which first stimulated and continue to stimulate our work. We all have our own 'questions'. Racker talks of his:

> [The patient's negativity awakens] in the analyst long-standing paranoid and depressive anxieties and senses of guilt. Faced with the aggressivity of the patient towards the ego and the effects of this aggression, he turns inside and confronts his primitive crimes on a conscious level. Often it is these infantile conflicts, with their aggressive charge, that push the analyst to choose his profession, with which he tries to repair the objects of his aggression and to overcome or deny his sense of guilt. Because of the strong masochism of the patient, the defence of the analyst, joined to the therapeutic action, collapses and the analyst finds himself threatened by the return of the catastrophe, in other words, the encounter with the destroyed object.
>
> (Racker 1953: 105–106)

What reason would the analyst have (on an unconscious level) to want to cure if he were not himself responsible for the patient's illness? In this way the patient, simply by virtue of being a patient, is from the very beginning the creditor, the accuser, the super-ego of the analyst and the analyst is his debtor.

Speaking about 'social inequality in the society that is made up of the analyst and the person in analysis' (quoted by Goretti 1996: 393), Racker brings us to the edges of the Barangers' (1969) 'bi-personal field', which, as we know, has had a strong influence in delineating some of the contours of the landscape of Italian psychoanalysis over the last few years.

8

Italian landscape

The period between the Italian Psychoanalysis Congress in 1980 ('The Analytic Relationship') and the 1994 congress ('The Contribution of the Analyst to the Constitution and Maintenance of the Analytic Field') was both intense and controversial. The concepts of 'relationship' and 'field' (which appear in the titles of the congresses) contributed to defining the landscape of Italian psychoanalysis during those years. Often they overlap and shade into each other. In telling their story we shall try to clarify the two terms and, where possible, distinguish between them. My description will seek to respect the thinking of a range of different authors and schools. My personal point of view will be left in the background, as it can easily be inferred from the rest of this book.

Nonetheless, my description cannot make claim to objectivity, which remains a myth. I have been personally involved in this broad movement of thought which revolves around the concepts of relationship and field, and this contribution of mine, the history I shall trace, cannot but reflect a personal 'point of view', with all the partiality that implies. I leave it up to others to complement this vision with other points of view. Various authors and different research traditions have addressed these questions, traditions that start from very different assumptions. Nonetheless, there are numerous points of intersection, and we shall try to point them out whenever they emerge.

There are still some open and unresolved theoretical and clinical problems which need to be worked through together, and these I shall try to describe at the end of our path. The aim (hopefully not too utopian) of this reconstruction of mine is to broaden the basis for dialogue and research. Let us start from the Taormina Congress. I do not know what mythical and historical factors lay behind the choice of the title for this Congress, nor even who was personally responsible for it, but the choice of the title – 'The Analytic Relationship' – suggested that this relationship could no longer be taken as a 'self-evident' assumption of analytic practice based on the argument that since analysis unfolds in the relationship which exists between analyst and patient, there can be no analysis without the analytic relationship. Stripped of what was obvious and implicit in this assumption, the analytic relationship became the specific object of research, and as with all research, an object of doubt – the end point of a process of thought and experience which no longer considered transference–countertransference the only model capable of representing the analytic situation.

After the congress a book was published entitled *La Relazione analitica* [*The Analytic Relationship*] (Brutti *et al.* 1981) which brought together the papers presented by a number of psychoanalysts from the Rome Psychoanalytic Centre and the Naples Psychoanalytic Centre. The papers were then followed by a critical elaboration which defined and constituted a specific sector of psychoanalytic investigation that was to go on to involve other analysts over a period of some years. As the search went on for a new form in relation both to the changed model of reference and to an object of research that was both old and new, differences in use of language emerged.

In this first phase we might talk about two views of the 'analytic relationship', one narrow and the other general. In the narrow view, A. M. Muratori (1981) identified some phenomena which were not explicable only in terms of transference and countertransference. For example, how can we describe the 'style' of an analysis, which, even if it has a profound effect on its outcome, cannot be assigned either to patient or analyst but to the resulting whole? There was also the question of the different outcome of a second analysis with a different analyst from the first. This problem cannot be explained only in terms of the greater technical skills of the second analyst, as there can also be a different and unpredictable outcome when the same analyst provides extra analysis. Even in this case it is the whole which has changed, albeit in a form that is difficult to describe.

Parallel to this discussion of clinical issues, an epistemological and methodological reflection was set in motion which hinged around the impact of the observer on the phenomena he is investigating in the field that forms between subject and observed object. This line of research together with the broadening of the concept of the countertransference, whose limitations had been touched upon by Racker (1953) and overcome by the Barangers (1969), caused the concept of relationship to slip slowly from a narrow to a general use. If no cognitive and experiential act of the object (patient) by the subject (analyst) can be assumed beyond the relationship which exists between them, the 'relationship' represents a general phenomenon, whose functioning and laws one needs to begin to understand, and it is presumed that this will include but also transcend those of the individual subject.

The *relationship* came to be defined as a complex system, a structure whose direction and function could not be deduced and inferred only from the characteristics of the patient and the analyst, although their stories, ideologies and teleonomic plans contribute to forming it and determining its course.

Writers reflected not only on individual but also on ordinary thought. At the time Gaburri (1980) talked of the 'language of the couple'. The concept of 'collusion' was revisited and the phenomenon was considered not only in its generally negative meaning, but also assessed as an emotional and representational formation to which both analyst and patient contribute and which at some moments, by way of a secret pact, can guarantee the stability of the analytic system. The relationship was described in terms of the rites, myths and constructions it produces and the transformations of the relationship divided up into rapid and long-term transformations.

Some clinical phenomena, labelled in the literature as extrasensory perception (ESP), helped support these relational hypotheses (Chianese, Pozzi). In these phenomena the arrow of time seems to 'free itself of its obligatory trajectory: the past, the present and the future seem to collapse into each other in a kind of contemporaneousness, and the message appears to us with predictive qualities. The amazement that is felt is due to the realisation that a strict order has been infringed' (Muratori). This infringement, we would add, affected the separate identities of the two subjects.

There were also differences. For some (Brutti, Traversa, Galdo, Maccari), the relationship was unknowable, others (Giordanelli, Gragnani) defined attempts at modelling. To this end some (Muratori, Cargnelutti) used the 'general theory of systems' of Von Bertalanffy and others (Chianese) Lévi-Strauss's version of structuralism.

Metapsychology remained the theoretical framework albeit interpreted in an equivocal manner and with the deployment of other theoretical concepts. Already in 1980, for example, A. Vergine had talked about the relationship as a structure, using metapsychology but also a broadened and revisited concept of self.

Symmetrical areas ('relationship') of the analytic situation were identified and asymmetrical areas ('rapport') which were commensurate (Muratori, Cargnelutti, Napolitano) to the terms/concepts of 'continuous' and 'discrete' in mathematical logic, notably in the version proposed by Kuyk (1977, *The Discrete and the Continuous*).

At the 1984 Italian Congress of Psychoanalysis (Continuity and Discontinuity in the Analytic Process) these theses and hypotheses were presented and then later brought together in a book edited by A.M. Muratori (1987b), *Il continuo e il discreto in psicoanalisi* [*The 'Continuous' and the 'Discrete' in Psychoanalysis*].

The model of 'relationship' gave rise to a transformation of the concept and use of interpretation and a changed view of subjectivity. During that time interpretation was subjected to a profound critical revision. In 1978 Turillazzi Manfredi's 'Interpretazione dell'agire e interpretazione come agire' [Interpretation of action and interpretation as action] problematised the relationship between word and act (the interpretive word as opposed to acting out), pointing out that interpretation (in some situations) can be seen as action on the part of the analyst. The interpretive act was no longer a function solely of the analyst, designed to restore meaning to the patient's confused material but rather an act, sometimes encouraged by the patient himself, aimed at translating what emerged from a shared area, a speech act that speaks about and of the relationship.

So a distinction began to be made between two functions in the relationship: the function of the patient and the function of the analyst (which includes the function of interpretation), and these were not strictly speaking tied one to the person of the patient and the other to the person of the analyst. The patient is the bearer not only of suffering but also of interpretations of his suffering and the analyst not only has the privileged function of interpreting, but also feels empathy and sympathy for the patient and, as Pontalis says, he can, and in some ways must, recognise himself as a patient. In the relationship the interpretations, never absolute, offered by both analyst and patient, were considered by Vergine (1981) as 'codes of turn taking', 'point moments' of the relational structure, 'spatial-temporal indications to identify a topographical-dynamic detail of that structure'. Just as there is no single code, there no interpretation can be seen as something absolute, as any more 'true' than many other possible interpretations.

As for subjectivity, the question is too vast and goes beyond the scope of this book. Suffice it to say that the subject and crisis of the subject tormented western culture in the transition from the nineteenth to the twentieth century. Freud's psychoanalysis grew out of and expresses this crisis: the subject is divided, there is an unconscious dimension which eludes it. This motif will remain constant throughout his development.

This Freudian legacy was to be fully received by European psychoanalysis, especially the French school, notably Lacan. From the beginning, however, the *Weltanschauung* of the American psychoanalysts was different. Starting from Hartmann's self, with its autonomy and renewed centrality, passing through Kohut's concept of self, with its tendency to cohesion, and ending up with Shafer's 'agent', they have consistently restored or tried to restore the lost unity of the subject.

Each time, not only in psychoanalysis but also in other cultural fields, the subject is weakened, there is a reinforcement of the structure, the system, of intersubjectivity and the relationship; and vice versa each time a subject-centred position is reconquered, relationship and structure are pushed into the background. The (also logical) consequence of a relational vision is a different view, a changed vantage point on subjectivity. Reflections on the subject starting from the relationship, their articulation and their respective transformations, can be found compiled in Traversa (1987), *Soggetto, relazione, trasformazione* [*Subject, Relationship Transformation*]. At the end of the book, Vergine tries to bring together the various theses:

> The subject is elaborated as a transindividual concept [. . .] a function that cannot be defined simply in terms of the interacting components in the field [. . .] its boundary is shifting, as is its breadth [. . .] it is a pattern of 'bunches of relationship' [. . .] 'seams', archive, inventory of the dynamic variations of the system or actualisations of relational potential.

Parallel to the research described above, during the same period (the first half of the 1980s), F. Corrao and his Sicilian colleagues proposed the concept of 'field'. Their theory rested on a sober and solid epistemological reflection that draws on the physics of (among other authors) W. Pauli, the principle of complementarity advanced by Bohr (Corrao 1986) and the concept of space in H. Minkowski (Riolo 1986).

Their experience with groups facilitated an observation that sought to capture the whole rather than the individual elements in a field. In a group the individual elements (dreams, phantasies, etc.) 'are hardly ever traced back by the group to the private world of the subject, but are assumed as functions of the field: materials through which it is possible to build myths and group relations [. . .] the analytic field shares with the group field its "illusional" nature' (Riolo 1986: 202).

The favourite theoretical reference point was Bion, who considered psychoanalysis a relationship without related objects. It was Bion who said that only that which is common to analyst and patient can be the object of analysis. He had also valorised the function of the myth: in the works of the Sicilian colleagues there were frequent references to and use of Greek mythology. Finally, Bion was used partly because his theory had constantly avoided the prejudices and the tendency of analytic theory to fall into 'substantialism'.

Corrao wrote several works which aroused a great deal of interest in Italian psychoanalysis. He defined the analytic field (1986) as follows:

> In the broadest meaning of the term, the field is a system with infinite degrees of freedom, provided with infinite possible determinations which it assumes at every point in space and every moment of time [. . .] The model of the field does not appear to be delineated by any circumscribing horizon, nor does it appear to be bounded by any plane of factual perceptual observation but rather refers to possible phenomenological movements which although they are accidentally invisible can still be inferred and symbolised in a chosen language.

In a *non-substantialist* view, field was used as a method rather than content:

> If we are asked what is the nature of these characteristic properties [of the field], we can reply with sufficient certainty that the question is meaningless. We require only a method or a means for registering or recording them. If they change continuously, we think that we are dealing with a field.
>
> (Corrao 1986)

According to Riolo (1986: 81) 'In analysis we do not deal with objects or subjects but with a subjective field of mobile bi-personal or multi-personal relations.' Similarly to Vergine, he argued that 'subjects are *crucial points* on the field whose identity and position are constantly being re-established [. . ,] The analytic device can be assimilated to an artificial amplifying system like a lens or a screen; it is traversed by and reveals mental events but also, in the act of amplifying them, determines them as one of their possibilities.' It seems superfluous to point out how close Riolo's view of the analytic situation – as an artificial device, lens or screen – is to ours.

The concepts and models of relationship and analytic field were to be gradually deployed by individual analysts and study groups. Numerous works make reference to it. Here we shall mention only a few, with apologies to those authors who might (inevitably) have been omitted. A study group coordinated by A. Sollini (1987) published *Narcisismo, Sé, relazione* [*Narcissism, Self and Relationship*], with chapters by A. Sollini, F. Ferraro, A. Giuffrida, P. Scalzone and G. Maccari. The book is not a collection of contributions taking one single conceptual line but rather the trace of thinking around problematic questions of theory and analytic clinical practice. The study group, set up to investigate countertransference, encountered on its path the problem of narcissism which led to the problem of relationship. This line of research, close to Freud's path, dealt with the themes of self, destructivity and identity. The question of psychic suffering was not separate from a reflection on the analytic instruments designed to investigate that suffering and consequently the limits imposed on the analyst and his work.

Reflections and concepts of the analytic field make it possible to think of the analytic situation and the business of analysis with fewer constraints than in the past. According to L. Russo (1990), the analytic field presented the following characteristics: causality, interaction, contextuality, *après-coup*, over-determination, plurality and the provisional nature of levels, transformational potential:

> In the analytic field signs (verbal and pre-verbal signs, phrases, sound and visual images, gestures, intentions, etc.) are launched and projected. Immediately after being thrown into the field these signs appear like utterly undetermined elements which the ordering power of language contextualises and renders determinate.
>
> (Russo 1990: 70)

Using the difference between illocutory and locutory use of language

(Austin, Wittgenstein), Russo reflected on how language constructs and transforms the analytic field.

In 1990, *La situazione psicoanalitica come campo bipersonale* [*The Psychoanalytical Situation as a Bi-personal Field*] by Willy and Madeleine Baranger was published in Italy, edited by Stefania Turillazzi Manfredi and Antonio Ferro. The theories of the Barangers were to have a powerful influence on Italian psychoanalysis and in particular on a group of psychoanalysts who were members of the Centro Milanese.[1] This line of research had been preceded by a pioneering work by Nissim Momigliano (1984): '*Due persone che parlano in una stanza: Una ricerca sul dialogo analitico*' [Two people speaking in a room: a study of analytic dialogue], where the author pointed out the importance of the concepts of container and rêverie as a way of being able to see things 'with the eyes of the patient'. She used the difference Bion postulated between the psychotic and the non-psychotic part of the personality and again Bion's idea of working 'without memory and desire'. Nissim Momigliano's work was characterised by a deliberately non-academic style which made it possible to appreciate the depth of the analytic encounter. The study reflected the personality of the author and her long, rich experience as an analyst. It is most probable that there are no authors working in the Milan area (and beyond) who have not made reference to this work.

As with any research group, it is not easy to talk about, or especially to sum up, this group's characteristics and conceptual development. (Some years later, Robutti did so in the preface to a book we shall mention below.) Generally speaking, it seems to me that there is a basic common line and individual differences: Barale, for example, appears very responsive to Freudian contributions even though within a modified conceptual and experiential framework. The theory of the Barangers, Bion and Corrao appears to me to form a background shared by many authors. What I see as the greatest achievement of Ferro, Bezoari, Barale *et al.* is that they rescued the idea of field from abstraction and speculation (even though some of their works betray a certain penchant for sophisticated theorisation) and measured it against key and controversial points of psychoanalytical clinical practice and technique. Theirs was the attempt that came closest to being a working model. Here are some of their formulations. According to Ferro (1992: 21), the 'concept of field considerably expands that of relationship, because it extends it to the whole analytic situation, thus to the setting and the rules, also providing the possibility of a broader approach than that which looks at relationship'. Both the symmetrical and asymmetrical planes of the analytic field are considered, and the Barangers' concept of bi-personal phantasy is used. Very original is the concept of 'functional aggregates', which are represented through 'characters' in the field 'that come on stage [. . .] and are the expression of a continuous process whereby the two members of the couple tend to dream and communicate with each other what is happening between them almost moment by moment' (Bezoari and Ferro 1992: 72). This enables an adequate monitoring of the analyst's interventions. There is an articulation between relationship and transference:

> Not only is this process (which goes from transference to relationship) arduous and difficult, it is also never linear and uni-directional, as claimed by certain ideal schemas of treatment [. . .] The most common experience, and one we share, shows instead a movement of oscillation between these two regimes of the mental functioning of the couple: an analogous oscillation is that described by Bion between PS and D (and which, similarly, we represent with the symbols R↔T).
>
> (Bezoari and Ferro 1992: 77)

Within this conceptual framework the 'negative therapeutic reaction' is revisited (Bazoari and Ferro 1992). It is considered the product of a distorted relationship of the couple rather than solely the result of the patient's pathology. These are only some of the stimulating clinical ideas and theoretical hypotheses. These themes, closely examined and greatly enriched, are to be found in *L'esperienza condivisa. Saggi sulla relaziane psicoanalitica* [*Shared Experience. An Essay on the Psychoanalystic Relationship*] edited by Nissim Momigliano and Robutti (1992) with chapters by L. Momigliano, A. Robutti, E. Di Chiara, M. Bezoari, A. Ferro, F. Barale, R. Gagliardi Guidi, and F. De Masi. As mentioned above, Robutti reconstructs the history of the Centro Milanese di Psicoanalisi and its lines of research. The themes discussed are the analytic dialogue, the study of the mind of the analyst at work and applications in the clinical field. 'A fundamental line of our common thought,' affirmed Robutti (p. 17), 'unfolded around the idea that every human being, every subject is from the beginning in search of the other, an object, in order to construct what in the relationship with it will become its own internal containers. Such a way of seeing things has as its basis the theory of object relations (Ogden 1986).' According to Robutti: 'The aim of clinical psychoanalysis is no longer seen as revealing but rather as recovering and constructing what has not been able to develop in previous relationships. The present situation of psychoanalytic discourse can be seen as the continuous encounter or clash between two basic models, the "intrapsychic" and the "interpersonal" [. . .] We move in the area closest to the interpersonal pole.'

Within this framework the interpretation is no longer aimed at 'revelation, it acquires the function of constructing new meanings together with the patient'. Thus states Di Chiara, who sees as the three fundamental factors of the analytic experience 'the encounter, stories and leave-taking'. Gagliardi Guidi debated a hot subject that has been little dealt with: interrupted analyses. F. De Masi addressed the theme of 'transference psychosis' with special reference to work with borderline patients.

This rapidly sketched survey should still give an idea of the complexity and contradictory nature of the themes revolving around the concepts of relationship and analytic field on the eve of the 1994 Rimini Congress (*Il contributo dell'analista nella costituzione e mantenimento del campo analitico*; The Contribution of the Analyst to the Construction and Maintenance of the Analytic Field), which represented a chance to deepen and expand the debate. From my point of view, it was, at least to some extent, a missed opportunity. At the time, as scientific secretary of the Rome Psychoanalytic Centre, I was one of the organisers of the congress and had occasion to note a feeling of uncertainty. It was pointed out to me that even though we had not managed to agree on and formulate a 'conceptual model', over the years the themes of 'relationship' and 'field' had brought about a profound change in the mentality of analysts, in their way of relating to patients and colleagues. This transformation showed itself not so much in the content as in the 'style' of the interventions at the congress.

Although I can understand this point of view, I do not think it right to do without a further process of working through. We are reluctant to accept the wear and tear (which can rapidly reach the point of banality) to which terms/concepts that have opened up new territories of reflection and research in psychoanalysis are subjected. In this context, it did not seem to me to be a positive sign that at the congress one could come across more than ten definitions of 'field'. Even less encouraging was the limited number of works that tried to tell the history of concepts with a second-level reflection on them.

Among the few attempts in this direction we should mention the works by Bordi, Merendino, Bonaminio and De Renzis.

This overview of the notions of relationship and analytic field would be lacking in one point if we did not mention the relatively recent direction taken by American psychoanalysis, which has in the last few years reached these shores and has spoken through various colleagues: Bordi, Bonfiglio, Bonaminio. This branch of research has been given various labels: theory of the relational model (Mitchell 1988); theory of intersubjectivity (Stolorow *et al.* 1994). Boesky (1990), Renik (1993), Gill (1994) and Hoffmann (1991), to cite some authors, consider the American analytic situation as a relationship, an 'interaction' to which both patient and analyst contribute but where their positions are diversified and radicalised to varying degrees.

I do not think we can pass judgement or deliver a definitive opinion about an ongoing direction, nor is it easy to understand the extent to which adherence to these theories follows the trend of the fashionable systems from which analysts are not entirely free. We shall at any rate avoid speaking about the arrival of a 'new' paradigm – an occurrence as frequent in psychoanalysis (or rather as frequently proclaimed) as it is rare in the other sciences. More than paradigmatic changes, present-day psychoanalysis, even in the face of these themes, needs a long period of 'normal science' to enable communication between various languages which otherwise are unable to communicate with each other and thus generate closed systems both from the theoretical and clinical point of view.

We have already spoken (in relation to the relationship between history and psychoanalysis) of various psychoanalytic traditions. They are based on differences in the use of language, and the 'language obstacle' coincides with an epistemological obstacle, a cultural difference which, as Pontalis (1977: 151) says, is an 'ideological or philosophical divergence'; and 'we know about the whole impact of general culture on psychological [. . .] and psychoanalytic concepts. Likewise, however, we know that there is nothing more difficult than measuring this impact.' What needs to be avoided is the attempt at linguistic domination. The analyst is familiar with such 'violence' in his daily work, where it is common to find one language trying to impose itself on another – either that of the mother on the child or that of the analyst on the patient.

Dominance by or elimination of language is a historical-social problem: the history of culture and civilisation has offered us many examples, some of which either verge on the tragic or truly are tragic. The only possible solution lies in the coexistence of languages in their reciprocal 'translation': this is analytical work par excellence. Worthy efforts have been made in this direction: at the congress Bonaminio's paper sought to translate two analytic languages which speak to each other 'this side' and 'that side' of the Atlantic. There is a balance to be sought between a radical critique and an equally radical acritical adherence: translation and at the same time a link with tradition so as to preserve that 'essential quality' which matters so much to supporters of the interactive-relational point of view and to avoid the evident tendency towards reductionism, 'theoretical simplification' and 'practical simplicism' (Ponsi and Filippini 1996: 581).

This is a dialectical articulation with the psychoanalytic tradition (starting from Freud, who is often read with unacceptable simplicism) and in particular with the linguistic and psychoanalytic tradition which has been debating with undoubted profundity for some years about themes of field and relationship. 'In any cultural field it is *not possible to be original except on the basis of tradition*,' says Winnicott (1971: 134). 'The interplay between originality and the acceptance of tradition as the basis for inventiveness seems to me to be just one more example, and a very exciting one, of the interplay between separation and union' (original italics).

I have expressed my own position on numerous occasions: I am inclined to think of the encounter between analyst and patient not so much in terms of interaction as in terms of space; their encounter is not direct interaction but is still mediated by the respective 'intermediate areas'. If we are able to live inside and enjoy our own intermediate area, 'without making claims' (Winnicott 1971), we can recognise the intermediate area of the other, and the superimposition of the two areas which allows us to go through an experience which is both personal and common. Post Winnicott, we know that the 'intermediate area' is in contact with and open to culture, to that common base which unites us. By going down that road we can reflect on what unites analyst and patient, on the 'nature' of the analytic field and possibly on the laws that determine it:

> When one speaks of a man one speaks of him along with the summation of his cultural experiences. The whole forms a unit. [. . .] In using the word 'culture' I am thinking of the inherited tradition. I am thinking of something that is in the common pool of humanity, into which individuals and groups

> of people may contribute, and from which we may all draw *if we have somewhere to put what we find.*
>
> (Winnicott 1971: 133, original emphasis)

Loch (1977) starts from Wittgenstein and speaks of a 'common form of life' which unites us all, including analyst and patient, with its implicit anthropology, which inhabits any (even pathological) manifestation and is expressed in all activities, including psychotherapeutic ones. Being immersed in a cultural universe is a fact for man, as is his biological and instinctual constitution. In biological terms (originary immaturity), the subject needs another to survive and a cultural order (and an anthropological 'development' within that culture) to make his experience meaningful and profitable, starting from the biological experience (De Micco 1996). So for other authors (for example, Nathan) there is total equivalence between possessing a psyche and possessing a culture.

Linguists and anthropologists have tried to demonstrate the existence of structures that tend towards universality, such as kinship and language structures. Starting from this common foundation, historically determined differences have emerged between various cultures, beliefs, customs and 'mentalities', to use F. Braudel's excellent expression. 'Mentalities' are slowly transforming structures that determine the way in which we interact with ourselves, our sex, the sex of others, time, etc.

The human condition differs from the 'living order' (investigated by biology): its specificity lies in the relationship which unites man with his peers, a relationship mediated by languages and symbols. These relations constitute a specific foundation of the human order which is different from the vital order, relations which are supported by a (psychic) causality that is different from natural causality. The human subject is thus defined in relation to other subjects considered in terms of temporal differences (differences between generations) and differences between the sexes (Green 1996) – differences which are interrelated. It is in this sense that sexuality is at the centre of human relations and for this reason that it occupies a central position in analytic practice. In the transmission between generations the child receives, from the sexual adult, messages and 'enigmatic signifiers' (Laplanche) which will later be enclosed in the unconscious by the process of repression and then opened by the particular condition that is determined by the analytic situation: a singular experience which comes to occupy the point of intersection between bodies and culture, individuals and generations.

If psychoanalysis has unified the subject of anthropology, the group subject and the subject of the analytic field, the work that we have to do is reflect on their differences; that is to say, we have to think what joins individual subjectivity to the subjectivity of the whole. The psychical subject cannot be separated from intersubjectivity, which means 'psychical work', constraints and limits. This is the teaching of Freud, and Stolorow's often repeated remark that Freud's theory is a theory of the 'isolated psychic apparatus' seems to me incomprehensible. Rather we should be thinking of the fractures, the *telescopage* as Faimberg puts it, between these various 'spaces' of subjectivity (anthropology, group, analytic field) which have 'their own laws and rules of reciprocal substitution' (Kaës 1993: 31). I believe that, with regard to the analytic field, we are a long way from having identified these 'laws', even though we still intuitively know that they cannot replace those of the single individual.

'The analytic situation has its own spatial and temporal structure, it is orientated according to certain lines of force and dynamics and possesses its own laws of development' – this is how the Barangers put it in the Preface to their 1969 work. In the same volume we find:

> Up to now, by insisting on the existence of a *Gestalt* of the couple in the analytic situation and calling this *Gestalt* our specific field of work, all we were doing was saying that a melody was nothing other than the sum of its notes, that a group is the sum of its members. However, we need to go further and ask ourselves how this *Gestalt* is constituted, why it is not constituted in the same way as any couple and what processes contribute to its formation.

Since then we haven't progressed very much further on this point, despite some attempts to look at the 'field' using the theory of systems, structuralism or certain concepts taken from mathematical logic. Openings could be made, by those with the appropriate expertise (I do not see myself as belonging to this group), to models based on topology, the theory of groups and catastrophe theory (Thom). The study of groups has brought us to a more advanced point in Bion's proposed formalisation of 'basic assumptions'.

But these are not the only outstanding problems. Connected to the laws of the field is the problem of time or rather the timeframe (*tempi*) of the analytic field:

> What psychoanalytic theory suffers from most of all is an inadequate working through of temporality, which has the task of articulating the different concepts of development, maturation, chronology, *a priori* and *a posteriori*, repetition, the difference between the time of the subject and the time of the other, slowing down and haste, retrospection, etc.
>
> (Green 1990: 308)

To this list compiled by Green, from a relational perspective we could add, if it were not implicit in his words, the timeframe of the analyst and the patient, the timeframe of their respective elaboration, the timeframe of their synchrony and discord, the timeframe of their wholes, rites, 'chiasmuses' and ideologies, etc.

Finally, there is the question of writing, which we have talked about and which we can summarise as follows. Writing follows the analyst's technical modifications. The analysis can no longer be described as the history of an illness, or only as the development of the transference neurosis. Analyst and patient are co-authors and, to varying degrees, actors in the affair. What are the narrative forms which best express this changed landscape?

Research on the analytic field is open-ended; many questions remain up in the air. To conclude: no progress has been made from a descriptive level to a 'conceptual model', no general laws have been laid down from which to derive, as a logical consequence, technical modifications. We are not even certain whether this will in fact be possible and whether the driving force might not lie in a partial indeterminacy. We are nonetheless convinced that we cannot stop discussing these questions and must open up a broad-based debate under the sign of that 'intellectual communism' which Freud referred to in a letter to Jung (7 April 1907), where it should not be necessary to verify in minute detail what has been received and what has been given (Freud and Jung 1974). But the greatest obstacle is represented by analysts themselves. Starting from Bion, they have often spoken about 'thoughts without thinkers', but nothing is more difficult in psychoanalysis: thoughts remains too closely connected to 'thinkers' and their destinies. Rarely do they manage to come together in a common field of exchange, and this is a great shortcoming that restricts the development of psychoanalytic thinking.

The two 'clinical' essays that follow certainly do not resolve the problems which we have just finished expounding: they also fail to go much beyond the descriptive plane. Chapter 9 ('A Work by a Single Author with Two Heads and a Double Look') brings together experiences from some time ago and, despite their working through, perhaps bears the sign of its time, a way of thinking and modelling the relationship of that period (the early 1980s). Chapter 10 ('Chiasma') was written more recently and represents a different way of addressing the problem of the relationship both in terms of style and content. In Chapter 9 the modelling is explicit and follows from the case studies. In Chapter 10 it is inscribed in the narrative fabric, shadowing its movements and merging with it. Again we meet the lines that have run through our investigation: constructions, screen memories, repression, denial, the transgenerational approach, history, destiny, resignification. We do not think that we should abandon these valuable contributions from the tradition of clinical psychoanalysis in the name of the 'new' – the field and the analytic relationship. I am very fond of this short work and now entrust it with the future of research – for the moment intuitively represented by images and metaphors.

9

'A work by a single author with two heads and a double look'[1]

A nun

He felt tired and sleepy. He had often said to himself that early morning sessions cost him a great effort, although he realised that thinking that way was a reflection of certain stasis in the analytic work with the patient. That particular morning the monotony of what the patient was saying lulled him into a slight drowsiness. He woke up from this short dream: 'A young man was trying to seduce a young nun, everything took place in a highly erotic atmosphere. He followed the existential drama of this young nun who, in order to follow the man, "divested" herself of her religious garments.'

During the short time he had been asleep, the patient had been silent: 'At first I didn't say anything because I couldn't describe the phantasy I had had the day before. I had difficulty talking about a phantasy that upset me! I was walking up to my girlfriend's second-floor flat when as I passed the first floor, where an old nun lives, I had this phantasy of breaking down the door and raping her.'

This old nun reminded him of a nun who for reasons of age and illness had been given permission by her convent to be looked after at home by her family. For him she represented immobility, a timeless dimension, illness, a maternal figure. He thought that the phantasy probably meant that the maternal figure was the obstacle that prevented him from reaching the girl. The session went on and the patient gave no sign of having noticed or registered the analyst's little nap.

In the days that followed the analyst found himself thinking about that brief dream and remembered a period at the beginning of his working life when he had been employed at an institute for cerebropathics run by nuns. This had been shortly before the start of his personal analysis. He remembered the spicy comments and erotic fantasies about the young nuns at the institute that his friends and colleagues bandied about in typical student manner.

A few days earlier, the patient (a medical student) had once again spoken to him about his plans (seen as unlikely to be fulfilled in the near future given his inhibitions) to specialise in child neuropsychology once he had graduated, and possibly to work as a child psychotherapist. This young man had come to analysis after repeated panic attacks and episodes of depression which had started after his elder sister had got married. He had been a militant Catholic, meaning he had followed in the tradition of his mother's family, a family that included many priests and nuns. During the period when the episode we are recounting took place, every Sunday he used to visit an institute for cerebropathics with his girlfriend. A year before his birth his mother had given birth to a cerebropathic, who had died a few days after being born.

So before the analyst's eyes a particular interlacing pattern was taking shape which united him and the patient and which expressed themes of incest, reparation and separation. How had this strange phenomenon come about? In their relationship, all the facts of their personal histories (for example, the biography of the patient) seemed to flow together from both sides, from the side of the analyst and that of the patient: the patient's memory of the phantasy he had had some days earlier, the perception of reciprocal silence, various elements of the context. The whole contribution, both from analyst and patient, was put together to be worked through in dream form by the analyst (function of the relationship) to express latent thoughts in the relational area. The whole process related to the dynamics of the dream.

We have here two representations which highlight the twofold aspect of the system. Temporal contemporaneousness, the setting, the dovetailing narrative and the unifying symbol would confirm the hypothesis of a single structure, functioning as one 'semiotic formation' in which are highlighted, on the one hand, phenomena such as condensation, shifts and multidetermination (which give rise to manifest and latent content of representations), and on the other, opposing psychic forces.

One wonders where the astute selection of the term 'nun' took place. One might think that the notion 'nun' resided in the common relational structure, and that the two different plot lines were formed in the vertical dimension and in the transition to more differentiated structures. Alternatively the signifier 'nun' was to be found at the meeting point between the two areas (the patient and the analyst), which could perhaps find correspondence with what, in the model of the psychic apparatus, is described as preconscious (the seat of verbal representations).

Positioning the signifier 'nun' at the preconscious level is justified by the state of knowledge of the two of them, analyst and patient, at the moment when this signifier was forming in their common thought, a state of consciousness in which preconscious values predominate. We are faced with various levels and forms of thought. The way in which these levels (and/or forms) are articulated seems to me to be a characteristic of analytic thought (and analytic experience). If understood in its globality and unity, this modality appears to be distinct both from the modality of the dream and that of waking. The difference could lie in the various mixtures of level (and/or form) and in the increased possibility of their use. We hypothesise that in the formation of this particular thinking the analyst and patient continually define an area where it is possible that, while one of the two becomes the bearer of images, the other thinks in a logical-conceptual way and vice versa. We use the generic term 'image' to refer to a vast field which encompasses fantasy images, concept images and model images. For example, the nun, who can be interpreted in her quality as a phantasy image, also has a value as a model image of the analytic relationship in its generative potential and vicissitudes and in its breaking down of barriers and boundaries (incest).

Epistemologists have evaluated the contributions which images make to the construction of knowledge in different ways. Some have emphasised their value as a 'psychological aid' (Hesse 1966), while others point out how they lose their importance once the knowledge takes on logical conceptual form. In analysis, in the process of experience and knowledge, both moments are fundamental: the construction of knowledge and knowledge itself. They unfold before our eyes and we ourselves contribute to the various levels in the construction of knowledge, from the more germinal to the more structural. The formation and use of images in analytic thought is a stage along this path of permanent construction and reconstruction.

We are then seduced by the idea that since the origin of psychoanalysis (Anzieu 1975; Molinari 1979) analytic thinking has been formed from a set of propositions derived from so-called 'daydreams' constituted by the following sequence: (a) formation of images; (b) secondary cognitive elaboration, corresponding in some respects to the various cycles of the dream. A prototype of this procedure could be Freud's self-analysis. It is probable that these cycles are a function of the analytic relationship.

Already in its phenomenic occurrence, the image of the nun, both for analyst and patient, is inscribed in a story, a succession of events. In the working through and transition from experience to transcription, the narrative element becomes more evident. Following this path we note – among the stories of the analyst and the patient – oppositions and differences which are ordered according to this chiasmus.

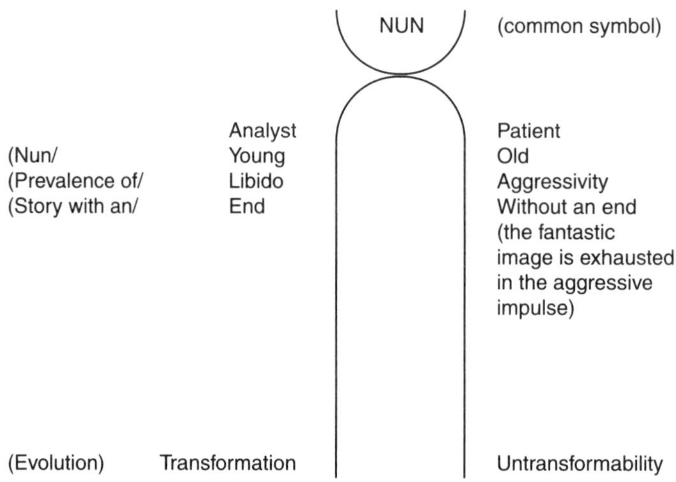

If we read the two stories separately, the analyst's story might appear as the vector of transformations. By doing this we assign a difference of function and role to the analyst and the patient. The alternative, however, is to try to read these two narrative versions at the same time, 'effecting a non-synthetic meeting of the two senses'. The global meaning around which the two texts centre is 'produced by the complex movement of the simultaneous affirmation and negation of another text' (Kristeva 1969).[2]

In this way it becomes more evident that the two stories reflect a common model based on the themes of Time–Incest–Separation. Thus I think it useful to consider the stories of the patient and the analyst not as two distinct stories but as two versions of the same narrative structure,[3] a structure nourished by thinking that operates by means of thematic opposites. As we have seen, many elements are connected by oppositions – oppositional gaps which present significant relations. If these elements are isolated and detached from the diachrony of the two versions of the analyst and the patient, they are laid down and come to occupy a place within an ideal framework which looks at the parameters of Past–Present–Invariance–Change according to this pattern.[4]

PAST	**PRESENT**
Old nun	Young nun
Old age	The young man
Illness	Pschoanalysis
Mother	Undressing
Before the analysis	Infantile psychotherapy
Timeless dimension	After the analysis
Immobility	
Cerebropathies	
INVARIANCE	**CHANGE**

This brings us to the basic narrative structure, where the two versions appear as (discursive-logical-affective) instruments that mediate between Past–Present–Invariance–Change, resolved in this case, considering the unitary nature of the structure, according to a formula along these lines: 'The past must be integrated into the present for change to be possible.'

The term 'nun' acts as a (semantic-logical-affective) mediator between all the oppositional poles since it traverses and mediates them all (for example, past and present, invariance and change). Moreover, in its quality as symbol the term itself (one thinks of the words 'mother' and 'sister', both used as equivalents to 'nun') tends to frame a general question which could be formulated thus: does duality come from unity? Does the other arise from the same? The narrative structure is founded on such aporias, which one tries to resolve via an exchange of terms and functions between the two versions.

The question belongs equally, and without any prejudices as to roles, to both the area of the analyst–patient in their distinct and historically determined individuality, and to that of the analyst–patient in 'relationship'. This event had much preoccupied the analyst, but the patient, even later, seemed to be unscarred by it. The analysis went on for many years and as it was approaching the end the analyst thought of looking again at his old notes about the episode of the 'nun'. He planned to use them to write an article about that remarkable event. It was then that the patient reported this dream:

> I was on my way to Cottolengo [Institute for Cerebropathics], but this time my sister was there and not my girlfriend, and she had a lovely, fair-haired, healthy small child on her arm. In the end it appeared that we stopped going towards Cottolengo. On the road I saw that a friend of mine – same age, reserved, introverted, inhibited – had married and gone to live in two rooms in the convent where I had spent my adolescence. I went in and was impressed by the historical importance of the place. Almost a library, small but old, lots of documents on the table, lots of sheets of paper. I was especially intrigued by a study about a nun who had lived there. Perhaps, I thought, those letters and documents might hide/reveal a secret love affair of the nun's. I was fascinated and I thought – one could spend one's whole life looking at these papers and trying to trace this story. It was a fascinating thought but it also expressed fear of immobility. Outside it was afternoon, one of those afternoons which I have described experiencing to you so many times – a timeless afternoon.

After a brief pause he went on:

> I remember a dream I had a long time ago about an act of violence against a nun – was it a dream or a fantasy? I can't remember, so much time has passed . . .; the nun reminds me of my mother, brought up by an uncle who was a priest, she was supposed to become a nun . . .; the nun of Monza . . .; my father's letters to my mother when they were going out; now they don't disturb me, it is as if I had accepted that they were in love . . .; I associate the library in the dream with his study, with the books, the old atmosphere, the papers and the books on the desk . . .; the study-analysis.

This dream occurred when the analysis was coming to an end, when it was felt that the 'moment to conclude' had come, which corresponds to the moment of concluding the time to understand (Lacan 1966). 'There are well-defined temporally limited 'windows' [. . .] there are definite moments when the end of the analysis can be decided. If you miss it, then you start on another cycle, a new twist in the spiral' – this is Laplanche (1987) talking about the end of the analysis. It seemed that the patient did not want to dwell on it and start a new cycle on a theme which he had reopened and which he wanted to conclude and which the analyst had reopened in order to write a scientific article: another 'chiasmus'. The dream was at any rate an open window through which the analyst could observe the changes that had occurred during the analysis.

Time–Incest–Separation were reformulated in a different composition of the whole which was the formal index (in the sense of a new and varied narrative emergence) of a structural transformation. All this shows that one could no longer subscribe to the dichotomy between old and young, libido and aggressivity, etc. The dream gave a model image of the relation that was substantially changed with regard to all its generative possibilities and the possibilities of breaking down borders and limits.

The theme of the nun, which had so struck the analyst on account of the unexpected irruption of the hypnagogic fantastiquerie and the correspondence with the patient's fantasy, did not seem to have struck the patient, at least not consciously. Nonetheless it had been one of the basic themes, which on several occasions (up to the dream of the end of the analysis) had come out in the analysis to signal both the changes in the mind of the patient and the transformations in the analytic relationship.

Events, like those described, which happen at such a great distance of time are 'emergences' of the same structure and can serve to describe the transformation of key themes. Seen, however, in the overall context of an analysis, the events are watered down and merge into the complex representation of the analytic process in which the transformation takes place – amidst contradictions, resistances, returns, openings.

Thus even the significant elements of an analysis, those we manage to isolate and link together and whose transformation we can follow, can always only give us a limited picture of the relational structure. This structure is never captured in its globality and continuity both because of the relativity of our instruments and our vantage points and due to the fact that the analyst is profoundly involved in the relationship. Behind the changing and discontinuous experience of an analysis made up of so many events, interpretations, constructions and experiences, we are at any rate aware of a plot, a connecting tissue, some basic continuity. Some analytic events, like those we described earlier, give us a glimpse of that continuity, but sometimes it is not signalled by big, remarkable events which happen during the session but by small no less remarkable events, which can happen both to analyst and patient during the moments that precede the session.

On the margins

An unexpected and sudden encounter on the street took place with the patient he was about to meet shortly afterwards in a session. The encounter takes them both by surprise. They show a mixture of courtesy and reserve, and in greeting each other both bow their heads slightly and symmetrically in an obsequious manner. The analyst goes on his way and in his mind's eye the scene appears to him tinged with irony. It reminds him of an etching by Paul Klee which depicts two naked gentlemen both with the typical physiognomy of members of the Central European middle class bowing to each other. Back in his office, he tracks down the title of the work: *Two Gentlemen Bowing to One Another, Each Supposing the Other to Be in a Higher Position* (1903, invention 6).

Hardly through the door, the patient says with a smile: 'Our meeting reminded me of a early Klee painting of two men bowing to each other, I can't remember the title.'

The title which both had forgotten comes as an interpretation (in the psychoanalytic meaning of the term) of certain areas of their relationship, areas in part hidden, characterised by narcissistic elements. This level is revealed by what happened while in another sphere, better known to both of them: a very fertile exchange was taking place in full respect of their individuality and differences – a libidinally invested sphere.

'On my way to the analysis today I walked down a dead end and I felt disorientated.' After these words, the analyst tried to listen for the metaphorical meaning of this description. The patient continued: 'That's what it's called, Vicolo Cieco, and it's parallel to the alleyway that leads here to your place. It's even similar; I noticed this strange name two weeks ago.' This communication came at the beginning of a session, in the third year of analysis with a patient who had recently started talking about his definite improvement. Even though the analyst could to some extent share his patient's opinion, his attitude also seemed to chime in with his vague hypomanical characteristics, with the analyst's fear of his patient's flight into healing and away from the analysis. He had previously refrained from communicating his doubts, considering them only hypotheses to be subjected to criticism. This time, however, by entering the dead end the patient seemed to both of them to be confirming the analyst's suspicions.

It often happens that an entire session can be taken up with a patient describing the period of time immediately preceding the session. Patients tell stories that begin 'On my way here' and talk of bizarre and unusual encounters, surreal collages of thoughts, actions, objects, people. Often we sense the echo and the taste of Breton's 'erring'. At other times the events are more hazy. In its factuality, analysis seems to be marked by discontinuity: distinct sessions, intervals, people with different roles and functions. Once we begin to move away from the surface phenomenic events and engage in a preliminary investigation of spatial-temporal experiences, immediately this simplification starts to give way. We notice two opposite and concurrent tendencies: on the one hand, strict adherence to chronological time (the appointment is fixed, analyst and patient keep to the convention), while on the other hand, experienced time expands, picking up multiple afferences inherent in symbol and memory. The events that precede the session cannot be described as solely historical, in the sense that they really happened, but they are also symbolic and paradigmatic ('dead end' as a 'double' of both analysis and life: a paradigm of existence).

Real actions seem to become one with their metaphorical meaning almost as if real space and the space of thought coincided. The meaning is general and configures the being in the world of this patient. In the first clinical example we found the theme of the double, a fundamental element in the structure of that patient. The chosen scenario was one of the many possible ones which he used from time to time. The choice, however, clearly celebrated the entrance of this theme into the, as it were, theatrical 're-production' (the performance) of the analysis, involving analyst and patient as actors and no longer simply as commentators on scenes-texts, an experience which was thus more likely to lead to transformations.

Moreover, even if attached to separate individuals, in both cases the codes were preferential and specific to the two relationships: in the one case the 'actions of the world' were the discursive plot on which the relationship with a more praxis-orientated patient was founded; in the other, painting was often used in communication with that particular patient as he was someone with an outstanding artistic sensibility. It is as if the codes formed by the respective individuals in some way also transcended them.

Two features characterise some of the events that precede the session: the importance of action and the objects that occupy that space. The delimitation of the field formed by the setting reduces the channels of communication and at the same time, precisely for that reason, intensifies its capacity and potential for communication. The session is the realm of the word, action is banned by statute, pact and theory. If we imagine a hierarchy of levels between word and action through the mediation of thought, emphasis on the first level accentuates and facilitates polysemy and symbolisation.

In the space of time that precedes the session such rules and hierarchies of levels do not apply. Equally, however, neither do the rules and levels which govern the everyday. As the session functions as a field of attraction, the actions can mime a discourse and the objects stand for words and symbols.

Actions cannot be assimilated to the concept of acting as it is commonly understood. They do not involve the crisis of mentalisation and symbolisation. On the contrary, we are offered the chance of catching actions as they are constituted with symbolic qualities. This could be read as a transition from 'action' outside the session to its working through inside the session, but I prefer to think of the co-presence of levels immanent to the action as it happens. The objects contribute to giving a sense of that co-presence – which in this case is co-presence of matter and symbol.

'How strange, as I came up the stairs to your place it was dark, the lights weren't working. Ten minutes ago I bought a present for my girlfriend – some elegant exotic candles.' When telling this story the patient also gives the name of the shop where he bought the candles. Ten minutes earlier, while waiting for the patient, the analyst had been uncertain whether to go downstairs and buy some candles in the very same shop, but had not done so, thinking he would not have enough time.

This episode lends itself to multiple interpretive combinations. The symbolic and real gift which is meant to illuminate the 'inside' and the 'outside' both symbolically and really was made at a period in the analysis when the transference was intrinsic, parallel to the patient's present love affair and his complex oedipal vicissitudes. Psychoanalytic interpretations implicitly make use of the category of the 'discrete'.

This is how we separate and isolate objects and phenomena. Taking the material briefly presented here, one could isolate the counter-transference of the analyst, the transference of the patient, the transference of the analyst, and so on. One could trace causal links to the patient and his history, causal links to the analyst and his story, both combining to determine the event.

Bivalent logic – non-contradiction – underlies and is implicit in this type of reasoning. A description or explanation linked to the discrete relies for its intelligibility on the notion of the succession of time, but this is at the same time also its limit. According to Von Wright (1969), Kant's theory could be called a causal theory of time 'according to which the objective order of events in a temporal sequence (of before and after) depends on subsuming these events under the category of cause and effect [. . .] we must describe events by making use of contradictory states in an order of succession, otherwise we have contradictions. Metaphorically speaking, time, one might say, is man's way out of contradiction'. Indeed it was Kant (1781) who said: 'Only in time can two contradictorily opposed predicates meet in one and the same object, namely, *one after the other*' (*Critique of Pure Reason*).

Our descriptions of the analytic field make use of such a concept of time and such logic. But it is equally evident that the category of 'continuous' would furnish a valid key to understanding the analytic events described above. We prefer to use the concept of 'continuous' in its extensive sense, as we think that it is not inscribed solely in the 'intellectual structures' but, paired with the 'discrete', contributes to bringing about not only thought but also, for example, the imaginary.

Let us consider in this context Muratori's metaphor (1987b) of the 'pattern of a brocade, hidden by the threads of the weave'. The 'continuous', on another level, refers to the 'connecting pattern' Bateson (1979) talks about: 'What pattern connects the crab to the lobster and the orchid to the primrose and all four of them to me? And me to you? And all the six of us to the amoeba in one direction and to the backward schizophrenic in another?'

The logical form founded on the principle of non-contradiction and the succession of time is no longer the most suitable form for thinking of the analytic field, as has been pointed out by the Barangers. In the second clinical example we gave earlier, it would be difficult to identify before and after, as they are at the very least un-decidable. According to the logic of isolated elements, 'buying candles' could be considered a 'property' which A (analyst) and P (patient) enjoy, but one could also say, taking on the concept of 'logical relationship' that 'buying candles' is the relationship that exists between A and P. The same explanatory criterion can be applied to our first clinical example, where analyst and patient make reference to a sole referent – which in that case was not an object but a painting.

In both these examples, the description and the transcription, in assigning a path, a before and after, circumscribe the oppositions within the timeframe of the story and relativise them, so that they form a whole and do not contradict each other. The complementarist theory sees the discrete and the continuous as simultaneously compatible and irreducible to each other. Adopting 'discreteness' undoubtedly produces an economy and utility which lies in the possibility of marking borders: in our case the distinction between observer and observed, analyst and patient appears to be very evident. That is excessively functional. Putting it reductively, we could say that the setting separates patient from patient. But how many times have we seen these boundaries broken down, making us see them as functional limits, forcing us to define other limits and boundaries.

But we think that the principle of complementarity applied to the discrete–continuous pair is useful to the analytic field because of another aspect that appears problematic in psychoanalysis both in theory and in clinical practice, namely what we can call 'events'. A powerful idea is suggested by Kuyk (1977), who lists examples of concepts founded in the discrete and their continuous counterpart and includes the pairing event (discrete) and process (continuous). Moreover in the same chapter he assigns to the continuous the 'process of thought' and 'historical continuity'.

We have been describing analytical events that occur in the space of time immediately before the session partly in order to point out the meaning, which can be extended to other analytic events, of surprise and wonder – the sensation of singularity which seizes us. At the same time or immediately afterwards, faced with events and surprise, we try to give them meaning by placing them in a 'historical continuity' or, according to point of view, we consider them as elements in a structure. In second level working out, which is what we have tried very briefly to do here, we can explain the present dynamics, both in reference to the patient's present life and in connection with the here and now of the transference – the starting point of investigations into historical and structural meaning.

The events are thus inscribed in a process or a structure, but as Bateson (1979) rightly says: 'The ongoing processes of change *feed on the random* [. . .] for the creation of new order, the workings of the random, the plethora of uncommitted alternatives (entropy) is necessary. It is out of the random that organisms collect new mutations . . . This difference is basic for any sort of theorizing behavioural science.'

Morin (1972) points out: 'A science of becoming should explore the necessary relationship between self-generated phenomena (which develop according to an internal logic and lead to events which ensure development) and hetero-generated phenomena, which need to be stimulated by events and accidents to develop.' From this point of view, it is the randomness of the events, the 'accidents' that advance the process of change.

These final albeit brief remarks about the opposition between events and process could lead on to remarks of a theoretical character and a reappraisal of the nature of the conceptual oppositions which have always dominated the scientific universe: being-becoming, part-whole, event-process, etc. With regard to this vast problem, which partly goes beyond the scope of these pages, we would like to make one brief point. The stimulus comes from Ceruti (1983), who asked himself what it meant to assume both poles of these oppositions, without taking them away as oppositions. He argued that this does not necessarily mean reaching synthesis.

According to Varela (1979, quoted by Ceruti): 'We have instead a direct evaluation of how things are put together through our descriptions, without losing sight of the fact that on a different level every "thing" can be seen as a process.' More generally, we can see how the concept of complementarity puts us at a distance from the classical way of understanding dialectics. In the classic (Hegelian) paradigm duality is connected to the idea of polarity, the clash of opposites. The fundamental form of duality of this type is symmetry; both poles belong to the same level. The framework of logic behind this dialectic is negation; the couples are of the form A/non-A.

The point here is that the qualities are represented by the overlapping of levels, whereby one term in the pair emerges out of the other:

> The fundamental form of this duality is asymmetry: both terms extend across levels. The framework of logic which is behind this dialectic is self-reference, that is, pairs of forms: 'thing'/process which leads to the 'thing'. [. . .] When

> we observe natural systems, *we do not in fact find oppositions anywhere unless in the values we wish to carry in them.*

Freud has taught us to discover a *whole* world in a small part – in a lapse, a parapraxis.

So the 'small' events which happen prior to the session can equally well pose the problem of how a part can represent the whole. On this point, Napolitano (1987) says:

> Trained as we are in the recognition of reality, we know that the session is only a small part of the patient's and the analyst's time. Trained as we are to recognise the sense of reality, we know that this part successfully represents the whole. The research conducted on a frontier area contiguous to the spatial-temporal setting raises questions concerning the irruption or dissolution of reality, and in parallel, the irruption or the dissolution of the sense of reality.

If we suppose that the analytic field extends well beyond its known spatial-temporal dimensions, the setting, by fixing borders, becomes the methodological expedient designed to make the field 'discrete'. Some events on the margins point to the possibility of its spatial-temporal extension. We then find ourselves following traces of a vaster field we assume to be continuous (*relationship*) – which could never be grasped as a whole, but only by the creation of further borders and limits.

10

Chiasma

History isn't flexible
like an unbroken link chain.
In any case,
many links don't hold.
History has no before and after,
nothing in it simmers
on a slow flame.[1]

Before the events I am about to relate, two young men had been meeting regularly, four times a week, for four months – engaging, that is, in psychoanalysis. Years later, one of the two, the doctor, recalled little of their first encounter. After finishing his story, the other had asked for 'order'. 'I want more order,' he said. Not that he had appeared to the young doctor to be particularly confused. In fact the doctor had been struck by his rigid comportment, a kindness he found excessive and, above all, his look. A white film covered one eye and gave him a fixed look, while the other eye, still filled with the melancholy of childhood, conveyed great gentleness. He claimed to be a Freudian Marxist long after that period in history had come to an end. He had taken a few exams at the faculty of psychology, found he couldn't go on and then started working in the civil service. The doctor will always remember one thing about their first encounter. He thought, and indeed said to himself: 'This man is going to study', or rather 'I'll make him study.'

The young man exuded this kind of optimism. He was going through one of the rare periods in life when 'order', a deep-seated trust in life and the future, marked his actions and encounters, lending them a tone of hope but also of naivety. About that time, a woman patient who had suffered much in her life had conveyed to him her impression that he had not yet had sufficient dealings with the 'dark side' of life.

Since its inception psychoanalysis has tried to pursue an objectivity and a scientific status that it has never fully achieved, and only recently has it begun to pay attention to the human characteristics of the psychoanalyst. It has never, however, made mention of the period in life when the first psychoanalytic encounter takes place. I think that Mme Sechaheye could only have offered the famous apple at that precise moment in her life – not before, not after, and with no other patient. It is said that other psychiatrists have tried with other apples and other psychotics but with little success.

So the young doctor, faced with that fixed infantile stare, thought to himself: 'He is going to study.' Yet he realised with hindsight that, the signs which might have justified other predictions were clearly present: for example, the sorrowful way the young man lay on the sofa holding his head away from the headrest. Two images – a dream and a memory – remained impressed on the analyst. Images, memories, dreams, eyes: from the very beginning, the 'visual' has been at the centre of the analytic encounter. I suggest that from now on the reader adopt this point of view as well, together of course with any he may discover on his own.

'A book opens, an illustration, a picture inside, a child, a child with a tense face holding his head in his hands . . . it was like a painting,' says the patient. *The Scream*, thinks the doctor, Edvard Munch's *The Scream*.

The patient describes a memory:

> An image often comes to my mind. I was perhaps six years old, I was convalescing. Outside it was raining. I looked out of the window and at that moment I thought, now I have understood. It must have been something very basic. Since then I have on many occasions made an effort to remember what I understood, but I've never succeeded.

The doctor quotes this description at the beginning of one of his first scientific articles as a paradigm of all analytic experience. The two elements that make up all analytic experience came together: memory ('I was six years old') and knowledge ('now I've understood'). This is the question and the enigma which every analysis faces: at the beginning is memory and loss of memory.

History is not made
by those who think about it, nor
by those who are ignorant of it. History
doesn't become manifest, it insists
it detests 'little by little',
it goes neither forwards
nor backwards, it changes platform
and its direction
is not on the timetable.
(*La Storia*, Montale)

That morning he arrived, punctual as always. He stood upright and as usual held a newspaper in his hands; his smile was a slight, involuntary caricature directed at himself and others. Towards the end of the session, he said: 'Last night I dreamt of a ophthalmologist, tall and thin, who was examining my diseased eye with some optical instrument. At the centre, in the chiasma, there was a flame.'

During his adolescence he had seen an ophthalmologist after a herpetic keratitis had left him with a white film over one eye. During that same period his hair had started to fall out as a result of alopecia. Months earlier he had talked about all of this without showing any real emotional involvement; he was a man who suffered no pain.

'Tall and thin' – the young doctor thought about the styleme his patients use to describe him in their dreams. 'And the flame . . .?' he asked. The flame meant nothing to the young man. He changed the subject. Eventually, the doctor tried again. 'What about the flame?'

'I don't know,' said the patient, almost absent-mindedly. 'Perhaps it's a votive flame. The votive flame in front of the photo of my brother, on the bedside table in my parents' bedroom. I saw it at night because I used to sleep in that room.'

'Which brother?' wondered the young doctor. This was the first mention of a brother. He felt suffused by a strange feeling, not sudden anxiety but a sinister, spreading immanent aura, an emotion he often felt in the silence of listening to this patient's dreams.

'Have I never told you about him? I didn't think it was very important. Before I was born, exactly one year before, in fact, my brother died. He was five. It was the period after the war. He was playing with some other children in the village where my grandmother lived.

They touched a bomb and they all died. My brother had the same name as me.'

Pontalis uses the expression 'to lose sight of' to refer to, among other things, the work of mourning which is expressed through the pain of no longer being able to see the lost object. This young man was not in a position to 'lose sight of' his brother.

There is a basic difference between visual perception and field of vision. What is achieved, for example, through painting or the reproduction of a dream is the possibility of rendering the 'invisible' visible, also through visual perception. The dream of the screaming child that holds his head between his hands, the analyst's recollection of the Munch painting, are ways of making the invisible visible.

Let us see what invisible things the dream of the flame allows us to see. In the dream the young man with the damaged eye does not report but recalls the photographic image of his brother. The enigma he faced as he came into the world does not only lie in the unresolved double. The analyst is faced with a flame, not an external flame, an object of visual perception, but an internal flame that follows an optic path and is at the centre of a chiasma, and which could easily be lost sight of. Behind the flame is the invisible hand that has placed it there, the hand of a mother who, in a moment of impossible mourning, put an eternal light in front of the image of a lost child – a gesture that sought to eternalise the moment. Being seen and at the same time not being able to be seen like (for) the other (death) – this is one of the fires that stoke his enigma.

It is impossible now to reconstruct what the doctor felt on hearing the dream. Many things separate me from him, but we do share a lasting fundamental conviction: namely, that the patient carries within him some unconscious knowledge – disguised, disfigured, partially disavowed – which the analyst must decipher and reconstruct together with the patient. 'The pathological factor is not his ignorance in itself, but the root of this ignorance in his *inner resistances*,' argued Freud (1910b: 225).

My previously expressed conviction has resisted the fashion of hermeneutics (with its danger of infinite hermeneusis), radical constructionism and narratology (with its potentially infinite series of analytical narratives). I believe that Freud's formula is still valid when we are in the presence of the hidden knowledge of the hysteric, the obsessive. This knowledge is contained within an unconscious phantasy. But can we talk of 'knowledge' in the presence of meta-historical events, or in the presence of the unresolved content of the other's unconscious (Abraham and Torok)? In what way or in what form can they enter history, become historicised? How can they be represented in transference?

> Archaic experiences have no structure, they have no figurative form. Discourse gives them a name that unifies and concretises them in a totally original way and in a form that doesn't exist in any place in the unconscious of the patient and in no other place in the analytic space through the language that gives them form.

Viderman's formula (1979) doesn't convince me as much now as it once did. I don't believe in the power of language and, unlike Viderman, I put my trust in figuration rather than language. Traces, images. The relationship of the visual with the unconscious is not contingent but essential. 'Art does not reproduce the visible; rather, it makes visible,' said Klee. Pontalis (1977) picks up Klee's point: 'so we have lost what we thought was before us. Perhaps we had never had it, never seen it, *never seen it being born*. The painter's vision, *transference in analysis* gives all of this a locus' (emphasis added).

Again, a place – not a verbal place (as in Viderman) but a place of vision: I have been trying to define this place for some time. Elsewhere, analytic space has been considered 'an apparatus for seeing'; the analytic space seen as 'virtual space', the ideal place for all optical instruments, including the human eye, essential for vision – patient, analyst, theory as reflecting lenses. The analytic space, I concluded, is the ground against which we see the unfolding of events and the worlds of analysis, events and ways which are otherwise invisible.

The patient, with his dream of the flame, indicated to the doctor where to look and what to look at; that was where his malaise lay. The bearer of an enigma, a question, an almost-knowledge that was suspended awaiting transference – not repetition but transference which gives rise to something, which brings into being, which sees. After that dream the eyes of the doctor slowly began to see his patient's failed existence. He had literally put on the clothes of someone else (those discarded by his brother-in-law). He had stopped studying and withdrawn into a civil service office. Files would pile up over time which this new Oblomov was unable to deal with or to close; cordial relations with his office colleagues, dinner at his mother's house. He retreated into his house where he lived alone, a house that was constantly dark, the shutters always broken. He took refuge in fantasy, hidden from the eyes of the world.

The doctor had to curb his inclination to make a connection between his patient's stories and the original double. He felt their fascination but was aware that the man had thrown away his life on this point. He had been taken there by the other, without force, without any apparent drama. Here is another image from his memory: 'I remember that my mother opened a drawer in a chest of drawers. In an old newspaper was wrapped one of my brother's eyes and a lock of his hair.' He had never thought of that memory as being strange or unreal. For his consciousness, before he talked about it with his doctor, it was something that had happened. He had seen his mother, the newspaper, the eye, the hair. He must have been about eight at the time. The doctor necessarily saw this delusional memory in relation to the loss of hair and the keratitis that afflicted the patient during his adolescence.

Talking about screen memory, Gaddini (1977) uses the following image: 'The phenomena which constitute and characterise it may appear to us, through their pathological expression, as on the same level, like the stars in the sky. But as with the stars, they can be on different planes and can represent different moments in a long process.'

We can never know whether false memory came before his keratitis and alopecia or whether, on the other hand, these dramatic events in his adolescence were projected backwards onto a screen of time and fixed in the delusional scene at the age of eight. Or alternatively – and this is the hypothesis I would subscribe to – possibly memory and illness meet, join up, communicate internally in an attempt to establish a relationship of symbolisation, an attempt which in this particular case partially failed. What they try to communicate and to represent is a maternal phantasy or rather the maternal unconscious and its lack of mourning.

Repetition compulsion and deferred action (*après-coup*) are constant forms of a psychic constructivism (and by derivation, of an analytic procedure) that, in fortunate cases, give order and meaning which can be conscious or unconscious and keep the person away from madness. In our case there is an excess that cannot be symbolised and which appears in reality (the hallucination-delusion of false memory) and the body. These excesses are not waste products; they contain fundamental elements of truth for the existence of the person. In *Constructions in Analysis* Freud states:

> The delusions of patients appear to me to be [. . .] attempts at explanation and cure, through it is true that these, under the conditions of a psychosis, can do no more than replace the fragment of reality that is being disavowed in the present by another fragment that had already been disavowed in the remote past [. . .] delusion owes its convincing power to the element of historical truth which it inserts in the place of the rejected reality.
>
> (1937b: 268)

Interestingly, in this passage Freud spoke of a truth that takes the place of a reality. In our case, a false, hallucinated reality contains an inexpressible truth which refers to the phantasy and the maternal unconscious. The opposite also happens: reality is repressed in order to repress the phantasy.

In the middle of the session there is a long silence:

> I don't know, confused and fragmented images of a dream, something vague; . . . I was in the waiting room to your consulting room . . . I remember very little. Like a veil that is torn . . . The door to your studio is ajar, you could just see something on the other side . . . A scene that could be frightening . . . It was as if the scene were repeated twice . . .

Long silence. He begins again to free associate: '. . . Waiting, waiting, expecting . . . pregnancy, but what's that got to do with it . . . the open door . . . who knows?' The young doctor thought of symbolic meanings centring on the analysis and kept quiet. After a while the patient contradicted the doctor's thoughts and spoke instead of a hypothetical reality. 'I don't know, it's vague, shreds of memory. Could my mother have had other pregnancies?'

He came back the next day after talking to his sister. There had been two miscarriages when the patient was in his early adolescence, a year apart. Both times it had happened during the night – painful, dramatic experiences. His mother had come out of the patient's bedroom shouting, there was blood, the half-closed bedroom door, the sister helping the mother. 'Shut up! Don't shout, or else you'll wake him up!' Someone closes the door.

History isn't
the devastating bulldozer they say it is
It leaves underpasses, crypts, holes
and hiding places. There are survivors
History's also benevolent, destroys
as much as it can: overdoing it
Sure
would be better, but history is short
of news, doesn't carry out all its vendettas.
(*La Storia*, Montale)

During that analysis the doctor came face to face with the dark side of life. It was an experience of solitude, at times one of terror, a kind of initiation. The young patient was constantly in danger of 'losing' his life. An eternal student, he had got to the point where either he took an exam or it would be as if he had never started, back to square one. This was a turning point in the analysis. A description of the unfolding of this analysis lies beyond the province of this book. There are far too many levels that have not been described: the father, the sister, a web of internal events and realities, transference and its unwinding. Later, I intend to put forward my hypothesis about the level we are examining here. However, one can only be in agreement with Pontalis when he says that it is always difficult to say, at the end of an analysis, what has happened and, above all, why it has happened. What did the young man get out of it? This is a hard question to answer. On the inside, quite a lot, but there is little one can say about his external life: he started studying again, cleaning up his house, opening the windows, cooking; he became the office cashier.

Looking at this analysis overall, I could say that he got what he was looking for and asked for at our first meeting: 'more order'. He abandoned the analysis some years later, announcing it a very offhand way, between one topic and another: 'I was thinking, that's OK for me. We can stop here.' Occasionally there was a kind of 'unconscious subject' talking in him which had some awareness of his pain and his limitations, an arena that was much wider than his conscious knowledge. The dream of the flame, the dream of the shout were expressions that belonged to that register. The laconic farewell was meant to be understood in all its depth, but he didn't want to let on.

A few months before leaving he had told the doctor he would soon be able to see again with his damaged eye. Some years earlier his eye specialist had told him to let time pass, and eventually the veil might be lifted from his eye. One of his final comments before leaving was: 'I used to have to pretend to be an intellectual in order to exist. Now I can exist without pretending.' He went away and the other never heard anything more about him.

The young doctor, who was slowly becoming a not-so-young doctor, at times found himself thinking of his patient; just fleeting thoughts, wondering how he was, what he was doing with his life. He toyed with the idea of writing something about the experience, but for years did nothing, adducing a series of objections. At first it seemed premature, he needed time to mourn. Later there was the fear of the patient's identity being recognised, although this was extremely unlikely. The fact remained, however, that the plan was repeatedly put off. Some time later he discovered a poem by Eugenio Montale ('History', *La Storia*, 1984), which seemed to him to provide an appropriate framework for the story of the man's life, but even then he let time pass, although he never gave up the idea altogether. He felt it as a commitment that he had made to himself, and secretly to the other.

He was forced to ask himself the question why he felt so tied to someone so different from himself, whose face was now blurred in the eye of his memory. He thought of the destiny of meta-historical events, of twin transference analysed and resolved in analysis, whose continuation and continuity beyond the analysis he happened to experience. He thought of the necessity of events, and for the first time he came to re-evaluate a favourite subject of Gaddini's, the post-analytic process, which as a student he had thought of as abstruse and audacious. Between analyst and patient, during the course of the analysis, there had been involvement and sympathy but also a basic difference not only in roles but also in lifestyles. There had, however, been a signal and a border post they had shared on a stretch of their path – Lietta's shop, in his grandma's village, was at the crossroads between the main road and small road that leads to the crag and the bottom of the valley where the bomb that killed his brother had exploded. Lietta's shop sold a little of everything and in his childhood it had been a safe and protected refuge.

In his dream the topography of that place was broken up and recomposed into a surreal unity. Lietta's shop was in the village, but at the same time, as can only happen in dreams, it was also in Rome, at the intersection of two roads with a large square in the middle. The streets and the square in Rome meant nothing at all to the patient but for the other, the doctor, they were laden with meaning and symbolism. It was the place where his analysis had taken place. The house of his analyst was there, the topography was unmistakable.

There has been a lot of discussion – perhaps even too much discussion – about relationship in analytic circles, and not all of it relevant. Relationship, if the term is still useful, is not revealed at first glance. At times one can see its traces, its underground course, one glimpses its profile when one looks back over a long period. Long periods. The passage of time in life and in analysis is subject to stops and gos, hiccups, expansion, returns. Time continues to ask us questions and we never stop asking ourselves questions about time. Let's try to read its forms in relation to psychic phantasies and structures: the unmoving time of the ideal ego, the zero time of megalomaniac delusions and omnipotence; the creation of the future in the ideal of self – the self follows in future time the realisation of the ideal until death.

Time and its double, we could say. In *The 'Uncanny'*, Freud says that Rank has:

> having gone into the connections which the double has with [. . .] shadows [. . .] with the belief in the soul and with the fear of death [. . .] but he also lets in a flood of light on the surprising evolution of the idea. For the 'double' was originally an insurance against the destruction of the ego, an 'energetic denial of the power of death', as Rank says; and probably the 'immortal' soul was the first 'double' of the body. This invention of doubling [is] a preservaion against extinction [. . .] The same desire led the ancient Egyptians to develop the art of making images of the dead in lasting materials. Such ideas, however, have sprung from the soil of unbounded self-love, from the primary narcissism which dominates the mind of the child and of primitive man. But when this stage has been surmounted, the 'double' reverses its aspect. From having been an assurance of immortality, it becomes the uncanny harbinger of death.
>
> (1919a: 234–235)

The young man's double had never been able to represent an assurance of immortality but had been from the very beginning a dark harbinger of death, of the disappearance or annihilation of self.

Continuing to live in the mind of the other (the doctor) amounted to maintaining in time a benevolent double, the first stage of the double, the stage that had never been established firmly in him before starting analysis: thinking of him, thinking of him as alive, the person whom the mother's unconscious had thought of as death/the dead one.

As time went on and the doctor became aware of his own fading youth, the double started to change and to become an 'uncanny harbinger of death'. Only then, or only now perhaps, the secret pact between those two men began to unravel, and each was restored to his own destiny. The literary artifice which divides up the narrator and two actors is the symbol of this farewell, this separation. This is all I can say.

The symbols arise self-generated from the depths. Language only plays a small part. They mediate between phases of life and analysis. If we insist on decoding them through language, reducing them to hypothetical prime units, this sometimes only serves to destroy their mediating function. At every turning point in life, being is restructured. Different sized faults open up; some make us lose our heads and others form the residue of injuries to body and mind. The analyst and the patient go round these circuits again. They try to restore sense and integrity. In their relationship symbols are created which assume a mediating function. We cannot take it for granted that the analyst will successfully protect these symbols, their formation and development.

I have spent many years reflecting on history and psychoanalysis, looking for the justification of both searching for laws and constants based on Freud and his 'constructions'. I do not know whether this story of mine marks a break with those experiences or rather is continuous with them. As psychoanalysts we are constantly in contact with history, not history with a capital H but intimate secret history far away from the clamour of large-scale history. The difference between the two was evident to Elsa Morante, who made it the premise for her novel, *History* (1974). To quote a passage taken from the Gospel According to Luke: 'You have hidden these things from the wise and understanding, and revealed them to little children.' What is the point, then, of writing a clinical 'history'? It is not simply a question of offering an objectifying, documentary account within the bare framework of a scientific discipline. Our accounts also have value as testimony, if not of redemption, of that secret history which we are privileged enough to have access to. At first we are the activators of this story and later, slowly, we become actors in it. Narration is thus 'an indispensable instrument for calling into question each time the regime of univocity into which closed theoretical and logical systems want to force the manifestation of human life' (Gargani 1987).

Maybe we need to relinquish something, we need to renounce the single method, the unifying theory without, however, abandoning the methodological and theoretical rigour that is innate to man. As long ago as 1966 Foucault said:

> Psychoanalysis cannot be deployed as pure speculative knowledge or as a general theory of man. It cannot span the entire field of representation, attempt to evade its frontiers, or point towards what is more fundamental, in the form of an empirical science constructed on the basis of careful observation; that breakthrough can be made only within the limits of praxis in which it is not only the knowledge we have of man that is involved, but man himself – man together with Death that is at work in his suffering, the Desire that has lost its object, and the language by means of which, through which, his Law is silently articulated.

He argued that all analytic knowledge is linked to a praxis, to the narrowing of the relationship between two individuals, one of whom listens to the language of the other, thus redeeming the desire of the object he has lost (making him understand that he has lost it), and freeing him from the constantly repeated proximity of death (making him understand that one day he will die).

Now, at a distance of many years, one can fully agree with this view and even see it as prophetic, considering the developments and achievements of contemporary psychoanalysis, as long as we don't see the psychoanalyst as 'subject-supposed-to know', who already knows what desire, law and death are even before the adventure of analysis with the patient begins. I go along with Bion when he says that there are two frightened people in the analyst's room: the experience I have described bears witness to this. Again in agreement with Bion I think that we can only analyse what analyst and patient share. Only at the point where their two gazes meet, on the borderline between the visible and the invisible, can we discover a piece of truth. The visible and invisible go together to create a chiasma, or a mesh, as Merleau-Ponty (1993) calls it.

> History scrapes the bottom
> like a torn dragnet

and more than one fish escapes.
Sometimes you meet the ectoplasm
of an escapee, and he doesn't seem particularly happy.
He doesn't know he is outside, nobody told him.
While the others in the bag think
they're freer than him.

(*La Storia*, Montale)

Postscript

What the image represents is its meaning.
But an image cannot illustrate its form of illustration; it exhibits it.
What can be shown cannot be said.

These three aphorisms from Wittgenstein's *Tractatus* (1921) could be taken to indicate my difficulty, my unease, at the moment when I entrust to this brief work the future of research which for the moment is represented through images, metaphors, the scenes of this story. Only a posteriori (this was not my intention) can it be read as a theoretical text with a narrative structure, a 'model' given the form of scenes and images. I shall start to 'say' what the story 'shows'. Chiasmus (or chiasma), comes from the late Latin chiasmus, χιασμος, taken from the name of the letter χ because of its cross-like form. It is a rhetorical form comprising four elements, where the first corresponds to the fourth and the second to the third. More generally speaking, chiasmus is a consistent rhetorical figure that arranges the elements of a proposition in reverse order to those of the previous conceptually related proposition. In most cases, more than syntactic inversion, there is a mutation, or even a reversal of the meaning of the words: 'Being unable to cause might to obey justice, men have made it just to obey might. Unable to strengthen justice, they have justified might' (Pascal). 'It is clear that the arm of criticism cannot replace the criticism of arms' (Marx).

From this brief preamble it is already clear that 'chiasmus' is not foreign to psychoanalysis. It can be found, for example, in the titles of many works by psychoanalysts. At any rate, the very number of these (at times somewhat mannered) titles indicates that psychoanalysis darkly recognises in chiasmus an important aspect both of psychic activity and clinical work. In contemporary philosophy both Heidegger and Merleau-Ponty have used 'chiasmus'. In Heidegger it is not a specific theme although it is clearly important in the different periods and systems of his thought (some examples: 'the question of the truth turns into the truth of the question'; 'the essence of language, the language of essence'). In Merleau-Ponty chiasmus is a central theme in his unfinished work *The Visible and the Invisible* (1993). This work is of particular importance for psychoanalysis (Pontalis was inspired by it when writing his *Losing Sight*, 1988), in that Merleau-Ponty puts seeing, the chiasmus between inside and outside, visible and invisible at the centre of his thinking.[2]

Seeing and saying, vision and rhetoric find themselves at the centre of the discovery of the unconscious starting from *The Interpretation of Dreams*. F. Roustang (1977), making specific reference to the seventh chapter of *Traumdeutung*, explored the psychoanalytic aspects of Freud's style and isolated four recurrent stylistic figures: concatenation, the repetition of words from the end of one paragraph at the beginning of the next; inclusion, repetition of the same words at the beginning and end of a paragraph; pericentre, moving one or more words from the edge of a paragraph to the middle of the next; chiasmus, repetition of words in inverted order ('the desire of dreams' and 'the dream of desire'). In the seventh chapter of *Traumdeutung* the activity of the psychic apparatus is at one and the same time the subject of the style and its object. Form and content are inseparable and, in effect, interchangeable.

According to P. J. Mahony (1987: 119–121), chiasmus in the description given by Roustang is a stylistic figure which remains localised and circumscribed to the primary process. For Mahony, it can be extended; chiasmus is a figure 'whose rich potential has not been fully exploited'. Chiasmus is to be found in *Studies on Hysteria* (1895b), in which Breuer, who wanted to address hysteria along psychological lines, ends up talking about intra-cerebral excitation and Freud, who had started to form physiological and clinical explanations, concluded by admitting that his case studies read like short stories. In *The Future of an Illusion* (Freud 1927), as in other writings, there is a chiasmus (characteristic of his discursive style) between Freud and a hypothetical interlocutor with whom he debates by thesis and antithesis; chiasmus between the 'familiar' and the 'unfamiliar' (the uncanny). Finally Laplanche (1970) in the last pages of *Life and Death in Psychoanalysis*, describes a much broader chiasmus which runs through the whole of Freud:

If the terms of the pairs of opposites, which are constantly present in psychoanalytic thought, are aligned with one another

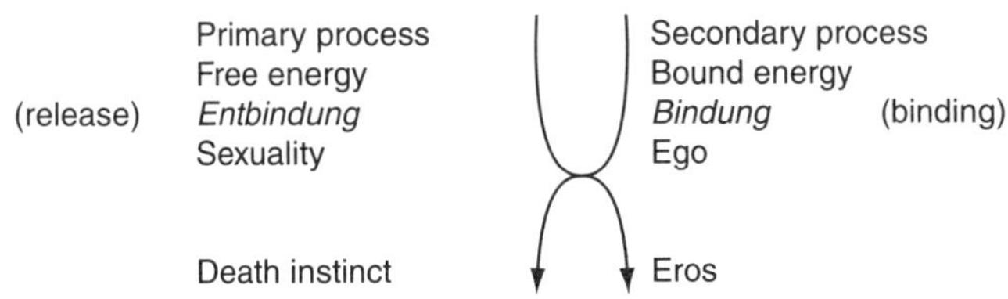

This genealogy is designed in a strange chiasmus, whose enigma we, as Freud's successors, are beginning to decipher.

Chiasmus is often found in our work, even though it is rarely made explicit; there is a reference to it, for example, in Baranes (1996), when he speaks of the psychology and therapy of adolescents. In the present work, in Chapter 9, a chiasmatic figure develops from two opposite and symmetric narrative versions – the analyst's and the patient's – around the theme of the nun. These themes, even though they derive from the patient and the analyst, depart from them and constitute images, scenes and stories which take form, meet, intersect and develop in the 'scenic space' of analysis.

Lionel Trilling called psychoanalysis 'a science of tropes'. Metaphors, metonymies, chiasmuses, points, ellipses, spirals, circles – 'tropes' and 'geometries' of the psychic space and the analytic space – awaiting a specific 'topology' of the analytic field, these geometries are apprehended intuitively in the course of analytic experience, perceived, for example, when our patients get ready to 'leave the stage' of analysis. If we do not go out through the 'temporal windows' of the end of analysis, Laplanche (1987) states that 'we start on a new cycle, a new twist of the spiral'. Flournoy (1985) suggests: 'The analytic field is conceivable only in its *circularity*. The problem of the end of the analysis lies in the necessity to leave this circularity, to come out of it passing from a circular spinning top movement to a circular wheel-shaped movement' (emphasis added).

We might think that there are specific 'typologies' which characterise some analyses and differentiate one analysis from another, but we can also suppose that there are courses of different 'tropes' and 'geometries' at various moments in every single analysis. We know that a metaphor can liberate or imprison. We might suppose that there are different (unconscious) strategies to 'get out of' a metaphor, a spiral, a chiasmus. Leaving the stage is a metaphor I have used to suggest not only the end of the analysis but a substantial aspect of the analytic method, not a specific act so much as a style.

11

Leaving the stage

> it is a melancholy of mine own, compounded of many simples, extracted from many objects, and indeed the sundry contemplation of my travels, in which my often rumination wraps me in a most humorous sadness.
>
> (Shakespeare, *As You Like It*)

Not only analysis but life itself can be seen as a 'multiple-entry scenario': the question is how to enter and leave the stage. *Hilflosigkeit*: we enter the scene of life too early. 'Originary' impotence is the permanent irresolvable condition of existence, but at the same time a potential source of greatness; the inclination to omnipotence and the complementary sensibility to the limit which exposes us to impotence and annihilation.[1] Because of this condition we always need an *other*: another 'object'; another 'environment' (Winnicott); another psychic agency (super-ego and ego ideal). The other, often not recognised as such, must be there at the right moment. There is always a gap, a 'difference', a dissymmetry, which varies in size, between the subject and the other, between the child and the adult, between the patient and the analyst, between the expectation of the object and its fulfilment.

This gap, this 'difference', exposes the human subject to the trauma that, within certain limits, remains inevitable. Thus man always has (albeit unreliable) access to everything that belongs to him and defines him as a human being. According to Laplanche (1987), sexuality is, for example, 'the privileged field of a dialectic between too much and too little, between too early and too late'. This dialectic runs through the patient–analyst relationship, whether it is considered under the heading of 'desire' or of 'need'.

The good mother is not a mother who is always present. Here again, there can be too much and too little. The analyst who identifies with this symbolic figure on the analytic scene must keep to appropriate timing and forms, and there is no fixed criterion valid for every moment and every occasion.

Narcissistic patients, who show more obvious signs of 'empathetic failures', provide fresh confirmation of Nacht's old 'adage' to the effect that 'the analyst treats more by being what he is rather than because of what he knows'. But in order for him to be transformed into an internal function, 'being what he is' should not be confused completely with the 'person' of the analyst. The analyst should let himself be used as a 'self-object', to borrow Kohut's term.

Earlier on, as I talked about the dynamics of transference and took Pontalis as my starting point, I reflected on the analyst as person and character, person and 'psychic person', 'vehicle and receiver'. Transference, as a false nexus, can lead to the analyst saying: 'You don't love (and/or hate) me but another (your mother, your father, etc.).'

Everything is seen in relation to the past and the figures that inhabited the past. But in analysis, sooner or later, the moment comes when it is no longer possible to 'return to sender', to the presumed legitimate 'addressee'. No longer 'there and then' but 'here and now': transference must halt, it must be celebrated in *praesentia*.

The oscillation between presence and absence, person and personage, substitute figure and addressee is what defines the paradox of the analyst's condition. And the paradox is not resolved (reassuringly) by making the obvious point that it depends on the point in time in the analysis, on the type of patient, etc. I am more tempted to think that the state of the analyst means that 'paradox is accepted, tolerated and respected and that it remains unresolved [. . .] one could resolve the paradox, but at the price of losing the value of the paradox itself' (Winnicott 1971).

> The conductor of the orchestra was standing there beside me. I could sense his presence and hear his voice but I couldn't see him. He was rather blurred, I can't say who he was. He showed me my place in the orchestra and at that moment I felt deeply moved: this is it, this is the place I have been seeking for such a long time.

This is the dream of a young musician who had suffered as a result of his father's death during his adolescence. A path had been interrupted and he had had difficulty finding his place in life. The analyst would have looked in vain for his own face in that faceless man, for his own words (or even his own 'accent', his own 'tongue') in the musician's words.

Although that tongue and that face had helped bring about that moment, he had to 'leave the stage' and watch things silently from the auditorium. 'After all, does not the paradox of the analytic situation lie in the fact that another (who is not another but a *neuter* removed from my gaze) is necessary if I want to find myself?' (Pontalis). There must be some reason why we carry on avoiding the gaze of the patient and being a faceless voice.

Transference is shot through with life and death; it arises out of a loss, out of 'losing sight of' the object. Transference is death (to the extent that one starts from the loss of object), and life (because it migrates towards other objects and we know how difficult analysis becomes in the presence of the tyranny of original objects that prevent this migration, this 'betrayal').

After the loss (in some cases the death) of an important person, one tries to replace that person. Even the analyst, the person of the analyst can serve this purpose. But in the long term he does not contribute to the working through of transference.

The young musician, recognising his emptiness, accepts his mourning for his father and takes over his function. For this to happen, the analyst too must accept emptiness and mourning – mourning for his own person, a person who serves as a support (*Anlehnung*) in the meaning that Freud gave this term. Just as drives 'lean on' a function, the sexual drive on self-preservation, transference leans on the person of the analyst while remaining distinguished from it.

Analysis cannot only take place in 'fullness', it is not resolved in continuous interaction, in running through step by step, moment by moment, that which has been done and said. We are at last beginning to open our eyes to the unsustainability, or at least the limits, of this position. We need to make room for the 'void', to create it. Laplanche states:

> A fullness is the positive repetition of behaviours, relationships, infantile imagos. A void is also a repetition but where the repeated infantile relationship finds its enigmatic character and where the imagos are not totally full [. . .] if transference only existed in fullness [. . .] nothing would ever permit us to get out of the fullness [. . .] it is only from that moment when a split

> appears in the heart of the imagos and the transferred scenes [. . .] that transference in fullness can evolve into the transference of the void and be worked through.
>
> (Laplanche 1987: 159–160)

Recognising the presence, the role of the analyst, his person, the interaction with the patient has undoubtedly been an advance on the unsustainable and unacceptable objectivisation of the patient and a defensive presumed neutrality. But it must also be recognised that empathy, hermeneutics, continual interaction may not only open up but also obstruct the analytical space. They may cover and negate the void, the mourning, the absence which also run through the analytical situation.

The analyst can thus be led to negate the most disturbing aspects of his work. He can fall under the illusion of being able to resolve the 'paradox' of his position with continuous 'fullness'. We need to leave an empty space. Our work lives in a 'virtual space' (which we must try to create) that both separates and at the same time connects me to the other, the past to the present, life to death; it is a space that at times is reduced to a line which is traced and then erased and moves elsewhere.

'I live as much with the dead,' said Paul Klee, 'as with the unborn. Somewhat closer to the heart of creation than usual. But not nearly close enough.' Only now, with the help of Klee have I managed to understand Bion's dialogue in his later work (*A Memoir of the Future*, 1975b) with the 'pre-born' and 'unborn'. This is not so much an inclination towards death or a sort of melancholy as a recognition of the complementary nature of presence and absence. Managing to live and cope with one's own and others' solitude (including that of the patient) is the pre-condition for building up that area of the game, that area of creativity, between analyst and patient. According to Winnicott that space makes possible 'memory, reliving, fantasying, dreaming, integrating past, present and future' (1971: 37).

I would not like to be misunderstood: after the disappearance of the analyst's 'supposed knowledge' I don't want to give birth to an analyst's 'supposed creation'. I don't attribute this particular talent to him, his work (*Arbeitung*) is something that has been chosen but also necessitated. We can't do without being analysts or doing analysis. We are subjected to this profound need and fortunately this condition does not entitle us to rise above anybody, least of all the patient. On the last page of *Les Mots*, Sartre states (1964):

> What I like about my madness is that it has safeguarded me, from the very first, against the blandishments of the 'elite'. I have never seen myself as the happy owner of a 'talent': my one concern was to save myself – nothing in my hands and nothing in my pockets – through work and faith. Now at last my unadulterated choice did not set me up above anyone: with neither tools nor equipment I gave my entire self to the task of saving my entire self. If I put away Salvation among the stage properties as impossible, what is left? A whole man, made of all men, worth all of, and anyone of them worth him.

Elsewhere in this book I highlighted the point Freud makes in *The Unconscious* (1915c) that our relationship with our unconscious is a relationship with 'another person', a person partly unknown to us. This image, this metaphor ought to be of fundamental value for the psychoanalyst. We never know ourselves fully. We never completely know who we are. This limit is for me a kind of ethical principle of our work, which is to be applied to us as well as to the patient we are analysing. As Vergine states:

> I think that the limit of our knowledge is a fundamental assumption of knowledge itself; I am also led to think that, if everybody can say something about the other, nobody will ever have the intellectual ability or the right to formulate who is another.
>
> (Vergine 1992: 30)

In the words of Winnicott:

> Psychotherapy is not making clever and apt interpretations; by and large it is a long-term giving the patient back what the patient brings. [. . .] if I do this well enough the patient will find his or her own self, and will be able to exist and feel real. [. . .] Even when our patients do not get cured they are grateful to us for seeing them as they are, and this gives us a satisfaction of a deep kind.
>
> (Winnicott 1971: 158)

There is a profound difference between 'seeing' what someone is like (and the other recognises himself, as in the young musician's dream) and asserting or 'saying' what another is. There can be 'violence' hidden in saying, interpreting (Aulagnier 1975).

The true self can be seen more than uttered in the analyst's room, since for Winnicott (and later for Kahn) the self is secret, private, hidden from the eyes of the world and in part from the eyes of the person himself. It is this core that the analyst must protect and defend. As Calvino states in *Mr Palomar* (1994):

> Each individual is made up of what he has lived and the way he lived it, and no one can take this away from him. Anyone who has lived in suffering is always made of that suffering; if they try to take it away from him, he is no longer himself. [. . .] But you yourself say that my illness is probably linked to my situation and to my destiny. You can't change that, so how do you expect to help me?

We also know Freud's famous reply (on the last page of *Studies of Hysteria*) to his hypothetical patient:

> No doubt fate would find it easier than I do to relieve you of your illness. But you will be able to convince yourself that much will be gained if we succeed in transforming your hysterical misery into ordinary unhappiness.
>
> (Freud 1895b: 305)

We are now back again with the analyst's project and his ethics – the starting point of our investigations. Although our project and our ethics start from Freud they depart from his pessimism.

The analyst's ethics forces him to reject what seems like a fact, someone 'who has always been like that', determinism, the fatality of destiny, but it also forces him to protect and respect the identity of the patient without distorting him, without wanting to treat him at all costs. Relieving the patient from suffering and allowing him to rediscover his own destiny, his own 'idiom' (Bollas 1989) and not the destiny that has been imposed on him is a task that is both ambitious and humble at the same time. Even though it has rarely been made explicit, the subject of destiny (the word itself appears in the title of this book) runs through and guides my research – this journey that is now nearing its conclusion.

Before leaving the stage, I have no last message. I am aware that the narrative and theoretical fabric of this book have not produced a unified and coherent text(ure) for the various topics we have examined, each of which could have been explored on its own. I am not convinced that coherence is always a virtue; it is better to contradict than to repeat yourself. Any research involves 'erring', in the sense that Breton gives the term – travelling without a fixed destination, but equally, falling into error, making mistakes, contradicting yourself. The scientific enterprise, and on a broader scale, the human enterprise is to err; error always has to be taken into account.

There remains a split between the first part of this book, where the focus is on 'psychic reality', and the latter part, which deals with the 'interpsychic'. This split corresponds basically to my vision. Between these two realities lies the virtual space of analysis. I am not troubled by the thought that I haven't been able to propose a unified and conclusive theory. I am comforted by Pontalis (1977: 131) who ironically argues: 'Like all apparatuses, the theoretical apparatus gains by not functioning well.'

As I am now about to turn the last page, I find myself once again 'at the point we started from', faced with those 'fundamental questions that are peculiar to each analyst [. . .] [which] designate the point both of resistance and fascination that marks his relationship with analytic theory' (Aulagnier 1975).

For many years this 'point of resistance and fascination' was for me the subject of *constructions*. I measured both myself and my patients, their pasts and their destinies, against it.

For me the pairing and the opposition between construction and reconstruction has represented the meaning of analysis which has been determined by history, its constraints and limits, but which is also propelled by a creative tension to surmount those constraints and those limits. The Old German term *baun* unites the meanings of *bauen* (to construct) *wohnen* (to live) and *sein* (to be).[2] The expression *ich baue* (I build) also means *ich bin* (I am). In Old German the same word indicates remaining, living but also, in a parallel sense, being and constructing. Surely this is the meaning and purpose of our acts and our words, our writing and our living?

Notes

Foreword

1 'Everything goes back to the reproduction of scenes, some of which can be arrived at directly, but others always by way of phantasies set up in front of them. The phantasies are derived from things that have been *heard* but understood *subsequently* and all their material is, of course, genuine. They are protective structures, sublimations of the facts, embellishments of them, and at the same time serve for self-exoneration. Their precipitating origin is perhaps from masturbation phantasies. A second important piece of insight tells me that the psychical structures which, in hysteria, are affected by repression are not in reality memories – since no one indulges in mnemic activity without a motive – but *impulses***3** which arise from the primal scenes' (Freud 1897. Letter 611 from Extract from the Fliess Papers, *SE*, Vol 1, 247).

2 See for example Antonino Ferro's books in this New Library of Psychoanalysis series (see pp. iii–v).

1 Turning over a new leaf

1 The Italian edition of the complete works of Freud, *Opere di Sigmund Freud* (C. L. Musatti, Ed. and Trans., Torino: Boringhieri, 1966–1980) dates 'From the History of an Infantile Neurosis' as 1914, whereas in the *Standard Edition of the Complete Psychological Works of Sigmund Freud* (J. Strachey, Ed. and Trans., London: Hogarth Press, 1953–1974) the same paper is reported with the date 1918.

2 Material reality, historical reality, psychic reality

1 The Italian edition of the complete works of Freud, *Opere di Sigmund Freud* (C. L. Musatti, Ed. and Trans., Torino: Boringhieri, 1966–1980) dates 'From the History of an Infantile Neurosis' as 1914,whereas in the *Standard Edition of the Complete Psychological Works of Sigmund Freud* (J. Strachey, Ed. and Trans., London: Hogarth Press, 1953–1974) the same paper is reported with the date 1918.

2 In 1911 Freud was one of the signatories, together with Einstein, David Hilbert, Joseph Petzoldt, Georg Helm, Felix Klein and others, of a manifesto, drawn up partly by Mach, to promote the foundation of a society of positivist philosophy. This has emerged from a recently discovered document (Henneck, *Nochmals über Einstein und Mach*) and been reported by Holton (1973).

3 Maryse Choisy's testimony can be found in Albano (1987).

4 I am indebted to J. M. Pré-Lavarrière and C. Rabant for the lexical and conceptual research they carried out on *Constructions in Analysis*, published in *Patio*, 'Constructions dans l'analyse et crise de la langue', 1985, Editions de l'Eclat.

3 Psychoanalysis and history: an interminable dispute

1 'What we initially call history is nothing more than a story. It all starts with the window of a *legend* [. . .] The term "history" oscillates between two poles: the history which is told (*Historie*) and the history which is done (*Geschichte*)' (De Certeau 1975: 303). In Freud there is an ongoing comparison between the formation of legends, ancient historiography (which hides the true origins of a people) and the patient's defensive constructions with regard to his own past. Some examples: *The Psychopathology of Everyday Life* (1901: 46); *Notes upon a Case of Obsessional Neurosis* (1909); *Leonardo da Vinci and a Memory of his Childhood* (1910a: 82–3).

2 The various schools of psychoanalysis can be distinguished according to the varying importance they assign to the biological and cultural organising principles. We are in debt to the French school for having pointed out the importance of structures of kinship and language. Conversely there is a complete strand of psychoanalysis which started from Bowlby and ended with the present Infant Research which implicitly or explicitly assigns overriding importance to biology. Most of this research is carried out with great rigour and pays particular attention to early aspects of mental functioning but, as M.L. Mascagni rightly points out when speaking of Lichtenberg, it amounts to the 'irremediably ethological translation of the language of psychoanalysis'.

3 The idea of historical as opposed to material truth comes out repeatedly during this period. See Freud's letter to Arnold Zweig dated 11 March 1934.

4 Hempel also thought about psychoanalysis. In *Aspects of Scientific Explanation, and other Essays in the Philosophy of Science* Hempel analysed the explanation Freud gave in *The Psychopathology of Everyday Life* (1901: 116–117) for a lapse of his. He had by mistake written the date of 20 October 'bracketed under the correct date of the month of September'. Freud's interpretation was that this expressed a wish to bring forward the moment when the patient was due to visit him (the patient had already announced his visit for 20 October in a letter). Freud was trying to cope with the financial anxieties of returning from the holidays with little prospect of work.

Hempel thinks this explanation partial:

> In other words, the *explanans* does not imply, and hence does not fully explain, that this particular lapse, let us call it *s*, made by Freud on this occasion, falls into the restricted category, let us call it *W*, of acts which consists in writing the words 'Thursday 20th October'; rather the *explanans* only implies that *s* falls into a broader category, let us call it *F*, which includes *W* as a particular sub-class, and which consists of all acts which would express and symbolically satisfy *Freud's unconscious desire in one way or another.* The argument that we are examining could be called a partial explanation; it offers a complete or conclusive motivation to expect that *s* is a member of *F* and, since *W* is a sub-class of *F*, it indicates that the *explanandum*, that is, *s* which is included in *W*, agrees with or confirms what one must expect on the basis of the *explanans*.
>
> (quoted in Lavagetto 1985: 218–219)

As Lavagetto points out (1985: 248) when commenting on this passage, Hempel's conclusions do not amount to a disavowal that 'partial explanations are also founded on laws nor do they cancel the value of these laws [. . .] it is worth asking oneself whether partial explanations are not the only ones available in the field of human sciences and if this is not due to the specific nature of events'.

5 Freud had recourse to the concept of primal phantasies on various occasions in his work: see *Introductory Lectures on Psychoanalysis* (1916: 370–371); also in the case of the Wolf Man (1918: 97, 119–120) primal phantasies were central to his thinking.

6 *Kairos* is an ancient Greek word meaning the right or opportune moment. It is now used in theology to describe the qualitative form of time. Lysippus and artists of the Hellenistic period depicted *kairos*

as a winged young man in the full vigour of his youth ready to spring into action to capture the fleeting moment. In the fourth century BC Callistratos wrote: 'The lock of hair on his forehead indicated that while he is easy to catch as he approaches, yet, when he has passed by, the moment of action has likewise expired, and that, if opportunity (*kairos*) is neglected, it cannot be recovered.' Extensive documentation on *kairos* can be found in *Lisippo, l'arte e la fortuna*, Fabbri Editore 1995, the catalogue accompanying the exhibition held in Rome that same year.

4 Psychoanalysis and narrative: a controversial relationship

1 It was Meltzer's *The Psychoanalytic Process* (1967) that brought the term process to the fore and expanded it, and for a long time it stood for the analytic experience *tout court*. Meltzer set up an isomorphism between the structure of the mind and the nature of the psychoanalytic process which was considered a 'natural' product of the former. The process was described in terms of a sequence and order which was also 'natural' and which was deduced from the sequence of child development. There was thus an analogy (which went beyond a simple metaphor) between the model of treatment and the model of child growth. It later became clear that this – essentially Kleinian – model could not be considered natural, that is, objective and unchangeable, as it was like all models historically determined and has since been subjected to profound criticism by recent research on child development. But this also makes us cautious about research which in its turn can, in the most ingenuous formulations, propose data observed as objective and unchallengeable. We need to consider that all concepts based on supposed 'naturalness' can be strongly deontic. We deduce a deontology from an underlying ontology, a realistic ontology which conceives knowledge as the discovery of the objective laws of nature. A deontology founded on such an ontology tends to derive its imperatives and prescriptive propositions from observational propositions. In this way an often cryptic theory of values tries to impose itself prescriptively because it claims to be a deontology based not only on the contingency of subjective preferences or research traditions but on the rationality of a natural order (Zolo 1988).

2 (*The Question of Lay Analysis*, 1926b: 248): 'For we do not consider it at all desirable for psycho-analysis to be swallowed up by medicine and to find its last resting-place in a text-book of psychiatry under the heading 'Methods of Treatment', alongside of procedures such as hypnotic suggestion, autosuggestion, and persuasion, which, born from our ignorance, have to thank the laziness and cowardice of mankind for

their short-lived effects. It deserves a better fate and, it may be hoped, will meet with one. As a 'depth-psychology', a theory of the mental unconscious, it can become indispensable to all the sciences which are concerned with the evolution of human civilization and its major institutions such as art, religion and the social order [. . .] The use of analysis for the treatment of the neuroses is only one of its applications; the future will perhaps show that it is not the most important one. In any case it would be wrong to sacrifice all the other applications to this single one'. It must have been one of his constant concerns at the time, for two years later (22 April 1928) he wrote to Ferenczi (Jones 1953–57): 'The internal development of psychoanalysis, contrary to my intentions, is drifting everywhere further from that practiced by laymen, to become a medical specialty, and I consider that to be fatal for its future!'

3 Steven Marcus (1976) was of the same opinion. He considered Dora (together with other Freud case studies) a new literary genre in which the narrative contains analysis and interpretation. In his view, the unfolding of the story reveals to the attentive reader that the main character is not Dora but Freud himself – the narrator and at the same time the archaeologist of psychic structures.

4 I am using the distinction made by Laplanche (1987) between *Erfahrung, Erlebnis* (in which the object disappears in the subject) and *Experiment* (in which the subject disappears in the object).

5 The crisis of history and the creation of 'analytical space'

1 'And just as divine truth is what God orders and produces as He comes to know it, so human truth is what man arranges and makes as he knows it. In this way knowledge is cognition of the genus or mode by which a thing is made, and by means of which, as the mind comes to know the mode, because it arranges the elements, it makes the thing.' Gianbattista Vico (quoted by von Glaserfeld 1981), together with Kant, Hume and Dilthey, can be considered as one of the precursors of today's constructionism: a movement of thought which can, however, be traced back to the Pre-Socratics who were the first, at the dawn of western thought, to have raised the question of the relationship between mind and world. Does the world we know exist as such independently of the thought that thinks and creates it? Common sense, which we know is often fallacious, tells us that what we know is what really exists: the knowledge of how things really are. This way of seeing things presupposes a thought that reflects, that reproduces reality (as we have seen, we can find this point of view in Freud's thinking, at least in part of it). According to constructionism, however, our vision of reality is not a

true image of what we find outside ourselves. So-called reality is a 'construction' of those who believe they have discovered it; more than a discovery, then, it is an 'invention' (Watzlawick 1984). Constructionism asks questions about the most radical problems of knowledge, both ontological and epistemological: it does not so much investigate what is known (the ontological problem) or only how it is known (the epistemological problem) but rather it interrogates itself on how reality itself is constructed – and in its more radical version, how reality is invented.

In the twentieth century, thinkers such as Husserl, Wittgenstein, Piaget, Schrödinger and Heisenberg are among the most significant representatives of this complex epistemological movement. More specifically, by 'philosophical constructivism' we mean an epistemological current present in Germany in the 1960s and 1970s, whose exponents include F. Kambastel, J. Mittelstrass, P. Lorenzen and Kuno Lorenz. Philosophical constructivism tries to re-found general non-contingent propositions (for example, the principle of causality, traditionally considered to be necessary). These propositions are the linguistic formulation of rules that are tacitly accepted in a community. Philosophical constructivism accepts and extends the ideas of mathematical constructivism to be found in L. Brouwer, who emphasises the constructed character of mathematical entities. Contemporary constructivism moves out of the mono-disciplinary radius and traverses other fields, other sciences, including linguistic, historical, anthropological, biological and cybernetic (to mention only a few). A useful reference work is *The Invented Reality* (1984), edited by P. Watzlawick, which brings together articles by R. Breuer, G. Elster, H. von Foerster, E. von Glaserfeld, R. Redl and F. Varela. The constructivist point of view in the field of biology, for example, suggests a reflection on biological and cognitive adaptation, not in terms of an environment that conditions biological structures (progressive optimisation of correspondence with the environment), but rather as an active response by the organism to environmental 'constraints'; the organism thus constructs its own reality inside so-called constraints, creating its own viability (Varela 1979). (Elsewhere in this book we have made use of Varela's constructivist concepts.)

In the sociological field, social constructivism is the current of thought (embodied in American sociologists such as A. Schultz, B. Berger, T. Luckmann and E. Goffman, who is very well known in Italy and was an important influence on Basaglia and Italian antipsychiatry) which tends to emphasise the role of 'social constriction' (which, they argue, produces constraints and oppositions typical of associated life; well-known examples include rigid male–female roles, sanity–madness). A significant thinker is T. Luckmann, a student of A. Schultz's, who together with B. Berger published *Reality as a Social Construction* (1966), which presented Weber's point of view (society as the product of social action) and Durkheim's (social events are external and coercive vis-à-vis the individual) as complementary, going on to propose a process whereby society is constructed around original attributions of meaning, which are subsequently institutionalised in social interaction.

In psychoanalysis, I. Z. Hoffmann (1991–1992) proposes the so-called 'new paradigm' of 'social constructivism'. Hoffmann's thoughts point to different epistemological and theoretical–clinical problems in the analytic situation. As we cannot go any further into this field for reasons of spaces, let us point out a few: the difference between positivism and constructivism, authenticity in psychoanalysis, the paradox of the analytic situation, the problem of choosing between a uni- and bi-personal theory. We can deduce from the fact that T. Luckmann was cited in Hoffmann's works that this author was one of the sources of inspiration for Hoffmann's concepts and terminology. And it is precisely the terminology which causes some perplexity. He uses the word 'social' to refer to the reciprocal interaction between the analyst and the patient: 'The term social has the connotation of participation and interpersonal influence' (1991: 78). It is difficult to understand why this interaction (in which analyst and patient 'construct' meanings) should be called 'social' (in society, constructed meanings are still institutionalised). This term confuses rather than clarifies Hoffmann's arguments. Only in a general and non-specific sense do analyst and patient constitute a 'social' interaction. There is a specificity in the 'analytic field' which needs to be distinguished from 'society' (with which the analytic field obviously cannot be in relation) – a 'society' which however has its own laws, 'constrictions' and 'constructions' investigated by the social constructivism of Luckmann, Goffman and Schultz. What's more, the term 'new paradigm', which is among the most often abused expressions in recent psychoanalysis, does not seem to be appropriate. Hoffmann (1992: 288) says that he uses the term 'paradigm' in an 'informal' sense, as a synonym for 'model' or 'point of view'. But why then use such a weighty term as paradigm? 'Paradigm', 'model' and 'point of view' are three very different terms.

In conclusion, we think that there should be a wide and deep discussion about constructivism in psychoanalysis. The constructivist point of view opens up broad prospects but we also need to know how to recognise its limits. In the mathematical field, for example, according to Kuyk (1977: 157): 'Brouwer's constructivism ran the risk of solipsism and obscurantism.' Constructivism is a broad field and certainly not new. It encompasses some radical points of view (von Glaserfeld) and other more moderate ones which take into account the influence of reality on the mind's perception of it. In an earlier chapter we described two aspects or functions of the mind, one delegated to the perception of reality, the other to its creation. We consider these to be complementary functions. We used constructivism as an important theoretical support when dealing with the mind–reality relation (Chianese 1988) in the construction of a theory. We referred to 'repetition compulsion and *après-coup*' (Chianese 1993) to link constructivism to the specific language of psychoanalysis and connected it to *topoi* that are in our view central to psychoanalytic clinical practice.

2 The Italian edition of the complete works of Freud, *Opere di Sigmund Freud* (C. L. Musatti, Ed. and Trans., Torino: Boringhieri, 1966–1980) dates 'From the History of an Infantile Neurosis' as 1914, whereas in the *Standard Edition of the Complete Psychological Works of Sigmund Freud* (J. Strachey, Ed. and Trans., London: Hogarth Press, 1953–1974) the same paper is reported with the date 1918.

3 Theory lives on a paradox. It exists as a body of doctrine with its own statutes and laws and also exists independently of the subjects who in their theorising must make reference to these common rules and laws. This is the fundamental function of theory: to protect against theoretical solipsism that can reach the point of delusion. But theory is embodied in the subject, in our case the analyst. It is the object of his cathectic drive, his transference. In it the analyst places (to quote an expression from Einstein) 'the centre of gravity of his own emotional life'. It is this dual aspect of theory that lies behind the contradiction we see in analytic circles: theory is considered both a cold and glittering show that gets in the way of clinical work and a constant object of conflict, tension and passion.

7 On the traces of countertransference

1 In *The Analysis of the Self* (Kohut 1971) countertransference was seen primarily in connection with the residual narcissistic disturbances of the analyst which might interfere with the development and analysis of the transference of the object-self. Again in *How does Psychoanalysis Work?* (1984) Kohut comes back to countertransference and argues that if we want to see clearly, we must keep the surfaces of our magnifying glasses clean. In particular, we must recognise our countertransference and thus attenuate the influence of factors which distort the precision of our communications, on the part of the analysand and his personality. Some post-Kohutians have critically revised Kohut's thinking. Donna M. Orange (1994: 250–51) maintains that countertransference in the broadest sense of the term is essential to empathy; it is a necessary condition for empathy and therefore has an important place in the psychology of self.

In our view the opposition between empathy and countertransference remains. Indeed Orange suggests renaming the countertransference which facilitates empathy as 'co-transference' and leaving the term countertransference to apply to the emotive memories of the analyst which interfere with his empathetic understanding and optimal ability to respond.

8 Italian landscape

1 Considering the importance of the Barangers' book, it is worth looking at it more closely, in particular at the article (written at the beginning of the 1960s) entitled 'The Analytic Situation as a Dynamic Field', which embodies the heart of their theory. The model is introduced as follows: 'The analytic situation must therefore be formulated [. . .] as a situation of two people inextricably connected and complementary. The members of this pair are not mutually intelligible inside this situation without each other [. . .] The analytic situation has its own spatial and temporal structure [. . .] force lines and lines of development' (pp. 28–29). The Barangers then go on to describe the characteristics of the analytic field and the (personal, spatial and temporal) ambiguity of the analytic situation. Basing themselves on Isaac's concept of unconscious phantasy they put forward the concept of 'couple phantasies' fed by both partners in the analytic situation, and describe the 'points of emergence' of these phantasies in the development of the analytic process. They introduce the concept of a 'bastion' of resistance. These are just some of the numerous, original ideas advanced by the Barangers.

I would like to reflect on two ideas which in my view remain problematic: the concept of person and the mechanism of projective identification, which represents, in their view, the basic link between the two people (the analyst and the patient). The Barangers see the 'bi-personal psycho-therapeutic relation' as the basic configuration, explaining that this relation is 'bi-personal on a simply perceptual level [. . .] a background against which tri- and multi-personal structures are made and unmade'. Despite this premise and delimitation, the concept of 'person' seems to me to be too binding and conceptually problematic, too strong a bond in view of the wavering, the plurality, the heterogeneity, the non-personal phantasies, the partial objects, etc. that characterise the analytic field. The concept of projective identification, borrowed from individual psychology, is ill-suited to represent a field situation which is supposed to be regulated by transpersonal mechanisms. I believe that the Barangers are, however, conscious of this. Indeed they say that 'obtaining from the bi-personal situation a theoretical reconstruction of the case in uni-personal terms by definition and then imagining that one can regulate the bi-personal situation according to this reduced and impoverished scheme is a true paradox'. I believe that work on the analytic relationship and situation is still static and caught up in this paradox.

Coming back to projective identification, there is not enough time or space here to talk about this concept in depth, which like many analytic concepts has been subjected to 'entropy' all too soon: its use has extended and impoverished it. Turillazzi Manfredi (1994) has dedicated two chapters to this question in *Le certezze perdute della psicoanalisi clinica* [*The Lost Certainties of Clinical Psychoanlysis*]. In 1985 Di Chiara and Flegenheimer dedicated a long, in-depth historical-critical paper to the concept of projective identification. As a guide, here is the original definition as given by Klein: 'Mechanism which [. . .] consists in the phantasied projection of split-off parts of the subject's own self – or even his whole self (not just partial bad objects) – into the interior of the mother's body, so as to injure and control the mother from within' Laplanche and Pontalis (1967: 356). In this form it is ill-suited to represent a relationship between two people who are distinct and recognised as such. On the contrary, it is a mechanism of the alienation of the relationship between two people and the alienation of the individual. It is no accident that Klein and Rivière invoke projective identification in referring to phenomena of 'de-personalisation'. Despite these objections, the Barangers' contribution is in my view of remarkable importance. I share their view of the field as a space of phantasies, of representations rather than interaction. There is methodological rigour to their approach: theirs is not an attempt to translate psychoanalytical terminology into a different lexis. It is rather a respect (neither sacred nor formal) for the foundations of psychoanalysis, such as the unconscious, *après-coup,* etc; a valuable reminder of how it is possible to bring about modifications in the fabric of psychoanalysis without impairing the foundations of the discipline.

9 'A work by a single author with two heads and a double look'

1 Comment by L. Aragon on *Magnetic Fields*, text written by Breton and Soupault, the result of automatic writing.

2 This type of reading is called 'paragrammatic' by Kristeva (1969) and she applies it to poetic language. I felt justified in using the term even though I am aware of the difference between the signifying practices of poetry and analysis.

3 There are two studies that we have taken into particular account for this description: (a) 'The structure of myths' by Lévi-Strauss (1958, *Structural Anthropology*); (b) 'Project outline for a study of the analytic relationship' by Ferrari and Garroni (1979).

4 The concepts of 'continuous' and 'discrete' are used in a broad sense. The continuous represents that which lasts in time and/or is composed of non-separate parts which are not exhausted in the division; the qualities of the concept of the 'discrete' are isolation, separability and finite divisibility. A mathematical example is the set of entire natural numbers between each of which there is a leap. For these concepts, see Kuyk (1977, *The Discrete and the Continuous*).

10 Chiasma

1 I shall in the course of this account borrow some lines from the poem *La Storia* by Eugenio Montale, a poem Barale was particularly fond of and which he referred to in two of his books (Barale and Ucelli 1992, Barale, 1996).

2 According to Merleau-Ponty, the world is 'visible', but not for this reason compact and stable. The 'visible' is unstable; the 'invisible' opens up in the world and is dug out of the visible. The invisible, then, is not another dimension opposed to the visible, a dimension which can lead to the irrational, the religious, the mystical; it lives in the visible, is inscribed as a 'cavity' in the fabric of the visible. The chiasmus between visible and invisible is connected to language, to the words we use to designate the visible and the invisible. Merleau-Ponty reflects on the word 'see' and says that we need to distinguish between 'gaze' and 'sight'. Sight is something external, even though we have always supposed that it was something internal (optical, psychological). Internal and external are for Merleau-Ponty always interwoven into a single phenomenon and this gives us a measure of the modernity, the topicality of his thinking. Merleau-Ponty's speculation influenced Lacan (one need only think of the 'mirror stage', the dynamic of seeing and being seen), Foucault, Deleuze, Derrida and Pontalis, who dedicated his *Losing Sight* to Merleau-Ponty. A reading of *The Visible and the Invisible* (1993) can be useful in rethinking the problems of seeing in psychoanalysis. Just to mention some points: the analyst is always in contact with the 'invisible', with invisible objects, so how is it possible to make them visible? What devices are most appropriate? What does 'seeing' mean in psychoanalysis? What difference is there between 'seeing' and 'observing'? How are internal and external related? The list could on.

11 Leaving the stage

1 This is how the physicist Robert Oppenheimer (1953), one of the 'fathers' of the atom bomb, described the 'complementary' nature of the human condition: 'The wealth and variety of the natural sciences taken

as a whole, the more familiar, yet still strange and far wider wealth of the life of the human spirit, enriched by complementary, not-at-once compatible ways, irreducible one to the other, have a greater harmony. They are the elements of man's sorrow and his splendour, his frailty and his power, his death, his passing and his undying deeds.'

2 These thoughts about the term *baun* come from Heidegger and are mentioned by Gargani (1987).

Bibliography

Abraham, N. and Torok, M. (1987) *The Shell and the Kernel*, Chicago: University of Chicago Press, 1994.

Albano, L. (ed.) (1987) *Il divano di Freud. Memorie e ricordi dei pazienti di Sigmund Freud*, Parma: Pratiche.

Anthi, R. (1983) 'Reconstruction of preverbal experiences', *Journal of the American Psychoanalytic Association*, 31: 3–32.

Anzieu, D. (1975) *Freud's Self-Analysis*, Madison, CT: International Universities Press, 1976.

Arlow, J.A. (1991) 'Methodology and reconstruction', *Psychoanalytic Quarterly*, 60: 539–563.

Artaud, A. (1958) *The Theatre and its Double*, New York: Grove Press.

Assoun, P.L. (1981) *Introduzione all'epistemologia freudiana*, Rome: Theoria, 1988.

Aulagnier, P. (1964) 'Remarques sur la structure psychotique', in P. Aulagnier *Un interprete en quete de sense*, Paris: Ramsay, 1986.

—— (1969) 'Societes de psychanalyse et psychanaliste de societe', *Topique*, 1: 7–46.

—— (1970) 'Un probleme actuel: les constructions psychoanalytiques', in P. Aulagnier *Un interprete en quete de sense*, Paris: Ramsay, 1986.

—— (1975) *The Violence of Interpretation. From Pictogram to Statement*, London: Routledge, 2001.

—— (1984) *L'apprenti-historien et le maftre-sorcier*, Paris: PUF.

Austin, J.L. (1975) *How to Do Things with Words*, Cambridge: Harvard University Press.

Bachelard, G. (1978) *The Formation of the Scientific Mind*, Manchester: Clinamen Press, 2001.

Bakan, D. (1958) *Sigmund Freud and the Jewish Mystical Tradition*, London: Free Association Books, 1990.

Balsamo, M. and Napolitano, F. (1994) *Costruire e Ricostruire* [*Constructing and Reconstructing*], Rome: Borla.

Barale, F. (1990) 'Riflessioni a partire dal Mosè: Trauma e storia dall'ultimo Freud a noi', *Rivista di Psicoanalisi* 4: 897–921.

—— (1996) ' "Si prega di chiudere gli/uno occhi(o)". Appunti su agire e ricordare', *Rivista di Psicoanalisi*, 3: 425–454.

Barale F. and Ferro A. (1992) 'Reazioni terapeutiche negative e microfratture della comunicazione analitica', in L. Nissim Momigliano and A. Robutti (eds) *L'esperienza condivisa. Saggi sulla relazione analitica*, Milan: Cortina.

Barale, F. and Ucelli, S. (1992) 'Il racconto della storia e lo strato roccioso della memoria', *Gli Argonauti*, 52: 35–45.

Baranes, J.J. (1993) 'Diventare se stessi: Vicissitudini e statuto del transgenerazionale', in R. Kaës, H. Faimberg, M. Enriquez and J.-J. Baranes *Trasmissione della vita psichica tra generazioni*, Rome: Borla, 1995.

—— (1996, 30 March) *Temporalita. E funzionamento psichico in adolescenza*, paper presented at the Second Congress on Child Neuropsychiatry, Rome.

Baranger, W. and Baranger, M. (1969) *La situazione psicoanalitica come campo bipersonale* [*The Psychoanalytical Situation as a Bi-personal Field*], Milan: Cortina, 1990.

Bartolomei, G. (1972a) 'Soggettivita e obiettivita nell'ermeneutica psicoanalitica. Un motivo di riflessione per lo storico', *Nuova Rivista Storica.*

—— (1972b) 'Psicoanalisi e storiografia: prospettive per un dibattito', *Nuova Rivista Storica.*

Bateson, G. (1979) *Mind and Nature. A Necessary Unity*, Cresskill, NJ: Hampton Press, 2002.

Becker, C. (1958) *Detachment and the Writing of History*, Ithaca: Cornell University Press.

Benveniste, E. (1956) 'Remarques sur la fonction du langage dans la decouverte freudienne', *Psychoanalyse*, 1: 1–15.

—— (1966) *Problems in General Linguistics*, Miami: University of Miami Press, 1973.

Berger, P.L. and Luckmann, T. (1966) *La realtà come costruzione sociale* [*Reality as a Social Construction*], Bologna: IL Mulino, 1969.

Bertalanffy, L. Von (1968) *General System Theory*, New York: George Braziller.

Besancon, A. (1971) *Storia e psicoanalisi*, Naples: Guida, 1975.

Bezoari, M. (1995, 8 March 1996) *Funzioni e disfunzioni del campo analitico*, paper presented at the Rome Psychoanalytic Centre, Rome, Italy.

Bezoari, M. and Ferro, A. (1992) 'Percorsi nel campo bipersonale dell'analisi. Dal gioco delle parti alle trasformazioni di coppia', in L. Nissim Momigliano and A. Robutti (eds) *L'esperienza condivisa. Saggi sulla relazione analitica*, Milan: Cortina.

Bion, W.R. (1962) *Learning from Experience*, London: Heinemann.
—— (1975a) *Two Papers: The Grid and Caesura*, London: Karnac, 1989.
—— (1975b) *A Memoir of the Future: The Dream*, London: Ronald Harris Educational Trust, 1993.
Blum, H.P. (1994) *Reconstruction in Psychoanalysis*, Madison, CT: International Universities Press.
Bodei, R. (1979) 'Comprendere, modificarsi. Modelli e prospettive di razionalita trasformatrice', in *Crisi della ragione*, Turin: Einaudi.
Boesky, D. (1990) 'The psychoanalytic process and its components', *Psychoanalysis Quarterly*, 59: 550–584.
Bollas, C. (1988, 24 June) *La funzione multipla dello psicoanalista: la regressione nel controtransfert*, paper presented at the Eleventh Congress on Child Neuropsychiatry, Rome, Italy.
—— (1989) *Forces of Destiny*, London: Free Association Books, 1991.
Bolognini, S. (2002) '*Costruzioni e campo analitico. Storia, scene e destino* [*Constructions and the Analytic Field. History, Scenes and Fate*]: Domenico Chianese. Rome: Borla. 1997, p. 267, *International Journal of Psycho-Analysis*, 83: 519–521.
Bonaminio, V. (1994) 'Intersoggettività e individualità', *Proceedings of the Tenth National Congress of the Italian Psychoanalytical Society*.
Bonfiglio, B. (1993) 'Gli aspetti relazionali nella teorizzazione psicoanalitica: le origini', *Rivista di Psicoanalisi*, 2: 301–320.
—— (1994) 'Gli aspetti intersoggettivi nel pensiero psicoanalitico da Ferenczi alle teorie costruttiviste', *Proceedings of the Tenth National Congress of the Italian Psychoanalytical Society*.
Bonomi, A. (1968) 'Prefazione', in J. Piaget *La Strutturalismo*, Milan: Il Saggiatore.
Bordi, S. (1994) 'Lo stato attuale del concetto di neutralità analitica', *Proceedings of the Tenth National Congress of the Italian Psychoanalytical Society*.
Bori, P.C. (1979) 'Una pagina inedita di Freud, la premessa al romanzo storico su Mosè', *Rivista di Storia Contemporanea*, 1: 1–17.
—— (1989) 'Introduzione', in P. Gay *Un ebreo senza dio*, Bologna: IL Mulino.
Bouveresse, J. (1975) 'Wittgenstein antropologo', in L. Wittgenstein *Note sul 'Ramo d'oro' di Frazer*, Milan: Adelphi.
Bouvet, M. (1967) *Opere psicoanalitiche, Vol. I: La relazione oggettuale*, Rome: Astrolabio, 1975.
Brenman, E. (1980) 'The value of reconstruction in adult psychoanalysis', *International of Journal Psychoanalysis*, 61: 53–60.
Brutti, C. (1981) 'Relazione-rapporto: raccordi e antinomie', in C. Brutti *et al.* *La Relazione analitica*, Rome: Borla.
Brutti, C. et al. (1981) *La Relazione analitica*, Rome: Borla.

Calvino, I. (1994) *Mr Palomar*, London: Vintage.

Cargnelutti, E. (1987) 'I concetti di "continuo", "discontinuo", discreto": convenienza del loro uso in psicoanalisi', in A.M. Muratori (ed.) *Il 'continuo' e il 'discreto' in psicoanalisi*, Rome: Borla.

Cargnelutti, E., Cerletti, A., Giordanelli, L., Gragnani, C. and Muratori, A. M. (1981) 'Dal "non-comunicato" alla "comunicazione": alcune ipotesi sul cambiamento', in C. Brutti *et al. La Relazione analitica*, Rome: Borla.

Ceruti, M. (1983) 'Prefazione', in S. Korner *Sistemi di riferimento categoriali*, Milan: Feltrinelli.

—— (1986) *Constraints and Possibilities*, Lausanne: Gordon and Breach, 1994.

Chatman, S. (1978) *Story and Discourse*, Ithaca, NY: Cornell University Press.

Chianese, D. (1983) 'Note sul rapporto narcisismo-transfert in Freud e Lacan', in N. Ciani (ed.) *Il Narcisismo*, Rome: Borla.

—— (1987a) 'La "relazione analitica" come struttura', in C. Traversa (ed.) *Soggetto, relazione, trasformazione*, Rome: Borla.

—— (1987b) 'L'intervallo che precede la seduta: un vertice di osservazione sul "continuo-discreto" in analisi', in A.M. Muratori (ed.) *Il 'continuo'* e *il 'discreto' in psicoanalisi*, Rome: Borla.

—— (1988) 'La costruzione di una teoria. Einstein–Freud: un confronto tra modelli', *Rivista di Psicoanalisi*, 3: 475–503.

—— (1990) 'Erkenntnis als Umwandlung. Die Funktion von Durcharbeitung und Konstruktion in der Psychoanalyse', *Jahrbuch der Psychoanalyse*, 26: 31–63.

—— (1992) 'Una "querelle" interminabile e una conciliazione possibile', in E.R. Wallace *Storiografia e causalità in psicoanalisi*, Rome: Borla.

—— (1993) 'Il Mosè e le costruzioni: itinerari interrotti', *Rivista di Psicoanalisi*, 2: 213–238.

—— (1994) 'Il Chiasma', *Rivista di Psicoanalisi*, 3: 517–531.

Clarke, R.W. (1980) *Freud. The Man and His Cause*, London: Jonathan Cape and Weidenfeld and Nicholson.

Collingwood, R.G. (1946) *The Idea of History*, Oxford: Oxford University Press, 1993.

Conforto, C. and Rossi, R. (1980) 'Problemi della "costruzione" rileggendo Freud', *Rivista di Psicoanalisi*, 1: 81–87.

—— (1995) 'Pulsione o relazione: una opposizione irriducibile?', *Rivista di Psicoanalisi*, 4: 583–610.

Contardi, R. (1996) 'Il cerchio e l'ellisse. Figure della soggettivita', *Rivista di Psicoanalisi*, 1: 47–78.

Corrao, F. (1986) 'Il concetto di campo come modello teorico', *Gruppo* e *Funzione Analitica*, 1: 9–21.

—— (1988) 'Morfologia e trasformazioni nei modelli analitici', *Rivista di Psicoanalisi*, 35: 513–543.

Croce, B. (1912–13) 'Filosofia come scienza dello spirito', in B. Croce *Teoria e storia della storiografia*, Vol. 4, Bari: Laterza, 1948.

Dazzi, N. and Conte, M. (eds) (1988) *La verifica empirica in psicoanalisi*, Bologna: Il Mulino.

De Certeau, M. (1975) *The Writing of History*, New York: Columbia University Press, 1988.

De Masi, F. (1992) 'La psicosi di transfert. Prospettive cliniche nel lavoro con pazienti borderline', in L. Nissim Momigliano and A. Robutti (eds) *L'esperienza condivisa. Saggi sulla relazione analitica*, Milan: Cortina.

De Micco, V. (1996) 'Psicoanalisi: un sapere che sostiene l'esistenza?', in W. Loch *Psicoanalisi e verità*, Rome: Borla.

De Renzis, G. (1990) 'Prefazione', in P. Lacoste *La strega e il transfert*, Rome: Borla.

—— (1993) 'Da Freud alla psicoanalisi: un problema di fondazione', *Psicoterapia e Scienze Umane*, 1: 37–63.

—— (1994) 'Sul concetto di campo analitico in psicoanalisi', *Proceedings of the Tenth National Congress of the Italian Psychoanalytical Society.*

Derrida, J. (1967) *Writing and Difference*, London: Routledge, 2001.

—— (1976) 'F(u)ori', in N. Abraham and M. Torok *Il verbario dell'uomo dei Lupi*, Naples: Liguori, 1992.

De Silvestris, P. (1992) 'Baratto e metafora, economia ed etica della trasformazione', *Quaderni di Psicoterapia Infantile*, Vol. 24, Rome: Borla.

—— (1994) 'Transfert come vita e destino', in M.L. Algini, P. De Silvestris, C. Farina, and M. Lugones *Il transfert nella psicoanalisi dei bambini*, Rome: Borla.

De Toffoli, C. (1992) 'Trasformazioni e divenire del reale nel campo analitico', *Rivista di Psicoanalisi*, 3.

—— (1996) 'Origine intersoggettiva ed inconscia dell'esperienza di se come individuo', *Rivista di Psicoanalisi*, 1: 79–98.

Devereux, G. (1967) *Dall'angoscia al metodo nelle scienze del comportamento*, Rome: Istituto della Enciclopedia Italiana, 1984.

Dewey, J. (1938) *Logic. The Theory of Inquiry*, New York: Henry Holt.

Di Chiara, G. (1992) 'L'incontro, il racconto, il commiato. Tre fattori fondamentali dell'esperienza psicoanalitica', in L. Nissim Momigliano and A. Robutti (ed.) *L'esperienza condivisa. Saggi sulla relazione analitica*, Milan: Cortina.

Di Chiara, G. and Flegenheimer, F. (1985) 'Identificazione proiettiva', *Rivista di Psicoanalisi*, 2: 233–246.

Duby, G. (1980) *Il sogno della storia*, Milan: Garzanti, 1986.

Eco, U. (1979) *Lector in fabula*, Milan: Bompiani.

Einstein, A. (1954) *Ideas and Opinions*, Pinebrook, NJ: Dell.

Ekstein, R. and Rangell, L. (1961) 'Reconstruction and theory formation', *Journal of the American Psychoanalytic Association*, 9: 684–697.

Enriquez, M. (1988) 'Incidenza del delirio dei genitori sulla memoria dei discendenti', in R. Kaës, H. Faimberg, M. Enriquez and J.-J. Baranes *Trasmissione della vita psichica tra generazioni*, Rome: Borla, 1995.

Faimberg, H. (1983) 'Il "telescopage" delle generazioni', in R. Kaës, H. Faimberg, M. Enriquez and J.-J. Baranes *Trasmissione della vita psichica tra generazioni*, Rome: Borla, 1995.

Ferrari, A. and Garroni, E. (1979) 'Schema di progetto per uno studio della relazione analitica', *Rivista di Psicoanalisi*, 2: 282–330.

Ferro, A. (1992) *La tecnica nella psicoanalisi infantile*, Milan: Cortina.

Ferro, A. (1994) 'Il dialogo analitico: costituzione e trasformazione di mondi possibili', *Rivista di Psicoanalisi*, 3: 389–409.

Filippini, S. and Ponsi, M. (1993) 'Enactment', *Rivista di Psicoanalisi*, 39: 501–518.

Flournoy, O. (1985) *L'atto di passaggio*, Milan: Cortina, 1992.

Flumerfelt, J.M. (1962) 'On reconstruction', *Bulletin Phil. Ass. Psa.*, 12: 53–68.

Forrester, J. (1990) *The Seductions of Psychoanalysis: Freud, Lacan, and Derrida*, New York: Cambridge University Press.

Fossi, G. (1993) *Teoria e tecnica della interpretazione*, Rome: La Nuova ltalia Scientifica.

Foucault, M. (1963) *Madness and Civilization: A History of Insanity in the Age of Reason*, London: Tavistock, 1967.

—— (1966) *The Order of Things*, London: Tavistock, 1970.

—— (1969) *The Birth of the Clinic*, London: Tavistock, 1973.

Freud, S. (1886–99) *Pre-Psycho-Analytic Publications and Unpublished Drafts*, Standard Edition, Vol. 1.

—— (1895a) *Project for a Scientific Psychology*, Standard Edition, Vol. 1.

Freud, S. (1895b) *Studies on Hysteria*, Standard Edition, Vol. 2.

—— (1895c) *A Reply to Criticisms of my Paper on Anxiety Neuroses*, Standard Edition, Vol. 3.

—— (1896a) *Further Remarks on the Neuro-psychoses of Defence*, Standard Edition, Vol. 3.

—— (1896b) *The Aetiology of Hysteria*, Standard Edition, Vol. 3.

—— (1897) *Extracts from the Fliess Papers*, Standard Edition, Vol. 1.

—— (1899) *Screen Memories*, Standard Edition, Vol. 3.

—— (1900) *The Interpretation of Dreams*, Standard Edition, Vol. 4.

—— (1901) *The Psychopathology of Everyday Life*, Standard Edition, Vol. 6.

—— (1905a) *Fragment of an Analysis of a Case of Hysteria*, Standard Edition, Vol. 7.

—— (1905b) *Three Essays of the Theory of Sexuality*, Standard Edition, Vol. 7.

—— (1909) *Notes upon a Case of Obsessional Neurosis*, Standard Edition, Vol. 10.

—— (1910a) *Leonardo da Vinci and a Memory of his Childhood*, Standard Edition, Vol. 11

—— (1910b) *'Wild' Psychoanalysis*, Standard Edition, Vol. 11.
—— (1912a) *The Dynamics of Transference*, Standard Edition, Vol. 12.
—— (1912b) *Recommendations to Physicians Practising Psycho-analysis*, Standard Edition, Vol. 12.
—— (1913a) *The Theme of the Three Caskets*, Standard Edition, Vol. 12.
—— (1913b) *Totem and Taboo*, Standard Edition, Vol. 13.
—— (1913c) *Further Recommendations on the Technique of Psycho-Analysis*, Standard Edition, Vol. 2.
—— (1914a) *On the History of the Psycho-analytic Movement*, Standard Edition, Vol. 14.
—— (1914b) *Remembering, Repeating, Working-through*, Standard Edition, Vol. 12.
—— (1914c) *On Narcissism*, Standard Edition, Vol. 14.
—— (1915a) *Observations on Transference Love*, Standard Edition, Vol. 12.
—— (1915b) *Instincts and their Vicissitudes*, Standard Edition, Vol. 14
—— (1915c) *The Unconscious*, Standard Edition, Vol. 14.
—— (1916) *Introductory Lectures on Psychoanalysis*, Standard Edition, Vol. 15.
—— (1917) *Mourning and Melancholia*, Standard Edition, Vol. 14.
—— (1917–1919) *Introduction to Psycho-Analysis and the War Neuroses*, Standard Edition, Vol. 17.
—— (1918) *From the History of an Infantile Neurosis*, Standard Edition, Vol. 17.
—— (1919a) *The 'Uncanny'*, Standard Edition, Vol. 17.
—— (1919b) 'A Child is being Beaten', Standard Edition, Vol. 17.
—— (1920) *The Psychogenesis of a Case of Female Homosexuality*, Standard Edition, Vol. 18.
—— (1921) *Group Psychology and the Analysis of the Ego*, Standard Edition, Vol. 18.
—— (1922) *Beyond the Pleasure Principle*, Standard Edition, Vol. 18.
—— (1923a) *Remarks on the Theory and Practice of Dream-Interpretation*, Standard Edition, Vol. 19.
—— (1923b) *The Ego and the Id*, Standard Edition, Vol. 19.
—— (1925a) *A Note upon the 'Mystic Writing Pad'*, Standard Edition, Vol. 19.
—— (1925b) *An Autobiographical Study*, Standard Edition, Vol. 20.
—— (1925c) *Negation*, Standard Edition, Vol. 19.
—— (1926a) *Inhibitions, Symptoms and Anxiety*, Standard Edition, Vol. 20.
—— (1926b) *The Question of Lay Analysis*, Standard Edition, Vol. 20.
—— (1927) *The Future of an Illusion*, Standard Edition, Vol. 21.
—— (1930) *Civilization and its Discontents*, Standard Edition, Vol. 21.
—— (1933) *New Introductory Lectures on Psychoanalysis*, Standard Edition, Vol. 22.
—— (1934) *L'uomo Mosè. Un romanzo storico, O.S.F.*, Vol. 11.
—— (1936) *A Disturbance of Memory on the Acropolis*, Standard Edition, Vol. 22.
—— (1937a) *Analysis Terminable and Interminable*, Standard Edition, Vol. 23.

—— (1937b) *Constructions in Analysis*, Standard Edition, Vol. 23.
—— (1938a) *An Outline of Psychoanalysis*, Standard Edition, Vol. 23.
—— (1938b) *Splitting of the Ego in the Process of Defence*, Standard Edition, Vol. 23.
—— (1938c) *Findings, Ideas, Problems*, Standard Edition, Vol. 23.
—— (1938d) 'Constructions in analysis', *International Journal of Psycho-Analysis*, 19: 377–387.
—— (1939a) *Moses and Monotheism*, Standard Edition, Vol. 23.
—— (1939b) 'If Moses was an Egyptian. . . .' *International Journal of Psycho-analysis*, 20: 1–32.
—— (1986) *Lettere a W. Fliess (1887–1904)*, Turin: Boringhieri.
—— (1990) *Lettere alla fidanzata e ad altri corrispondenti (1873–1939)*, Turin: Bollati Boringhieri.
Freud, S. and Ferenczi, S. (1993) *Lettere*, Vol. I, Milan: Cortina.
Freud, S. and Jung, C.G. (1974) *Lettere tra Freud e Jung*, Turin: Boringhieri.
Freud, S. and Zweig, A. (1970) *The Letters of Sigmund Freud and Arnold Zweig*, E. L. Freud (ed.), New York: Harcourt Brace and World.
Friedlander, S. (1975) *History and Psychoanalysis* (Susan Suleiman, Trans.), New York: Holmes and Meier, 1978.
Gaburri, E. (ed.) (1997) *Emozione e interpretazione. psicoanalisi del campo emotivo*, Turin: Bollati Boringhieri.
—— (1980) 'Protocomunicazione e comunicazione nel rapporto analitico', *Rivista di Psicoanalisi*, 1.
Gaddini, E. (1977) 'Formazione del padre e scena primaria', in E. Gaddini *Scritti*, Milan: Cortina, 1989.
Gagliardi Guidi, R. (1992) 'Le analisi che si interrompono', in L. Nissim Momigliano and A. Robutti (eds.) *L'esperienza condivisa. Saggi sulla relazione analitica*, Milan: Cortina.
Galdo, A.M. (1981) 'Sul "conoscere" la relazione analitica', in C. Brutti *et al. La Relazione analitica*, Rome: Borla.
Gallie, W.B. (1955) 'Explanations in history and the genetic sciences', *Mind*, 14.
Garella, A. (1994) 'Le complicazioni di un'implicazione', in M. Balsamo and F. Napolitano *Costruire e ricostruire*, Rome: Borla.
Gargani, A.G. (1985) *La stupore e il caso*, Bari: Laterza.
—— (1987) 'Filosofare, narrare', *Alfabeta*, 93.
Gay, P. (1985) *Freud for Historians*, Oxford: Oxford University Press.
—— (1988) *Freud. A Life for Our Time*, New York: Norton.
—— (1989) *A Godless Jew*, Yale: Yale University Press.
Geberd, E. (1969) 'Introduction to panel of child psychoanalysis. The separation–individuation phase: direct observations and reconstructions', *International Journal of Psychoanalysis*, 50: 91–94.

Gill, M. (1994) *Psychoanalysis in Transition*, Hillsdale, NJ: Analytic Press, 1996.

Ginzburg, C. (1986) 'Freud, the Wolfman and the Werewolves', in C. Ginzburg *Myths, Emblems, Clues*, London: Hutchinson, 1990.

Giordanelli, L. (1987) 'Scissioni e significato nella "relazione analitica"', in C. Traversa (ed.) *Soggetto, relazione, trasformazione*, Rome: Borla.

Glasersfeld, E. von (1981) 'Introduzione al costruttivismo radicale', in P. Watzlawick (ed.) *La realtà inventata*, Milano: Feltrinelli, 1988.

Godelier, M. (1990) 'Inceste, parente et pouvoir', *Psychanalystes*, 36: 61–72.

Goffman, E. (1961) *Asylums: Essays on the Social Situation of Mental Patients*, New York: Doubleday.

Goretti, G. (1996) 'La domanda dell'analista', *Rivista di Psicoanalisi*, 3: 393–404.

Green, A. (1973) *The Fabric of Affect in the Psychoanalytic Discourse*, London: Routledge, 1999.

—— (1975) 'The analyst, symbolization, and absence in the analytic setting', *International Journal of Psychoanalysis*, 56: 1–22.

—— (1990) *Psicoanalisi degli stati limite*, Milan: Cortina, 1991.

—— (1993) 'Discussion of "The inner experiences of the analyst" by T.J. Jacobs', *International Journal of Psychoanalysis*, 74: 1131–1136.

—— (1995) *Seminari romani*, Rome: Borla.

—— (1996) 'Misconoscimento dell'inconscio (scienza e psicoanalisi)', in *L'inconscio e la scienza*, Rome: Borla.

Greenacre, F. (1975) 'On reconstruction', *Journal of the American Psychoanalytic Association*, 26: 693–771.

—— (1981) 'Reconstruction: its nature and therapeutic value', *Journal of the American Psychoanalytic Association*, 28: 27–46.

Hamon, P. (1972) 'Pour un statut semiologique du personnage', *Litterature*, 6.

Heimann, P. (1950) 'On counter-transference', in P. Heimann *About Children and Children No Longer*, London: Routledge.

Hempel, C.G. (1942) 'The function of general laws in history', *Journal of Philosophy*, 34.

—— (1953) 'Reasons and covering laws in historical explanation', in P. Gardiner (ed.) *The Philosophy of History*, Oxford: Oxford University Press, 1974.

—— (1962) 'Explanation in science and in history' in Colodny, *Frontiers in Science and Philosophy*, Pittsburg: University of Pittsburg Press, 1963.

Hesse, M. B. (1966) *Models and Analogies in Science*, Notre Dame, IN, University of Notre Dame Press, 1966.

Hjelmslev, L. (1943) *Prolegomena to a Theory of Language*, Madison, CT: University of Wisconsin Press, 1961.

Hoffmann, L.Z. (1991) 'Discussion: toward a social-constructivist view of the psychoanalytic situation', *Psychoanalytic Dialogues*, 1: 74–105.

—— (1992) 'Some practical implications of a social constructivist view of the psychoanalytic situation', *Psychoanalytic Dialogues*, 2: 287–304.

Holton, G. (1973) *The Scientific Imagination*, Harvard: Harvard University Press.

Jacobs, T. (1991) 'The relationships between transferences and reconstruction', in T. Jacobs *The Uses of the Self*, New York: International Universities Press.

Jones, E. (1953–57) *The Life and Work of Sigmund Freud*, London: Hogarth Press.

Kaës, R. (1993) 'Il soggetto dell'eredita', in R. Kaës, H. Faimberg, M. Enriquez and J.-J. Baranes *Trasmissione della vita psichica tra generazioni*, Rome: Borla, 1995.

Kernberg, O. (1965) 'Notes on countertransference', *Journal of the American Psychoanalytic Association*, 13: 38–56.

Khan, M.R. (1964) 'Ego distortion, cumulative trauma, and the role of reconstruction in the analytic situation', *International Journal of Psychoanalysis*, 45: 272–279.

—— (1978) 'Prefazione', in D. Winnicott *Frammento di un 'analisi*, Rome: Il Pensiero Scientifico, 1981.

Klauber, J. (1976) 'Some little-described elements of the psychoanalytical relationship', *International Review of Psycho-Analysis*, 3: 283–290.

—— (1981) *Difficulties in the Analytic Encounter*, New York/London: Jason Aronson.

Kohut, H. (1971) *The Analysis of the Self*, London: Hogarth Press.

—— (1984) *How Does Psychoanalysis Work?*, Chicago: University of Chicago Press.

Kris, E. (1956) 'The recovery of childhood memories in psychoanalysis', *Psychoanalytic Study of the Child*, 11: 54–88.

Kristeva, J. (1969) *Sémeiotikè: recherches pour une sémanalyse*, Paris: Seuil.

Kuyk, W. (1977) *Il discreto e il continuo* [*The Discrete and the Continuous*], Turin: Boringhieri, 1982.

Lacan, J. (1966) *Ecrits: A Selection*, New York: Norton, 1977.

—— (1978) *Seminario. Libro II*, Turin: Einaudi, 1991.

Laplanche, J. (1970) *Life and Death in Psychoanalysis*, Baltimore, MD: Johns Hopkins University Press, 1985.

—— (1987) *Nuovi fondamenti per la psicoanalisi*, Rome: Borla, 1989.

—— (1991) *Elementi per una metapsicologia*, Rome: Borla.

Laplanche, J. and Pontalis, J.-B. (1967) *The Language of Psychoanalysis*, London: Karnac, 1988.

—— (1985) *Fantasme originaire, fantasme des origines, origins du fantasme*, Paris: Hachette.

Laudan, L. (1977) *Progress and its Problems: Toward a Theory of Scientific Growth*, London: Routledge and Kegan Paul.

Lavagetto, M. (1985) *Freud, la letteratura e altro*, Turin: Einaudi.

Leclaire, S. (1971) *Smascherare il reale*, Rome: Astrolabio, 1973.
Lévi-Strauss, C. (1947) *The Elementary Structure of Kinship*, Boston: Beacon Press, 1969.
—— (1955) *Tristes Tropiques*, Penguin: Harmondsworth, 1992.
—— (1958) *Structural Anthropology*, Penguin: Harmondsworth, 1968.
—— (1964) *The Savage Mind*, Oxford: Oxford University Press, 2004.
Lewin (1953) 'Reconsideration of the dream screen', *Psychoanalysis Quarterly*, 2.
Little, M. (1951) 'Counter-transference and the patient's response', *International Journal of Psychoanalysis*, 31: 32–40.
Loch, W. (1977) 'Some comments on the subject of psychoanalysis and truth', in J. H. Smith (ed.) *Thought, Consciousness, and Reality*, New Haven and London: Yale University Press, 1986.
Lorenzer, A. (1975) *Crisi del linguaggio e psicoanalisi*, Bari: Laterza.
Lotman, J. (1973) *Ricerche semiotiche*, Turin: Einaudi.
Lowenstein, R.M. (1951) 'The problem of interpretation', *Psychoanalysis Quarterly*, 24: 169–199.
Luchetti, A. (1985) 'Considerazioni sul punto di vista genetico della metapsicologia psicoanalitica', *Rivista di Neurologia, Psichiatria, Scienze Umane.*
—— (1994) 'Il "grado zero" della rappresentazione', in P. Aulagnier *La violenza dell'interpretazione*, Rome: Borla.
Maccari, G. (1987) 'La parola "detta" e "ascoltata" nella "relazione analitica" ', in C. Traversa (ed.) *Soggetto, relazione, trasformazione*, Rome: Borla.
Mahony, P.J. (1987) *Freud as a Writer*, New York: International Universities Press.
Malmquist, C.P. (1963) 'Problems of methodology and theory construction in psychoanalysis', *International Revue of Psychoanalysis*, 50: 3–23.
Mancia, M. (1989) *Memoria, costruzioni e ricostruzioni*, Naples: Istituto Italiano per gli Studi Filosofici.
—— (1990) 'Costruzioni e ricostruzioni nell'analisi', *Rivista di Psicoanalisi*, 4: 923–933.
Mann, T. (1956) *Tutte le Opere di Thomas Mann*, Milano: Mondadori.
—— (1968) 'Freud und die Zukunft', in T. Mann *Schriften und Reden zur Literatur, Vol II*, Frankfurt: Fischer, p. 230.
Mannoni, O. (1972) *La funzione dell'immaginario*, Bari: Laterza.
Marcus, S. (1976) *Freud and Dora: Story, History, Case History, Psychoanalysis and Contemporary Science*, New York: International Universities Press.
Mascagni, M.L. (1995) ' "Infant research e psicoanalisi. Alla ricerca del bilinguismo". Note in margine al secondo libro di Lichtenberg', *Psicoterapia psicoanalitica*, 2: 114–134.
Maturana, H.R. and Varela, F. (1980) *Autopoiesi* e *cognizione*, Venice: Marsilio, 1986.

McDougall, J. (1985) *Theaters of the Mind*, New York: Norton.
—— (1989) *Theaters of the Body*, New York: Norton.
Meghnagi, D. (1992) *Il Padre* e *la Legge*, Venezia: Marsilio.
Meltzer, D. (1967) *The Psychoanalytic Process*, Perthshire: Clunie Press, 1978.
—— (1981) *La comprensione della bellezza* e *altri saggi*, Turin: Loescher.
Merendino, R.P. (1994) 'Sul concetto di campo analitico: per una definizione del concetto di "soggetto analitico" ', *Proceedings of the Tenth National Congress of the Italian Psychoanalytic Society*.
Merleau-Ponty, M. (1993) *The Visible and the Invisible*, Evanston: Northwestern University Press.
Micati, L. (1993) 'Quanta realtà può essere tollerata?', *Rivista di Psicoanalisi*, 1.
Mitchell, S. (1988) *Relational Concepts in Psychoanalysis*, Harvard: Harvard University Press.
Molinari, S. (1979) *Notazioni sulla scienza dei sogni di Freud*, Bologna: CLUER.
Montale, E. (1984) *Collected Poems*, New York: Farrar Straus and Giroux, 2000.
Morante, E. (1974) *History: A Novel*, Harmondsworth: Penguin, 2002.
Morgan, L. (1877) *Ancient Society or Researches in the Lines of Human Progress from Savagery through Barbarism to Civilization*, Somerset, NJ: Transaction Publishers, 2000.
Morin, E. (1972) 'Il ritorno dell'evento', in E. Morin *Teoria dell'evento*, Milan: Bompiani, 1974.
Morris, H. (1993) 'Narrative representation, narrative enactment, and the psychoanalytic construction of history', *International of Journal Psychoanalysis*, 74: 33–54.
Muratori, A.M. (1981) 'Rappresentazioni fantastiche della "relazione analitica" come struttura-funzione', in C. Brutti *et al. La relazione analitica*, Rome: Borla.
—— (1987a) 'Invarianza e cambiamento nella relazione analitica', in C. Brutti *et al.* Traversa (ed.) *Soggetto, relazione, trasformazione*, Rome: Borla.
—— (1987b) 'Il continuo e il discreto in psicoanalisi: contributo alla teoria della conoscenza', in A.M. Muratori (ed.) *Il 'continuo'* e *il 'discreto' in psicoanalisi*, Rome: Borla.
Musil, R. (1930, 1932) *The Man Without Qualities*, London: Picador, 1979.
Napolitano, F. (1987) 'Linguaggio e relazione analitica, una ricerca attraverso le categorie continuo-discontinuo-discreto', in A.M. Muratori (ed.) Il '*continuo*' *e il 'discreto' in psicoanalisi*, Rome: Borla.
—— (1988) 'Un approccio coerentista a un problema metapsicologico', *Rivista di Psicoanalisi*, 3: 429–453.
—— (1990) 'La confrontabilità in psicoanalisi', *Rivista di Psicoanalisi*, 1: 97–123.
Nathan, T. (1986) *La folie des autres. Traité d'ethnopsychiatrie clinique*, Paris: Dunod.
Neyraut, M. (1974) *Le transfert*, Paris: Presses Universitaires de France.

Nissim Momigliano, L. (1984) ' "Due persone che parlano in una stanza". Una ricerca sul dialogo analitico', in L. Nissim Momigliano and A. Robutti (eds) *L'esperienza condivisa. Saggi sulla relaziane psicoanalitica*, Milan: Cortina, 1992.

Ogden, T.H. (1986) *The Matrix of the Mind*, Northvale, NJ: Jason Aronson.

Oppenheimer, J.R. (1953) *Science and the Common Understanding*, New York: Simon and Schuster.

Orange, D.M. (1994) 'Countertransference, empathy and the hermeneutical circle', in R.D. Stolorow, G. Atwood and B. Brandchaft (eds) *The Intersubjective Perspective*, Northvale, NJ: Jason Aronson, 1996.

Orlando, F. (1973) *Toward a Freudian Theory of Literature*, Baltimore, MD: Johns Hopkins University Press, 1978.

Pauletta, G.M. (1983) 'Relazione e relatività nella conoscenza psicoanalitica: da Mach a Freud a Einstein', *Rivista di Psicoanalisi*, 2: 334–351.

Petrella, F. (1985) *La mente come teatro*, Turin: Centro Scientifico Torinese.

—— (1990) 'L'archeologia analitica nell'ultimo Freud', *Rivista di Psicoanalisi*, 4: 956–971.

Pirandello, L. (1921) *Six Characters in Search of an Author*, New York: Dutton, 1922.

Pomian, K. (1981) 'Struttura', in *Enciclopedia*, Vol. 13, Turin: Einaudi.

Ponsi, M. and Filippini, S. (1996) 'Sull'uso del concetto di interazione', *Rivista di Psicoanalisi*, 4: 567–594.

Pontalis, J.-B. (1977) *Frontiers in Psychoanalysis. Between Dream and Psychic Pain*, New York: International Universities Press, 1981.

—— (1988) *Perdere di vista* [*Losing Sight*], Rome: Borla, 1993.

—— (1990) *La forza d'attrazione*, Bari: Laterza, 1992.

Popper, K. R. (1963) *Conjectures and Refutations*, New York: Harper.

Pozzi, O. (1987a) 'Dalla realtà della seduzione alla astinenza della realtà: il fantasma della relazione nel testo freudiano', in C. Traversa (ed.) *Soggetto, relazione, trasformazione*, Rome: Borla.

—— (1987b) 'Coazione e ripetizione', in A.M. Muratori (a cura di) *Il 'continuo'* e *il 'discreto' in psicoanalisi*, Rome: Borla.

Predaval Magrini, M.V. (ed.) (1979) *Filosofia analitica e conoscenza storica*, Firenze: La Nuova Italia.

Pré-Lavarrière, J.M. and Rabant, C. (1985) 'L'article de Freud: "Constructions dans l'analyse" ', *Patio*, 4: 11–16.

Rabant, C. (1985) 'Constructions, interpretations', *Patio*, 4: 28–35.

Racamier, P.C. (1989) *Antiedipo e suoi destini*, Milan: CERP, 1990.

Racker, H. (1953) 'Il significato e l'impiego del controtransfert', in C. Albarella and M. Donadio (eds) *Il controtransfert*, Naples: Liguori, 1986.

Rangell, L. (1967) 'The metapsychology of psychic trauma', in *Psychic Trauma*, New York, Basic Books.

Rella, F. (ed.) (1977) *La critica freudiana*, Milan: Feltrinelli.

Renik, O. (1993) 'Analytic interaction: conceptualizing technique in the light of the analyst's irreducible subjectivity', *Psychoanalysis Quarterly*, 62: 553–571.

Resnik, S. (1982) *Il teatro del sogno*, Turin: Boringhieri.

Ricoeur, P. (1984) *Time and Narrative*, Chicago: University of Chicago Press, 1985.

Rieff, P. (1953) 'History, psychoanalysis and the social sciences', *Ethics*, 63: 107–120.

—— (1959) *Freud: The Mind of the Moralist*, Chicago: University of Chicago Press, 1979.

Rinaldi, L. (1990) Verità storica e psicoanalisi', *Rivista di Psicoanalisi*, 3: 560–605.

Riolo, F. (1983) 'Sogno e teoria della conoscenza in psicoanalisi', *Rivista di Psicoanalisi*, 29: 279–295.

—— (1986) 'Dei soggetti del campo: un discorso sui "limiti" ', *Gruppo e Funzione Analitica*, 3: 195–204.

Robert, M. (1974) *From Oedipus to Moses*, Garden City, NY: Anchor/Doubleday, 1976.

Robutti, A. (1992) 'Incontro a un crocevia', in L. Nissim Momigliano and A. Robutti (eds) *L'esperienza condivisa. Saggi sulla relazione analitica*, Milan: Cortina.

Rosolato, G. (1969) 'Interpretation et construction', *Bulletin of the Ass. Psa. Fran.*, 5: 44–50.

Rossi, P.L. (1992) 'Relazione reale e comportamento dell'analista', *Rivista di Psicoanalisi*, 38: 491–511.

Roustang, F. (1977) 'Du Chapitre VII', *Nouvelle Revue de Psychanalyse*, 16: 65–95.

Rubinfine, D. (1962) 'Notes on a theory of reconstruction', *Bull. Phil. Ass. Psa.*, 12: 89–91.

Russo, L. (1986) *Nietzsche, Freud e il paradosso della rappresentazione*, Rome: Istituto della Enciclopedia Italiana.

—— (1990) 'Ipotesi sul campo analitico', *Rivista di Psicoanalisi*, 4: 1113–1149.

Sachs, O. (1967) 'Distinctions between fantasy and reality elements in memory and reconstruction', *International Journal of Psychoanalysis*, 48: 416–423.

Sartre, J.-P. (1964) *Words*, Harmondsworth: Penguin, 1967.

Schafer, R. (1968) *Aspects of Internalization*, New York: International Universities Press.

—— (1978) *Language and Insight*, New Haven, CT: Yale University Press.

—— (1981) *Narrative Actions in Psychoanalysis*, Worcester, MA: Clark University Press.

—— (1983) *The Analytic Attitude*, London: Karnac, 1993.

Schur, M. (1972) *Freud Living and Dying*, New York: International Universities Press.

Searles, H.F. (1959) *Collected Papers on Schizophrenia and Related Subjects*, London: Karnac, 1965.

Seganti, A. (1995) *La memoria sensoriale delle relazioni*, Turin: Bollati Boringhieri.

Segre, C. (1984) 'Il caso Dora: anamnesi e romanzo', in C. Segre *Teatro e romanzo. Due tipi di comunicazione letteraria*, Turin: Einaudi.

Sollini, A. (ed.) (1987) *Narcisismo, Sé, relazione*, Rome: Borla.

Spence, D.P. (1982) *Narrative Truth and Historical Truth. Meaning and Interpretation in Psychoanalysis*, New York: Norton.

Stein, C. (1971) *L'enfant imaginaire*, Paris: Denoel.

Stolorow, R., Atwood, G. and Brandchaft, B. (1994) *The Intersubjective Perspective*, Northvale, NJ: Jason Aronson.

Sulloway, F.J. (1979) *Freud, Biologist of the Mind: Beyond the Psychoanalytic Legend*, New York: Basic Books.

Tower, L.E. (1955) 'Countertransference', *Journal of the American Psychoanalytic Association*, 4: 224–255.

Traversa, C. (1981) 'La relazione analitica e Freud', in C. Brutti *et al. La relazione analitica*, Rome: Borla.

—— (ed.) (1987) *Soggetto, relazione, trasformazione*, Rome: Borla.

Trilling, L. (1950) *The Liberal Imagination*, New York: Viking.

—— (1955) *Freud and the Crisis of our Culture*, New York: Beacon.

Turillazzi Manfredi, S. (1978) 'Interpretazione dell'agire e interpretazione come agire' [Interpretation of action and interpretation as action], *Rivista di Psicoanalisi*, 24: 223–240.

—— (1994) *Le certezze perdute della psicoanalisi clinica* [*The Lost Certainties of Clinical Psychoanalysis*], Milan: Cortina.

Tylor, E. (1874) *The Origins of Culture*, New York: Harper, 1958.

Varela, F. (1979) *Principles of Biological Autonomy*, New York: Elsevier.

Vergine, A. (1980) 'La relazione analitica come struttura: una ipotesi metapsicologica del funzionamento psichico come "relazione" ', *Rivista di Psicoanalisi*, 1.

—— (1981) 'Relazione analitica, codice, processo di significazione', in C. Brutti *et al. La relazione analitica*, Rome: Borla.

—— (1987) 'Riepilogo e prospettiva', in C. Traversa (ed) *Soggetto, relazione, trasformazione*, Rome: Borla.

—— (1992) 'La relazione analitica e il caso clinico', *Koinos*, 1: 19–36.

Viderman, S. (1970) *La construction de l'espace analytique*, Paris: Gallimard.

—— (1979) 'The analytic space: meaning and problems', *Psychoanalysis Quarterly*, 48: 257–291.

Von Wright, G.H. (1911) *Explanation and Understanding*, Ithaca: Cornell University Press, 2004.

—— (1969) 'Tempo, cambiamento, contraddizione', in G.H. Von Wright *La logica del tempo*, Turin: Boringhieri, 1974.

Wallace, E.R. (1985) *Historiography and Causation in Psychoanalysis*, Hillsdale, NJ: Analytic Press.

Wallerstein, R. (1967) 'Reconstruction and mastery in the transference psychosis', *Journal of the American Psychoanalytic Association*, 15: 551–583.

Walsh, W.H. (1951) *An Introduction to Philosophy of History*, London: Hutchinson.

Watzlawick, P. (ed.) (1984) *The Invented Reality. How Do We Know What We Believe We Know? Contributions to Constructivism*, New York: Norton.

Winnicott, D.W. (1971) *Playing and Reality*, London and New York: Routledge, 1991.

—— (1986) *Holding and Interpretation: Fragments of an Analysis*, New York: Grove Press, 1989.

Wittgenstein, L. (1921) *Tractatus Logico-Philosophicus*, London: Routledge and Kegan Paul, 1961.

—— (1967) *Bemerkungen über Frazer's The Golden Bough*, Rush Rhees (ed.), *Synthese*, 17: 233–253.

Yerushalmi, Y.H. (1991) *Freud's Moses*, New Haven, CT: Yale University Press.

Zerbino, E. (1981) 'Conoscenza clinica e metodo storiografico: una lettura di Lucien Febvre', in *Psichiatria e psicoterapia analitica*, Rome: Il Pensiero Scientifico.

Zippin, D. (1967) 'Constructions in analysis: implication for methodology', *International Review of Psychoanalysis*, 54: 697–705.

Zolo, D. (1988) 'Epistemologia riflessiva e complessita sociale', *Micro-Mega*, 1.

INDEX